ADAPTATIONS

What happens to popular texts, both novels and movies, when they are transformed into an entirely different medium? *Adaptations* considers the theoretical and practical issues surrounding the adaptation of a text into a film, and also looks at the reverse process: the novelization of movies.

Adaptations surveys the key approaches and debates surrounding adaptation, and explores why adaptations of both 'high' and 'low' cultural texts have become increasingly popular. Beginning with the history of Shakespeare on film, from Olivier's *Hamlet* to Branagh's *Hamlet*, contributors examine screen versions of literary classics, from Nathaniel Hawthorne's *The Scarlet Letter* and Louisa May Alcott's *Little Women*, to Thomas Keneally's *Schindler's List* and Irvine Welsh's *Trainspotting*.

Adaptations goes on to consider adaptation in reverse, explaining how writers like Virginia Woolf incorporated cinematic elements into their work, and why there had to be a novel of Jane Campion's *The Piano*. Contributors examine adaptations from comics to film, such as the *Batman* movies, *Star Trek*'s incarnations as a long-running television series, and then as a sequence of movies, and *101 Dalmatians*' move from children's novel to cartoon to live-action film.

Contributors: Roger Bromley, Will Brooker, Deborah Cartmell, Ken Gelder, Ina Rae Hark, Pat Kirkham, Julian North, Sharon Ouditt, Derek Paget, Mark Rawlinson, Esther Sonnet, Sarah Warren, Paul Wells, Imelda Whelehan, Nicholas Zurbrugg.

Deborah Cartmell is Senior Lecturer in the School of Arts and Humanities at De Montfort University, Leicester.

Imelda Whelehan is Principal Lecturer in English and Women's Studies at De Montfort University, Leicester.

D0302190

ADAPTATIONS

From text to screen, screen to text

*Edited by Deborah Cartmell
and Imelda Whelehan*

London and New York

First published 1999
by Routledge
11 New Fetter Lane, London EC4P 4EE

Simultaneously published in the USA and Canada
by Routledge
29 West 35th Street, New York, NY 10001

Routledge is an imprint of the Taylor & Francis Group

Typeset in Galliard by Routledge
Printed and bound in Great Britain by
Biddles Ltd, Guildford and King's Lynn

British Library Cataloguing in Publication Data
A catalogue record for this book is available from the British Library

Library of Congress Cataloging in Publication Data
Adaptations: from text to screen, screen to text / edited by Deborah Cartmell and
Imelda Whelehan.
p. cm.
Includes bibliographical references and index.
ISBN 0–415–16737–X (hardcover : alk. paper). — ISBN
0–415–16738–8 (pbk : alk. paper)
1. Film adaptations. 2. Motion pictures and literature.
PN1997.85.A32 1999
791.43'6—dc21   98–49576
                                                           CIP

ISBN 0–415–16737–X (hbk)
ISBN 0–415–16738–8 (pbk)

TO JAKE BRADLEY,
MIRIAM SADLER, HESTER BRADLEY
AND LAURENCE SADLER

CONTENTS

CONTENTS

ILLUSTRATIONS

CONTRIBUTORS

Roger Bromley is Director of the Humanities School of Graduate Studies and Research at Nottingham Trent University. He has written extensively on popular culture, is the author of numerous scholarly articles, and has contributed chapters to twenty books. He was the co-editor of *A Cultural Studies Reader: History, Theory, Practice* (Longman, 1996) and the author of *Lost Narratives* (Routledge, 1988) and *Narratives for a New Belonging* (forthcoming).

Will Brooker is co-editor, with Peter Brooker, of *Postmodern After-Images: A Reader in Film, Television and Video* (Arnold, 1997). He is currently engaged on PhD work on Batman at the Tom Hopkinson Centre for Media Research, University of Wales, Cardiff.

Deborah Cartmell is Senior Lecturer in English at De Montfort University, Leicester. She is presently working on a book on Shakespeare on screen, is co-editor of the *Film/Fiction* annual journal (Pluto Press, 1996–) and has written on Spenser, Shakespeare and Afro-American literature.

Ken Gelder is Associate Professor and Reader in English at the University of Melbourne, Australia. His previous books include *Reading the Vampire* (Routledge, 1994) and – with Jane M. Jacobs – *Uncanny Australia: Sacredness and Identity in a Postcolonial Nation* (Melbourne University Press, 1998).

Ina Rae Hark is Director of the Film Studies Program and Associate Dean of the College of Liberal Arts at the University of South Carolina. Her film scholarship includes two edited volumes of essays, *Screening the Male* (Routledge, 1993) and *The Road Movie Book* (Routledge, 1997), as well as articles in *Cinema Journal, Literature/Film Quarterly, Film History, South Atlantic Quarterly, Journal of Popular Film* and *Hitchcock's Re-Released Films*.

Pat Kirkham (formerly of De Montfort University) is Professor at The Bard Graduate Center for Studies in the Decorative Arts, New York, where she teaches and is director of a major research, exhibition and publishing project related to women designers working in the USA 1990–2000. She has written and lectured widely on gender, design and film.

Julian North is Senior Lecturer in English at De Montfort University, Leicester. She has published on De Quincey and on Victorian drug culture. Her book, *De Quincey Reviewed* (Camden House, 1997), is a study of De Quincey's critical reception from the 1820s to the 1990s. She is currently working on the construction of Romantic reputation and on nineteenth-century representations of the drug experience.

Sharon Ouditt is Senior Lecturer in the Department of English and Media Studies at Nottingham Trent University. She is author of *Fighting Forces, Writing Women: Identity and Ideology in the First World War* (Routledge, 1994) and has published essays and articles on women's writing, autobiography and feminist theory.

Derek Paget is Reader in Drama at University College, Worcester. He is the author of *True Stories? Documentary Drama on Radio, Screen and Stage* (Manchester University Press, 1990) and *No Other Way to Tell It: Dramadoc/ Docudrama on Television* (Manchester University Press, 1998).

Mark Rawlinson teaches at the University of Leicester. He has written on the Holocaust and post-war British culture. His book, *British Writers of the Second World War*, is forthcoming from Oxford University Press.

Esther Sonnet is Senior Lecturer and Research Fellow in the Faculty of Media Arts at Southampton Institute. She has published widely on postmodernism and cinema, with a specific interest in feminist and postfeminist theory. Her current research is on women's erotica within the contemporary cultural production and consumption of popular fictional genres.

Sarah Warren read English and Media Studies at De Montfort University. She recently obtained her PGCE at Leicester University and now teaches reception class at Forest Lodge Primary School, Leicester. Her interests include issues of class and gender, literature for children, and early-years education.

Paul Wells is Subject Leader for Media Studies at De Montfort University in Leicester. He is author of *Art and Animation* (John Wiley/Academy Group, 1997) and *Understanding Animation* (Routledge, 1998), and is currently preparing books on British and American animation and its relationship to cultural history.

Imelda Whelehan is Principal Lecturer in English and Women's Studies at De Montfort University, Leicester. Her publications include *Modern Feminist Thought* (Edinburgh University Press, 1995) and she is co-editor of the *Film/Fiction* annual journal (Pluto Press, 1996–). She is currently writing a book examining the re-emergence of anti-feminist thought in politics and popular culture.

Nicholas Zurbrugg is Professor of English and Cultural Studies and Director of the Centre for Contemporary Arts in the Faculty of Humanities and Social Sciences at De Montfort University, Leicester. His books include *Beckett and Proust* (New Jersey: Barnes and Noble, 1988), *The Parameters of Post-modernism* (London and New York: Routledge, 1994), *Jean Baudrillard: Art and Artefact* (London: Sage, 1997) and *Critical Vices: The Myths of Postmodern Theory* (New York: G + B Arts, forthcoming).

ACKNOWLEDGEMENTS

We are indebted to the people and archives below for permission to reproduce the following stills. Every effort has been made to trace copyright holders, and any omissions brought to our attention will be remedied in future editions.

3.1   *Hamlet* (1990) © Paramount, courtesy of the Kobal Collection.
6.1   *The Scarlet Letter* (1995) © Cinergi, courtesy of the Kobal Collection.
7.1   *Little Women* (1949) © MGM, courtesy of the Kobal Collection.
7.2   *Little Women* (1994) © Di Novi/Columbia, courtesy of the Kobal Collection.
10.1   *Trainspotting* (1996) © PolyGram/Pictorial Press.
15.1   *Batman,* © Twentieth Century Fox Television/ABC, courtesy of the Kobal Collection.
15.2   *Batman and Robin* (1997) © Warner Bros, courtesy of the Kobal Collection.
17.1   *101 Dalmatians* (1996) © Walt Disney, courtesy of the Kobal Collection.

The editors wish to acknowledge De Montfort University for giving us the time to complete this project and Stephen Gamble and John Mackintosh for their expert computing advice. Special thanks to David Sadler and Ian Bradley.

Part I

AN OVERVIEW

1

ADAPTATIONS

The contemporary dilemmas

Imelda Whelehan

Although the study of literary adaptations on film and TV is becoming more common and indeed more 'acceptable' as a feature of English and/or Media Studies in higher education, it is still surrounded by knee-jerk prejudice about the skills such study affords, its impact on the value and place of the literary 'original' and the kind of critical approach it demands. Apart from analytical work on narratological perspectives, *auteur* theory and genre, there is little that unites the study of visual and written narratives in academic work – even though there are clearly shared processes in the study of both. Studying both fictional and filmic sources can be fraught with problems – particularly in making decisions about giving the 'appropriate' amount of attention to each medium, and fostering the skills specific to each form; but perhaps the chief problem lies in teasing out our own and others' conscious and unconscious prejudices about this kind of 'hybrid' study.

This book picks up on an interest in the process of adaptation from text to screen which has increased in the past two decades, but in a sense emerged with the popularity of films based on works of fiction and particularly the development of the Hollywood film industry. Many commentators[1] have focused on the process of the transference from novel to film, where often a well-known work of great literature is adapted for the cinema and expectations about the 'fidelity' of the screen version come to the fore. For many people the comparison of a novel and its film version results in an almost unconscious prioritizing of the fictional origin over the resulting film, and so the main purpose of comparison becomes the measurement of the success of the film in its capacity to realize what are held to be the core meanings and values of the originary text. These commentators have already charted the problems involved in such an exercise and the pitfalls created by the demands of authenticity and fidelity – not least the intensely subjective criteria which must be applied in order to determine the degree to which the film is 'successful' in extracting the 'essence' of the fictional text. What we aim to offer here is an extension of this debate, but one which further destabilizes the tendency to believe that the origin text is of primary importance. To do this we move from a consideration of 'literary' adaptations (where the text is so well known that a potential cinema audience would have an idea of the 'authentic' version regardless of whether they'd ever actually read it) to a focus on adaptations more broadly.

We may expect to recognize the 'essential' Dorothea in the BBC TV adaptation of *Middlemarch* (1994), to find our two-dimensional heroine metamorphosed into celluloid intact and judge the version accordingly, but what of the graphic narrative, such as *Batman*, made film? Or the film which generates a novel? Or the novelist who attempts the methods of the director on the page? Even when a literary text is the subject of an adaptation it may not be a text that many potential viewers are familiar with: it may be a misremembered children's story or an obscure work of fiction that only became widely known through the process of realization on screen. In any case, the potential cinema audience of even the most widely read classic will be largely made up of individuals who haven't read the text, and any critical consideration of an adaptation's reception might benefit from recognizing some of the practical realities involved in producing a commercially successful film – such as pruning culturally anachronistic features, trimming sophisticated narrative strategies into a recognizable popular film genre which is, in turn, an adaptation of other films, with intertextual links with its contemporary filmic counterparts.

Critics on adaptations

The critical literature on adaptations is not extensive, but there has been a steady stream of publications since the 1960s which have been devoted to this 'hybrid' study. Caught between literary criticism and film studies, such work has not, even now, reached a happy compromise in its approach to the two media – despite the fact that, as early as 1969, Robert Richardson was arguing that 'literary criticism and film criticism can each benefit from the other' (Richardson 1969: 3). However, most critics seem to want to assert some congruence between the two narrative forms, which may explain the popularity of comparisons between authors and *auteurs*, most notably in the linkage between Joseph Conrad and D.W. Griffith. Conrad claimed in his 1897 preface to *The Nigger of the Narcissus* that above all his aim was to make the reader 'see', and D.W. Griffith asserted that 'the task I'm trying to achieve is above all to make you see' (quoted in Spiegel 1976: 4). The attempt to inspire the visual responses of the reading audience is therefore held up as the key link between late realist and modernist novelists and the film-maker. This parallel has been so often cited in works of this nature that Giddings *et al.* cannily observe in their opening to the chapter on 'The literature/screen debate' that: 'it has become traditional in books concerned with screening the novel to open with the statements by Joseph Conrad, the novelist, and D.W. Griffith, the film-maker, which seem almost to echo one another' (Giddings *et al.* 1990: 1). Earlier, Sergei Eisenstein drew a parallel between Dickens and Griffith in his 'Dickens, Griffith and the film today', asserting that Griffith had been led to the technique of montage through Dickens' use of the device of parallel action (see Richardson 1969: 17).

The link between Conrad and Griffith and Griffith's work on Dickens adaptation obviously serves to confer some respectability on an art-form which in its earlier years was regarded as lacking. Perhaps more interestingly, Alan Spiegel cites a statement by Leo Tolstoy made in 1908 that suggests a genuine respect for the opportunities that film technology offers:

> You will see that this little clicking contraption with the revolving handle will make a revolution in our life – in the life of writers. It is a direct attack on the old methods of literary art. We shall have to adapt ourselves to the shadowy screen and to the cold machine. A new form of writing will be necessary....But I rather like it. This swift change of scene, this blending of emotion and experience – it is much better than the heavy, long-drawn-out kind of writing to which we are accustomed. It is closer to life. In life, too, changes and transitions flash by before our eyes, and emotions of the soul are like a hurricane. The cinema has divined the mystery of motion. And that is greatness.
>
> (Quoted in Spiegel 1976: 162)

Tolstoy sees the advantage of the film medium lying in the more enhanced representation of reality – the speed by which mood and action can be communicated. Just as Tolstoy's remarks suggest a respect, even awe, for this developing technological medium, other writers such as Virginia Woolf reflected on the impact of the cinema (see Ouditt, Chapter 12 in this volume), and some critics have been keen to demonstrate that modernist writers in the early part of this century were actually experimenting with 'cinematic' techniques in their prose fiction. While accepting that the two media operate within different constraints, some argue that the two forms are becoming more and more interdependent through the course of the twentieth century. Keith Cohen, for example, argues that the novel had itself developed 'cinematic' tendencies at a point when the form seemed to have exhausted itself – 'our century has put more rigorously into practice than ever before certain theories concerning the interrelatedness of the arts which were formulated in the nineteenth century, in an effort precisely to strengthen the specific effects of single arts' (Cohen 1979: 1). Here Cohen is primarily concerned with the modernist tradition and its realization in the avant-garde cinematic tradition, but Geoffrey Wagner also picks up Cohen's point that modernist writers used the 'cinematic' in their writing and argues that novelistic trends can tell us much about film: 'cinema is at its most convincing when it declines to be a dramatic mode and leans, rather, on its immediate antecedents in the aesthetic representation of reality (or irreality) – namely the novel' (Wagner 1975: 26). Wagner also picks up on another effect of the success of the literary adaptation and that is the drive to concretize successful films into print and notes that the 'first screenplay to be commercially published in America was *All About Eve* (1950)' (Wagner 1975: 29). The business in published screenplays has expanded and in contemporary times is most evident in the best-selling scripts of Quentin Tarantino; even the existence of a work of literature which engendered a film does not prevent the production of a screenplay, film diary or further film spin-offs about the making of the adaptation.

Gabriel Miller controversially states that 'the novels' characters undergo a simplification process when transferred to the screen, for film is not very successful in dealing either with complex psychological states or with dream or memory, nor can it render thought' (Miller 1980: xiii). This position demonstrates both an ignorance of film narrative strategies and an assumption that fiction deals with psychological dramas, thought, dream and memory in a transparent way that needs no artificial mediation. The assumption that fiction is more 'complex' than film is another way of privileging 'art' in fiction and undermines the possibility of serious study of the verbal, visual and audio registers of the film, as well as suggesting that film is incapable of metaphor or symbolism. While other critics aren't quite so obviously prejudiced against film, they tend to begin with the observation that the novel is a linguistic medium, whereas film is a primarily visual mode of communication, and that both are subject to differences in production and circulation:

> The reputable novel, generally speaking, has been supported by a small, literate audience, has been produced by an individual writer, and has remained relatively free of rigid censorship. The film, on the other hand, has been supported by a mass audience, produced co-operatively under industrial conditions, and restricted by a self-imposed Production Code. These developments have reinforced rather than vitiated the autonomy of each medium.
>
> (Bluestone 1957: viii)

As Bluestone notes, the differences between the novel and film extend from formal considerations to their very conditions of production – which themselves have quite distinct meanings attached to them. There is still the preconception that the novelist produces a work of quality, of 'high' art as it emerges from the solitary efforts of the individual to express their distinct vision, untrammelled by concerns about the commercial value of the product which is deemed subsidiary to aesthetic value. A film is, conversely, produced and packaged under a company logo, the high price of production necessitating the guarantee of box-office success. Somewhere between these two polarized views, of course, lies the recognition that the literary market is overwhelmingly guided by market forces (and what better boost can there be to a book's sales than a TV or film tie-in?) and the film industry has *auteur*-directors who rise to the challenge of classic adaptation in order to realize ambitions of producing the most compelling, truthful and authentic version – or a radical revisioning – of a particular text (we need only think of Kenneth Branagh's project with *Henry V* (1989), *Mary Shelley's Frankenstein* (1994) and *Hamlet* (1996), or the work of Laurence Olivier and Orson Welles before him).

Bluestone asserts that the relationship between novel and film has been 'overtly compatible, secretly hostile' (Bluestone 1957: 2): the most readily detectable hostility lies in the responses to adaptations which are deemed to 'betray' the original in some way, although a more interesting manifestation of hostility might be apparent in many adaptations' resistance to the idea of them as inferior or shadowy copies of the original. Commercially it is obvious that a popular film adaptation of a novel can transform the text's value, from esoteric object to object of mass consumption, but while a guiding concern remains with the privileging of the literary text other issues are evaded or marginalized to the extent that 'the novel is a norm and the film deviates at its peril' (Bluestone 1957: 5) even though the necessity of transference across the two media is universally acknowledged as inevitable. Hortense Powdermaker, in her anthropological investigation of Hollywood, gives clear reasons why the popular movie adaptation simply must deviate:

> The original source may be a novel or play the studio has purchased, and the writer is employed to do an adaptation from it. He makes the changes necessary for dramatic effect in another medium, those required to conform to the producer's personal fantasies and his notions of what the public wants, and to meet the taboos of the Production Code, and tailors it all to the screen personalities of the actors who will play the star roles. Sometimes only the title of the original novel or play is left.
> This 'adaptation' then becomes the source for the 'screen play' – probably done by another writer.
>
> (Powdermaker 1951: 153)

Interestingly, although what Powdermaker points to are the conflicting demands of the producer or director/*auteur*, censorship and social mores and the personalities of the actors, there are echoes of the processes of literary criticism in transforming the meanings available to the reader of the classic novel or the Shakespeare play. As our opening chapters on classic adaptation show, the adaptation process in these instances is already burdened by the weight of interpretations which surround the text in question, and which may provide the key to central decisions made in a film's production (see Cartmell, Chapter 3; Kirkham and Warren, Chapter 7; and North, Chapter 4, all in this volume).

What is clear is that certain features of novelistic expression must be retained in order to guarantee a 'successful' adaptation, but clearly the markers of success vary depending largely on which features of the literary narrative are deemed essential to a reproduction of its core meaning. In the case of the Shakespeare film, interpretation, awareness of academic critical debates and imaginative filmic translation of stagey scenes is essential; classic nineteenth-century novel film adaptation or TV serialization require historical veracity and authenticity of location and costume – to the extent that central characters may seem lost in the 'background', which assumes a pivotal role in the drama itself. Bluestone observes that:

> The film-makers still talk about 'faithful' and 'unfaithful' adaptations without ever realizing that they are really talking about successful and unsuccessful films. Whenever a film becomes a financial or even a critical success the question of "faithfulness" is given hardly any thought. If the film succeeds on its own merits, it ceases to be problematic.
>
> (Bluestone 1957: 114)

The question is left open, however, as to how successful films are determined, but it raises the issues of the relationship of box office success, target audience, and how, in particular, 'high' literature becomes popular culture with a corresponding effect on book sales and the perception of literary value and 'high' cultural tastes in the eyes of the mass viewing audience.

It is clear that the impetus for most adaptations rests with the relationship between characters rather than the overarching themes of the novel in question, and that those characters, taken from their original context, may to some extent carve out a separate destiny.

> What happens, therefore, when the filmist undertakes the adaptation of a novel, given the inevitable mutation, is that he does not convert the novel at all. What he adapts is a kind of paraphrase of the novel – the novel viewed as raw material. He looks not to the organic novel, whose language is inseparable from its theme, but to characters and incidents which have somehow detached themselves from language and, like the heroes of folk legends, have achieved a mythic life of their own.
>
> (Bluestone 1957: 62)

This can be witnessed in the 'Darcy' effect after the production of the BBC's *Pride and Prejudice* (1995) (see Sonnet, Chapter 5 in this volume), but is actually more obvious when we move into the realms of popular culture with the figures of Batman and the original cast of *Star Trek* (see Hark and Brooker, Chapters 14 and 15 in this volume).

Wagner is perhaps one of the first commentators to identify three types of adaptation: transposition – a novel 'directly given on screen' (Wagner 1975: 222); commentary – 'where an original is taken and either purposely or inadvertently altered in some respect' (Wagner 1975: 223); and analogy (e.g. a film that shifts the action of the fiction forward in time or otherwise changes its essential context; analogy goes further than shifting a scene or playing with the end, and must transplant the whole scenario so that little of the original is identifiable). In his following examples of the different types of adaptation, Wagner seems to associate transposition with the 'classic' adaptation, for example

Wyler's *Wuthering Heights* (1939). He observes that all such 'classic' adaptations are made into heightened love stories on film.

> Apart from the advantage of being able to flourish CLASSIC on the hoardings, and lure in some unsuspecting souls who will have the vague feeling that they have experienced *Wuthering Heights* by seeing it on the screen, the perennial answer [to the question why bother to adapt *Wuthering Heights*] seems to be that a love interest is held to construe to audience interest almost exclusively.
>
> (Wagner 1975: 234)

The example of *Wuthering Heights* as a transposition suggests some problems attached to these categories since, as Wagner himself notes, half the book is immediately chopped. Judgements about transposition seem as subjective as past determinants of success – here *Wuthering Heights* is condensed to 'a love story'.

Robert Giddings, Keith Selby and Chris Wensley in *Screening the Novel* (1990) are more interested in the interdependency of film and the literary tradition – 'Film may have been a non-verbal experience, but it based its narrative on the Western European cultural experience of literature' (Giddings *et al.* 1990: x). They identify the fact that film emerged at the height of realist traditions in the novel and in drama, and claim that there has been a perhaps unconscious tendency to attempt to translate classic realist texts into 'authentic' historical realism.

The narratological approach to adaptation

While the act of judging authenticity or textual fidelity may become an inexact science, dogged by value judgements about the relative artistic worth of literature and film (particularly when a classic is being translated for the popular cinema audience), the practice of comparing narrative strategies in order to better establish what key shifts are made in the process of transition may be quite comforting. After all, the process of presenting a literary text on film is one in which the stock formal devices of narrative – point of view, focalization, tense, voice, metaphor – must be realized by quite other means, and this is where the creative mettle of the adapter is put supremely to the test. Brian McFarlane's work in *Novel to Film* (1996) is the most complete example of the implementation of such an approach. As McFarlane notes, there needs to be a critical distinction made between those narrative features that can be transferred from one medium to another and those that can't. To clarify this distinction McFarlane returns to Barthes's classic essay, 'The structural analysis of narratives' (1966; reproduced in Barthes 1977: 79–124). Barthes's assertion that 'narrative is international, transhistorical, transcultural: it is simply there, like life itself' (Barthes 1977: 79) reminds us of his key role in establishing a form of structural analysis which was able to embrace fiction, cinema, history, painting and so forth *as narrative*. Following in the footsteps of the Russian formalists, structural anthropology and linguistics, Barthes aimed to produce a 'scientific' ordering principle by which the basic features of all narrative could be classified. With this in mind he broke down the segments of narrative into 'units', with the view that all units of narrative – the form and the content – are functional. Narrative units are further divided into distributional (functional) and integrational (or indices) – the former can be extracted as the 'story' in terms of actions, causes and effects, and the latter refers to psychological states, attributions of character, descriptions of location and so forth. Distributional functions are subdivided into cardinal functions (nuclei) and catalysers, with cardinal functions denoting those actions which are of direct consequence of the development of the story – '[a] nucleus cannot be deleted without altering the story' (Barthes 1977: 95). A catalyser on the other hand 'fills in' between key narrative events and is less pivotal: 'it accelerates, delays, gives fresh impetus to the discourse, it summarizes, anticipates and sometimes even leads astray' (Barthes 1977: 95) – any shifts, even if they did not alter the basic 'story', would certainly affect the narrative discourse.

In his preface, McFarlane states his clear intention to marginalize areas of analysis such as those which focus on the question of authorship and the influence of the industrial and cultural contexts on the process of adaptation, in favour of focusing on the structural effects of exchange and translation from one narrative form to another. As will rapidly become apparent to the reader of this volume, 'discussion of adaptation has been bedevilled by the fidelity issue' (McFarlane 1996: 8); the advantages of a narratological approach to the problem is a recognition that the differing conditions within which fiction and film narrative are situated depend upon the necessity of 'violating' the originary text. As McFarlane goes on to argue, a clear distinction needs to be made between those narrative features that can be readily transferred from one medium to another and those that require 'adaptation'. Returning us to Barthes's categories, he asserts that distributional functions can be to some extent transferred from one medium to the other, since they denote 'story' content and can be depicted audiovisually or verbally – indeed, to change a nucleus (he gives the example of changing a sombre ending to a happy one) would be to warrant the charge of tampering with the original and 'the film-maker bent on "faithful" adaptation must, as a basis for such an enterprise, seek to preserve the major cardinal functions' (McFarlane 1996: 14). Indices on the other hand – the means by which character information, atmosphere and location are presented – require adaptation since their verbal or audiovisual depiction requires quite different means of representation.

Important narrative features that produce 'atmosphere' and are essential to the shaping of the text would include the portrayal of point of view and focalization – yet it is of course much more difficult to signify ownership of the gaze through the camera lens than it is through first- or third-person narrative. As McFarlane admits,

In a sense, all films are omniscient: even when they employ a voice-over technique as a means of simulating the first-person novelistic approach, the viewer is aware...of a level of objectivity in what is shown, which may include what the protagonist sees but cannot help including a great deal else as well.

(McFarlane 1996: 18)

Similarly Bluestone notes that 'the novel has three tenses, the film has only one' (Bluestone 1957: 48), and here he earmarks a major distinction between the two forms: there is no past tense in the film. In the case of point of view, we move from narrative focalization to *mise en scène* and arguably the less discriminate 'eye' of the camera, which cannot help but afford us a sense of an omniscient perspective, even while it is depicting the viewpoint of single character. For Giddings *et al.* it is point of view which is particularly crucial in the shift from fiction to film: 'first-person novel point of view is not the same as seeing the action from the camera; in the novel, the narrator tells and the reader listens, but there is not equivalence, rather a warm intimate relationship' (Giddings *et al.* 1990: 14).

Implementing the kinds of narrative comparison between text and film that McFarlane undertakes in his case-studies can yield some interesting insights into both the liberating and repressive features of the processes of adaptation, as well as usefully side-stepping the temptation to be seen to prioritize the literary text (as in discussions about the role of the author and questions of fidelity). One problem that might be anticipated with such an approach could be witnessed in Barthes's project in *S/Z* (1970), which in its detailed focus on one short story serves to illustrate the obstacles preventing the same intimate analysis of a large piece of work – let alone a comparison across two narrative forms. Some of the 'codes' that McFarlane lists as part of the extra-cinematic fabric of the film are, like Barthes's own codes in *S/Z*, problematic in their actual interpretation and application. Most notably the 'cultural code' defined in McFarlane's taxonomy as 'involving all that information which has to do with how people live, or lived, at particular times and places' (McFarlane 1996: 29) raises issues about specta-torial relationship to the film, period in which it is being screened, the film's own possible changing status in film history (it may be revered as a classic in its own right some time later, or it may be cult viewing) and other broader factors which threaten to render the system unwieldy to the point of meaninglessness.

History, nostalgia, ideology

One aspect of the audience's relationship to the text that is of particular interest is their historical relationship – particularly in the case of the ever-popular costume drama, for which the nineteenth-century novel remains such a popular choice for adaptation:

> It can be no accident that the 'past' with which our media seemed particularly concerned, certainly as far as classic novels are concerned, is the nineteenth century – a major warehouse of historical commodities and evidence, and a period still almost within living memory in which culture we feel we have strong roots.
>
> (Giddings *et al.* 1990: 31)

Clearly the developing heritage industry itself revivifies our interest in the previous century and our past in general, but of course just as politicians are referring to an *idea* of the past when they talk of returning to 'Victorian values', so the past reproduced in the movies is a contemporary, even aspirational one:

> We look back to the past as travellers on a journey look back to the way they have come. If we modernize those staging-posts along our journey to our own way of thinking, it is in a sense a way of admitting they are no longer appropriate or relevant in their original form to speak to us of the twentieth century. If we slavishly endeavour to recreate them as we think they might have appeared in their own time we produce a fake antique.
>
> (Giddings *et al.* 1990: 34)

Giddings *et al.* note that this craving for recapturing the past is not necessarily a new thing – citing the early nineteenth-century Gothic Revival as one example and a later craze for pageants as another. This craving is firmly identified as an intense moment of nostalgia where greed for images of the past, even fictionalized ones through the vehicle of adaptations 'are all symptomatic of the condition of the national psyche which is shedding layers of modernity and reverting to its own past tones under the stress of contemporary economic, political and social crisis' (Giddings *et al.* 1990: 38). As is clear from these remarks, an examination of the investment in an idea of the past which certain adaptations foreground, allows a critical perspective which moves away from questions of fidelity and historical verisimilitude, and enables the criticism of the processes of ideology as a dominant shaping force in the production of popular adaptations. As Peter Reynolds observes:

> Animated images of literature in performance are seldom produced by accident or chance, nor are they natural and ideologically neutral. They have been designed and built (consciously or unconsciously) by their author(s) in order to project a specific agenda and to encourage a particular set of responses.
>
> (Reynolds 1993: 1)

Moving slightly away from the perspective that suggests the *mise en scène* in film cannot be as controlling as the focus of the omniscient narrator in fiction and therefore the viewer is more anarchic or liberated from desired readings, Reynolds asserts that 'what the spectator sees and hears is what he or she is allowed to see, and to set the agenda by foregrounding one issue or set of issues is to marginalize others' (Reynolds 1993: 1). In the case of television serializations, as Reynolds observes, the decisions about scheduling and timing enable a certain infusion of moral values.

Gender, class and other social differences are inevitably ideologically reconstructed in our own image more often than with reference to values of the past – one good example is that of the use of regional accents for the 'working classes', whereas the bourgeoisie and aristocracy are assumed to speak in received (modern southern) English. With adaptations of classic texts from earlier periods, therefore, it is not only a question of filling in the visual 'gaps' that appear to be suggested by the adapter's interpretation of the original. There is often the temptation to portray a scene from a late twentieth-century perspective in order, ironically, to sustain the adapter's sense of what is authentic to the text. Such decisions are often made on the basis of being faithful to what the author would have expressed had they possessed the freedoms to discuss certain subjects, or if they had had access to the same technology – one example of this kind of justification for certain production choices may lie in Laurence Olivier's claim that Shakespeare 'in a way "wrote for the films"' (preface to Olivier 1984). Recent examples of the adapter's decision to 'add' something in terms of tone are in the BBC's recent version of *Pride and Prejudice* (the character of Darcy is overtly sexualized, a clear object of the female gaze, culminating in the famous scene where Darcy strips to the waist to swim the lake at Pemberley) or the 'feminist' context of Ang Lee's *Sense and Sensibility* (1995) (see North, Chapter 4 in this volume). When seeking the adapter's moral or political view of the text, we often have to seek its manifestations in other production choices such as casting and choice of setting.

The question of the audience's historical relationship to the literary/filmic text is an interesting one, particularly if we take the 1990s as a case-study and note the rash of high-budget TV and film adaptations of nineteenth-century novels. It is legitimate to ask whether the preference for the nineteenth century emerges from the public interest in this period of British history, the growing dominance of the novel as a respectable and morally responsible literary form during this period, or the ideological and moral qualities of the texts themselves – particularly represented by their closure, and depiction of personal relationships and of history itself. It might be asserted that the nineteenth-century setting allows for the greater likelihood of some familiarity with a broader historical context on the part of the audience – not to mention the greater availability of 'authentic' settings in which to visualize the period. But is the choice of favoured authors itself telling? Have those writers whose subject matter can be deemed more 'lightweight' and digestible been selected – in preference to the more ponderous, complex or heavyweight – as being peculiarly compatible with commercial adaptation? This in itself raises questions about whether particular types of literary form appear to lend themselves to particular cinematic/televisual treatments. If adaptations of nineteenth-century novels have as part of their concern the bringing of the period 'to life', what choices are made about the depiction of the past in the will to produce 'authenticity'?

There is clearly a case for investigating the extent to which an idea of the past is what a classic adaptation seeks to capture, and how that idea of the past coalesces with the period in which the adaptation is made. In some cases, the will for historical veracity may overtake the will to realize a particular work of fiction – cleansing the narrative of features which might be actually historically anachronistic. In the case of films such as Spielberg's *Schindler's List* (1993), there is a danger that the Hollywood focus on spectacle and heroism replaces a sense of history altogether (see Rawlinson, Chapter 9 in this volume). It is apparent that adaptations also age, and even a classic 1980s television serial can seem anachronistic and dated because of the changing approaches to set design, costume, textual fidelity and production values which make the adaptation seem very much of its own time. Just as it is common to encourage students of literature to consider their own historical vantage point as readers of texts from an earlier period, it is fascinating to study the effect that the period in which a text is adapted has upon the representation of that text. Shakespeare adaptations tend to be much more heterogeneous in their uses of history and setting than novel adaptations – for obvious reasons. However, production choices seem to tie into 'trends' for performing the plays in certain ways – e.g. bringing them into the present – and although issues of historical fidelity may seem less relevant to Shakespeare adaptations, the choice of setting may often offer an insight into what the director wishes to tell us about the 'Shakespeare' effect in general – e.g. Branagh's realist *Henry V* (1989), or the Tuscan idyll as a backdrop to *Much Ado About Nothing* (1993). In the case of literary works that are repeatedly adapted – such as *Hamlet* – technological advances, shifting cinematic styles, changing critical responses are all legitimate areas of interest for the student of adaptations, in addition to the commonplace observation that subsequent adaptations often refer to earlier versions (either critically or as a homage) as much as they 'return' to the original.

In the case of classic serials of the 1990s at least, the past is not only 'brought to life', but the artefacts of the adaptation's production themselves also serve as links to a previous era – the costumes for Lee's *Sense and Sensibility* and the BBC's *Pride and Prejudice* have been touring stately homes and museums in Britain side by side with the 'genuine article', as if they stand as testimony to their historical accuracy. The settings for classic serials – particularly stately homes – have themselves become objects of nostalgic homage for the cinema/TV audience, improving their contemporary fortunes considerably. Lyme Hall in Cheshire, used to represent Pemberley in the 1995 adaptation of *Pride and Prejudice*, is a National Trust property accustomed to around 800 visitors a week late in the season; yet, in the autumn of 1995, 5,500 visitors arrived during the final two days of opening (Ward 1995: 10). The National

Trust, itself an organization concerned with capturing, preserving and restoring the 'past' in terms of authenticity and fidelity to period, contributes to its continuing livelihood by capitalizing on the use of its properties to celebrate the lives and loves of those who never existed. Lyme sells maps which enable visitors to trace the sites of key scenes from the television dramatization, so that part of the fascination merges with engagement in returning to the origins of the serial – rather than the text; this is borne out by the increasing trend for spin-off materials which 'dramatize' the making of serials and films themselves. The BBC's adaptation of *Middlemarch* managed to locate the majority of its scenes in Stamford and in doing so to have created a theme town, which further conflates past and present, fiction and the real, and allows visiting *Middlemarch* TV aficionados to produce an excess of 'readings' of a cultural site which is extra-textual and is ruled by no authorial or directorial intentions.

Audience, pleasure and intertextuality

In the quest to find a mode of expression that explains the point of collision between the two media, one alternative angle of investigation might lie in the area of research seeking explanations for the success with audiences (in particular) of classic adaptations, and to speculate on the ways that the interface between a literary text and its film tribute(s) is interpreted and used by its audience. Henry Jenkins' work on fandom might provide a point of access that throws up altogether different issues, considering the role of fan (following the work of Michel de Certeau) as poacher – a wilful appropriator of meanings for ends which could not be anticipated by a film's or television serial's producers. While the 'fan' is usually depicted as an extreme version of the average cultural consumer – someone who has a more than anorakish interest in rather trivial and debased productions – Jenkins reviews the work of fan cultures as more than bizarre subcultural formations, casting fans as active cultural critics who use the tools of academic investigation under a different guise and who are also often producers themselves of artwork, fanzines and other elements which point to their role as innovators as much as consumers. According to Jenkins, '[r]eading practices (close scrutiny, elaborate exegesis, repeated and prolonged rereading, etc.) acceptable in confronting a work of "serious merit" seem perversely misapplied to the more "disposable" texts of mass culture' (Jenkins 1992: 17). Fans of the 'Trekker' variety seem to have nothing in common with the classic adaptation viewer who (if one can generalize) may have little engagement with popular film outside of this 'genre', and whose choices may earn some kind of seal of 'value'; yet, as Jenkins remarks, 'taste is always in crisis; taste can never remain stable, because it is challenged by the existence of other tastes that often seem just as "natural" to their proponents' (Jenkins 1992: 16). For the fan, then, matters of 'value' extend far beyond the high/low cultural divide and – in opposition to the assumed pleasures of individual consumption accorded the literary reader – the fan produces communities of readers. What is clear from this, ironically, is that the original production which sparked off such adulation is perceived as lacking in some crucial way – 'Because popular narratives often fail to satisfy, fans must struggle with them, to try to articulate themselves and other unrealized possibilities within the original works' (Jenkins 1992: 23). Clearly the adapter 'poaches' from the original in most crucial ways, but perhaps the seasoned *consumer* of adaptations begins to find the process itself equally participatory, welcoming the opportunity to recapture the experience of a first encounter with the original text in a different formulation. Alternatively, perhaps there are pleasures to be found in first encountering a 'version' which appears to iconoclastically demolish the 'literary' shaping of its original. There is clearly room for an ethnographic study of consumers that would be well beyond the scope of this text.

Meanwhile, by looking at the conclusions of works which focus on the reader and the consumer group, we might begin to further unseat the primacy of focus which has been traditionally applied to author/authority and fidelity. Rather than a tendency to see the film/TV adaptation of a literary text as necessarily lacking some of the force and substance of its original, it might be more fruitful to regard this and subsequent adaptations of a novel in terms of *excess* rather than lack. Research into fandom in cultural studies documents the way that fan communities constantly produce new narratives about favourite characters or authors, as if what they find in the original text frustrates a quest for wholeness and completeness which can only be satisfied by the creation and dispersal of narratives which somehow fill in the 'gaps'. This feature of fan communities reminds us – among other things – of Shakespeare film versions, where the most successful and memorable filmic event simply does not and could not appear in the dramatic text. As Giddings observes,

> the memorable moments in Olivier's film [*Henry V* (1944)] are the lowering of the Constable of France on to his steed, the charge of the French cavalry and the exciting 'Whoooosh!!' as the English bowmen's arrows wing their deadly way on to the galloping French horsemen.
>
> (Giddings *et al.* 1990: xv)

The activity of fans in relation to cult texts reminds us that these readers/viewers automatically set themselves up as critics who feel that part of their critical activity is best expressed in a rewriting or reframing of the 'original'. In this they mimic the function of scholarly critics who always find more to add to their analyses of the text, until our academic understanding of a classic literary work becomes in more ways than one the sum of its commentaries. This view becomes crucial when, for example, we study a text such as *Hamlet* which has been subjected to countless adaptations, and recognize that in untangling one adaptation from another, we have recourse to many sources outside both the play and subsequent films. Fans may alight on a particular actor or style which they pursue across other films and TV serials and are therefore, in addition, sophisticated intertextual readers. Some adaptations – such as *Clueless* (1995), a free 'rewriting' of *Emma* – capitalize on the pleasures to be found in the recognition of intertextual citation; this film is also interesting because it was marketed to two quite separate audiences: the teen film-goer and the Austen reader (see Sonnet, Chapter 5 in this volume). Derek Paget, looking at 1995, divides audiences into two dominant types of British fan: 'Trainspotters' and 'Janespotters' (see Paget, Chapter 10 in this volume).

Readers of adaptations, in common with mass-media fans, can become more conscious of their active role as critics by evaluating both literary text and its adaptation, looking beyond issues of success or failure and considering, among other things, the choices made by the adapter, the conditions of those choices, other possible options and their possible effects. As well as considering their own historical vantage point, the adaptation's audience need to consider the historical context and technological constraints within which the adaptation is produced. It also may be fruitful to investigate how the historical 'authenticity' of the period represented by the literary text's setting is approached, and whether the ideological perspectives offered seem to echo those of the literary narratorial perspective – this investigation may extend to evidence of how scholarly criticism of the text is used by adapters. It is clear that various adaptations (of a single author or of one historical period) may be compared synchronically to some effect, particularly in the light of the current rash of Austen versions, and this allows the student of adaptations to look at the purposes and function of nostalgia, and the possibility of identifying trends in adaptation practices.

Conclusions

The field of adaptations has in the past been dominated by scholars working primarily from an 'English lit.' perspective, who may be inclined to privilege the originary literary text above its adaptations, thus favouring the slow individualized process of reading/interpretation above the 'immediate' short-term and often shared pleasures of visual spectatorship – despite a recognition that neither account of the process of reading/viewing, and more particularly of analysis, is accurate or enlightening. Cultural assumptions about the relative worth of the literary versus the film medium are still deeply entrenched enough to be likely to influence our approach to adaptation, and it might be worth considering as an intrinsic part of our study of the adaptation process what may seem on face value to be the most naive and obvious of preconceptions. To begin, it is possibly the 'literariness' of the fictional text which itself appears to give credence to the study of adaptations at all. This view – implied or otherwise – is clearly going to influence our approach to the analysis of the adaptation to the point where the outcome of analysis might be best summed up as the judgement of the 'success' or 'failure' of the film or TV version. To approach adaptations in this fashion does not simply throw us back into the speculative realms of authorial intention and 'appropriate' textual readings, it also raises the question of readerly intention and homogenizes the identities and desires of both film- and fiction-consumers, who may each experience their narrative pleasures quite differently.

The fear that the film medium could 'steal' the constituency of readers of literature has long proved unfounded, and indeed there is enough research on the consumption of film and TV tie-in titles to demonstrate that a successful film or TV interpretation of a literary text can bolster the sales of a novel substantially. It is well documented that more people who have enjoyed a film/TV adaptation will buy the literary version than will actually read it, but there is little research on how this potential new readerly community treat the novel or why they often never finish it. Another largely uninterrogated assumption is that film-goers seek out the authenticity of the original, recognizing that the visual interpretation cannot do justice to the depth and substance of the novel. But what if they find in the experience of reading the novel a sense that it is merely a failed 'version', or a pale shadow of the film/TV series? If we hold on to the 'literary' model of reading as the 'norm' in these cases, we are unable to account for those thousands of unfinished copies of *Middlemarch*, unless we take the pragmatic view that people have more problems finding the time and leisure to read a novel than they do to view one. If there were ethnographic studies of how spectators approach the novel version of a favourite film/TV series, we might also gauge the extent to which such an audience is also influenced by preconceptions of the nature of a high/low cultural divide between the consumption of films and of literature, and discover that the business of acquiring the literary original is part of the process of acquiring cultural 'capital' described by Bourdieu (see Gelder, Chapter 13 in this volume).

If the fear is that '[w]hat are now called departments of English will be renamed departments of "cultural studies" where Batman comics, Mormon theme parks, television movies and rock will replace Chaucer, Shakespeare, Milton, Wordsworth and Wallace Stevens' (Harold Bloom, quoted in Porter 1996: 2), there still needs to be further scrutiny about what we think the 'loss' of English to cultural studies would mean, or whether it is in any case within our power to stop the 'rot'. Since the 'crisis' in English studies emerged as a lively debate in the late 1970s, no one has been able to provide a convincing definition of what 'doing' English entails and where its boundaries lie. In this sense the practices of media and cultural studies have always been more self-reflective, more able to absorb seeming contradictions primarily because such studies rarely emanate from a sense of fidelity to a 'text'. A cultural studies approach foregrounds the activities of reception and consumption, and shelves – forever perhaps – considerations of the aesthetic or cultural worthiness of the object of study.

It is inevitable that with an increase in popularity of the study of the literary adaptation, there will be increasing laments about the 'dumbing down' (to use a debased Americanism) of culture expressing the fear that people will experience their literature at a 'baser' level. It is of course worth pointing out that effective textual comparisons across the literature/media divide demand acute skills of close reading and narrative analysis, as well as a good acquaintance with the general debates about the interface between 'high' and 'low' culture. Such a study allows us to acknowledge our actual reading practices in a postmodern cultural context, and inserts the reading of literary texts into the same critical sphere as the consumption of more explicitly commercial products. Perhaps encouraging more flexibility in analyses of literary texts through the study of adaptations will enable the audience to be more self-conscious about their role as critics and about the activities of reading/viewing that they bring to bear in an academic environment.

Note

1 See Bluestone 1957, Richardson 1969, Wagner 1975, Spiegel 1976, Cohen 1979, Miller 1980, Giddings *et al.* 1990 and Reynolds 1993.

Part II

FROM TEXT TO SCREEN

2

INTRODUCTION

Deborah Cartmell

This section aims to dispel the idea that literary adaptations are one-way translations from text – especially 'classic' texts – to screen. When we think of a literary adaptation, we tend to think of an adaptation from text to screen; indeed most studies of adaptation concentrate entirely on the novel, leaving dramatists like Shakespeare to be evaluated on their own. The following issues (among others) are addressed, taking into account the differences between book and screen adaptation in terms of narration, enunciation and narrative, as well as changes in audiences and/or reception:

Chapter 3	The establishment of a field of 'classic' adaptations within the academic curriculum and the consequence of this for other forms – Shakespeare on screen.
Chapter 4	The politics of adapting a nineteenth-century text: decisions about the application of twentieth-century values – *Sense and Sensibility* (1995).
Chapter 5	The relationship between 'high'/'low' culture and dual audience reception – Heckerling's 'free' adaptation of Jane Austen's *Emma*: *Clueless* (1995).
Chapter 6	Adaptations as social and cultural appropriations of the original literary text; questions of authenticity and authority – *Little Women* (1933, 1949, 1994).
Chapter 7	Film as 'emptying' a literary text and the imposition of Hollywood ideology – *The Scarlet Letter* (1995).
Chapter 8	The interaction between an author and film-maker – William Burroughs' *Naked Lunch* (1959) and David Cronenberg's *Naked Lunch* (1993).
Chapter 9	Ethical issues involved in adapting historical literature – *Schindler's List* (1993).
Chapter 10	The role of the author and the audience in adaptations of popular fiction – *Trainspotting* (1996).

As has been illustrated (Giddings *et al.* 1990: 4), the Academy Awards has

23

historically privileged adaptations of texts to screen (giving them three-quarters of its awards for Best Picture), and adaptations have an immediate commercial viability given that out of the top twenty highest-earning films, fourteen were adaptations. Wagner (1975: 222–6) has suggested three categories of adaptations: 'transposition', in which the literary text is transferred as accurately as possible to film (Branagh's *Hamlet*, 1996, for instance); 'commentary', in which the original is altered (as in Joffé's *Scarlet Letter*, 1995), and 'analogy', in which the original text is used as a point of departure (as in Amy Heckerling's *Clueless*, 1995). Dudley Andrew (1984) suggests adaptations be classified as 'borrowing', 'intersecting' and 'transforming': 'borrowing' makes no claims to fidelity (*Clueless*), 'intersection' attempts to recreate the distinctness of the original text (*The Scarlet Letter*) and 'transformation' reproduces the 'essential' text (Branagh's *Hamlet*). But these categories restrict the field of 'adaptation' where the figure of the author (Shakespeare, Austen, Hawthorne) is prominent in the film's publicity and reception. We often lose sight of the fact that other films, such as *Schindler's List* (1993) for example, are also adaptations, and that there are adaptations which cannot be categorized in the ways that Wagner and Andrew suggest. In fact the more we study adaptations, the more it becomes apparent that the categories are limitless.

Chapter 3 begins with an analysis of Shakespeare on screen and the implications of its now established place within literary studies. Looking broadly at the spate of adaptations in the last half of the century, we can see how Shakespeare on film has crept into the establishment by a seemingly public-spirited ambition to rescue Shakespeare from oblivion, respectfully preserving an idea of his conservatism for new generations. By looking at 'successful' films of Shakespeare's plays (defined here as those that are recycled in classrooms and academic debates), we can see that they all pay homage to Shakespeare's alleged conservatism and superiority. It seems to be the case that 'classic' adaptations, on the whole, tend to 'depoliticize' the 'original' literary text; the assumption is that if it is a 'classic', then it must uphold right-wing values. Nonetheless, Shakespeare on screen is at present 'academically respectable'; and where Shakespeare goes, others will invariably follow.

The first candidate must be Jane Austen, alongside Shakespeare, as a conservative literary icon. Both authors are identified by the word 'heritage', and screen adaptations of their work tend to perpetuate their assumed conservative ideology in spite of critical readings which suggest otherwise. The 'fidelity debate' – or the 'not as good as the book' argument – takes a different form insofar as production values of film adaptations are seen to smother the potentially radical critiques embedded within the original text. In her analysis of the 1995 screen adaptation of *Sense and Sensibility*, Julian North argues that this is ultimately the case. Although the film adaptation teases us into thinking that it's a radical rereading of Austen (through the privileging of Marianne's voice of radical over conservative ideology, and the expansion of the role of Margaret, whose presence throughout notionally challenges patriarchal values), such a reading is ultimately abandoned in the film's erosion of the distinctions between sense/sensibility and in its unequivocally romantic ending, re-establishing the patriarchal values which the novel questions. It seems that the film industry needs to confirm Austen and Shakespeare as belonging to 'British heritage'; accordingly, they must be marketed as conservative icons.

Similarly, Esther Sonnet reads the screen adaptations of Austen's novels as a symptom of a popular cultural anti-feminist desire for an unchallenged patriarchal order. Heckerling's updated 'free' adaptation of *Emma*, *Clueless*, is seen as a site which contests the value of high culture, yet ultimately affirms an Arnoldian belief that access to great literature is morally edifying. Even a diluted *Emma* – like the diluted Shakespeare and Dickens quoted in *Clueless* – is better than no *Emma* at all. For instance, Cher/Emma's correction of her stepbrother's 'cultured' girlfriend's misattribution of 'To thine own self be true' to Hamlet (maybe she doesn't know her *Hamlet*, but she does know her Mel Gibson) is, in many ways, the moral of the film.

Roger Bromley considers Roland Joffé's 1995 'free' adaptation of Nathaniel Hawthorne's *Scarlet Letter* as a half-baked attempt (like *Sense and Sensibility*) to impose a more overtly feminist reading onto the novel. Clearly, as Bromley argues, directors need to trace contemporary analogues in order to sell the films and to produce something more than just another 'period piece'. Instead of Pearl (as in the novel), Hester becomes unequivocally the oppositional figure; her quest for independence is a mission to liberate all women from the bondage of patriarchy: as Bromley notes, she wears her letter 'A' like the badge of Superwoman. Her bid for independence, however, is contradicted by her need for Dimmesdale, remodelled from weak hypocrite to passionate hero. He literally rescues Hester and – at the film's close – drives her and Pearl to a new life in the West. As Bromley observes, this adaptation, completely lacking in subtlety, is of value in exposing the ways in which Hollywood cannot resist imposing Romance and Western genres onto 'classic' texts, exchanging the novel's historical content for an ideology of the 'imperial self', an ideology which is backward-looking – in this case, both patriarchal and racist.

A text which explicitly focuses on the 'pre-patriarchal' space inhabited by Hawthorne's Pearl and Thompson's Margaret, is Louisa May Alcott's *Little Women*. Three film adaptations (1933, 1949 and 1994) are discussed by Pat Kirkham and Sarah Warren: they reflect on the ways in which the films sanitize poverty in keeping with the time of their production and in doing so construct different nostalgic representations of the past. For example, in the 1949 version, the Marches are paraded in extravagant dresses, emphasizing what had been missed during the previous period of wartime austerity. Unsurprisingly, the final coupling between Jo and Bhaer is romanticized in all three versions; the unattractive, awkward and older man is transformed into a Hollywood heart-throb, most noticeably in the most recent of the adaptations. Bewilderingly, Hollywood seems more insistent in 1994 than it was in 1933 to uphold the 'status quo', changing the originary text by offering Jo a romantic and conventional ending. In the 1994 film, aspects of the 'life' of Alcott herself are incorporated into the film, seemingly in an effort to accommodate new feminist readings of Alcott's novel. There seems to be a trend in the 1990s to include or allude to the author in adaptations of 'classic' texts – *Prospero's Books* (1990), *Wuthering Heights* (1992) and *Sense and Sensibility* (in which Elinor takes over Austen's role as ironic commentator). Authors' names are increasingly appearing in titles; although their names serve to distinguish the films from previous adaptations, they are also signifiers of a return to 'authenticity': witness *Bram Stoker's Dracula* (1992), *Mary Shelley's Frankenstein* (1994) and even *William Shakespeare's Romeo + Juliet* (1996) (in spite of the many liberties it takes with Shakespeare's play). The presence of the author privileges 'authority' and sanctions the adaptation as 'authoritative', faithful to the author because of their very presence within it.

All of these adaptations are considered 'classic' adaptations, and a question posed by John O. Thompson is pertinent here: 'Why should the market favour adaptation? And what does that...lead us to think about adaptation?' (Thompson 1996: 13). One reason, suggests Thompson, is 'the desire to concretize', to make books 'real' in the way that only the moving image can. But it is often the case that this is irrelevant, as many viewers will only be familiar with the adaptation and have no desire to read the book. Another possible reason adaptations of 'classic' texts are so popular is that they provide viewers with cultural capital, that is a viewer chooses an adaptation in order to become more 'cultured' or 'a better person'. However, as mass culture is increasingly becoming the subject of the same critical scrutiny as 'high culture', what constitutes 'culture' becomes increasingly problematic. It is clearly the case that 'classic' adaptations are as entertaining as they are 'educational', based on the emotions as much as on the intellect. In fact, adaptations offer an escape into another world, a time often portrayed as simpler and happier. These adaptations strip the original text of what is regarded as unpleasant, satisfying a nostalgic yearning for a sanitized version of the past, and are thus escapist in their overall appeal.

Rather than offering an analysis of appropriation, Nicholas Zurbrugg considers how we view the relationship of living writer to film director, using the example of David Cronenberg's film adaptation of William Burroughs' 'unfilmable' novel *Naked Lunch* (written in 1959 and adapted for cinema in 1993). The difference between author and *auteur* is so great that one wonders whether or not it is better to consider them apart rather than together. The author, in this case, plays less than second fiddle to the *auteur*; the literary text is far from sacred.

Emptying a literary text of its historical content in the translation from literary history to screen text is of a different magnitude when it comes to representations of the Holocaust. Indeed, it is difficult to conceive of Steven Spielberg's adaptation *Schindler's List* as 'escapist' in the way that adaptations of Shakespeare's plays or films of eighteenth- and nineteenth-century novels can be seen. In Chapter 9, Mark Rawlinson negotiates a pathway between the ways in which an adaptation desecrates and rescues memory in his analysis of adaptations of the history of Oskar Schindler's involvement in the Holocaust. In one respect, the adapter (like Schindler himself) rescues the memory from oblivion and, in this sense, serves a public function which exempts him from any form of critical scrutiny. As adaptations like *Prospero's Books* preserve and conserve Shakespeare, Spielberg's film keeps a memory alive. Yet the way in which the rescue of memory is achieved in *Schindler's List* is indeed problematic; the impossibility of visualizing or representing the 'Grey Zone' is indisputable, and any representation of man-made mass death can be regarded as a blasphemous transformation into fairy tale. Fairy tale, as Marina Warner has noted, is about magic and metamorphoses, where chopped hands and severed heads can be miraculously restored (Warner 1994: xv–xvi). The imposition of closure – or liberation – on the history necessarily closes off the past, leaving the audience with a cosy image of history as passed, possibly giving rise to commercial adaptations of the film, such as a Peugeot advertisement in which a girl in a red dress (a well-known image from Spielberg's *Schindler's List*, perhaps ironically originating from the film *Don't Look Now*, 1973) is miraculously plucked to safety from in front of an onrushing juggernaut. Adaptation can be seen to trivialize through commercialization to such an extent that a narrative of profound loss is processed into one of salvation.

Trivializing, diluting or forgetting the source is seen to be of little importance in Chapter 10. Derek Paget's 'Speaking out: The transformations of *Trainspotting*' completes the section on text to screen. Paget outlines the transformation of Irvine Welsh's 1993 novel into a play (adapted by Harry Gibson) and film (adapted by John Hodge, directed by Danny Boyle, 1996). Coming out at the same time as *Sense and Sensibility*, Boyle's film addresses a completely different audience; equally successful, the films can be seen to reflect two particular kinds of Britishness, and two kinds of adaptation. While audiences of both films would be alike insofar as they would have a common knowledge of the source books, their attitudes towards the sources couldn't be more unlike each other. The seriousness with which reviewers of Emma Thompson's version of *Sense and Sensibility* took the 'not as good as the book' argument reflects an inherent hierarchy of texts: those at the top of the canon (Austen, for one) must be treated respectfully and faithfully in adaptations of the canonical author's work. In adaptations of arguably 'oppositional' or 'counter-cultural' texts (like *Trainspotting*), little concern is given to fidelity. In fact, it's rarely mentioned that the film *Trainspotting is* an adaptation, while Ang Lee's film *Sense and Sensibility* is *always* referred to as an adaptation. Paget describes how Welsh made no attempt to interfere with the adaptations of his novel: in fact (in order to prevent his intervention) Boyle had Welsh appear in the film in a cameo role. Implicitly, the role of the author of the literary text in a film adaptation can be no more than that of a cameo. What is apparent from an analysis of adaptations of *Trainspotting* is that pleasure is derived from its intertextuality, which is inherent to all texts but perhaps the defining principle of any adaptation – the word 'adaptation', after all, crucially informs us that there is more than one text and more than one author.

Perhaps the search for an 'original' or for a single author is no longer relevant in a postmodern world where a belief in a single meaning is seen to be a fruitless quest. Instead of worrying about whether a film is 'faithful' to the original literary text (founded in a logocentric belief that there is a single meaning), we read adaptations for their generation of a plurality of meanings. Thus the intertextuality of the adaptation is our primary concern. This section of *Adaptations* progresses from Shakespeare to Irvine Welsh, as some might argue, from the sublime to the ridiculous. It demonstrates the need to open up the study of adaptation to extend to screen-to-text adaptations, as well as multiple adaptations where a multiplicity of sources is not bemoaned but celebrated.

3

THE SHAKESPEARE ON SCREEN INDUSTRY

Deborah Cartmell

Shakespeare on screen is now firmly placed within the literary canon. As Anthony Davies has argued (Davies and Wells 1994: 12), enlivened by the completion of the BBC/Time-Life project (1975–85) which televised the entire canon, critical discussion of screen adaptations of Shakespeare flourished. Although there were a handful of surveys of Shakespeare films before this (most notably, Jack Jorgens' *Shakespeare on Film*, 1977, and Robert Manvell's *Shakespeare and the Film*, 1971), by the late 1980s, Shakespeare on screen gradually became part of the establishment, reflecting its growing academic respectability.[1]

What I'm suggesting here is that Shakespeare on screen has successfully crept from 'low' to 'high' culture, clinched perhaps by the decision in 1987 to devote an issue of *Shakespeare Survey* to the topic. Produced from the Shakespeare Institute and co-edited by Anthony Davies and Stanley Wells, this 'highbrow' specialized annual implicitly announced in 1987 that Shakespeare on screen had achieved respectability and was now 'allowed' admission into the English curriculum. It is now the case that scholars – like Stanley Wells, general editor of the Oxford Shakespeare, or Ann Thompson, general editor of the Arden Shakespeare – can move, without losing face, between discussions of the original conditions of the production of Shakespeare's texts to accounts of filmic reproductions of the plays. Since 1996, Shakespeare on film – as a category like the tragedies, the histories, textual studies – is now included in *The Year's Work in English Studies*; Macmillan have put Shakespeare on film in their New Casebooks series (Shaughnessy 1998), and, at the time of writing, a *Cambridge Companion to Shakespeare on Film* is in production. It seems now obligatory to include at least one article on Shakespeare on screen in edited collections of Shakespeare's works.[2]

This chapter accounts for why Shakespeare on screen has achieved such success in a climate of growing concern regarding (to quote Allan Bloom) the universities' 'impoverishment of the souls of today's students' (from the subtitle of Bloom 1987) by considering how successful adaptations comment on their own constructions, either through self-reflective imagery or intertextual links to other screen adaptations of Shakespeare. Success is achieved not by rubbishing but by revering the original; the successful adaptation must make clear that it is – and can only be – a pale version of the Shakespearean text.

Shakespeare on screen is now in its second century and the reasons why Shakespeare has so long been considered adaptable to cinema have been variously discussed (Ball 1968; Collick 1989). According to Robert Hamilton Ball, Shakespeare's dramas were considered ideal material for cinema in the early twentieth century because the presence of Shakespeare on film raised the contemporary estimation of film as a low-culture medium. Shakespeare was chosen as a means of enhancing the cultural value of cinema (given the belief that 'Shakespeare' carried some guarantee of worth). Yet it took a long time for audiences – or at least academically-oriented audiences – to appreciate the translation of Shakespeare to the screen. Certainly, Laurence Olivier's *Henry V* (1944) – financed by the Ministry of Information to raise the nation's morale at a time of great uncertainty – succeeded in producing what was regarded as 'authentic' Shakespeare (Agee 1946) in spite of the many cuts and interpolations Olivier made. Its consensual acceptance by critics was, perhaps, due to its mobilization of a text to endorse national and cultural traditions at a moment of uncertainty. Certainly, the 'look' of the production (rather than the retention of the words) had much to do with whether or not it was seen as faithful to the 'essence' of Shakespeare. For the most part doublet and hose were seen as essentials; when Derek Jarman set his version of *The Tempest* (1979) in a derelict mansion (Stoneleigh Abbey in Worcestershire) and cast magician Heathcote Williams as Prospero (half the age of all previous Prosperos) and punk artist Toyah Wilcox as Miranda, audiences were shocked: as Jarman says 'it was like an axe-blow to the last redwood' (1984: 206). Jarman's film, although interestingly his most commercially successful, was disliked because it went too far – just as the Sex Pistols (from the same generation) did when they performed *God Save the Queen* – in its audacious, possibly blasphemous, irreverence for Shakespeare. It received an X-rating, ensuring that it would not be used in classrooms. The film contains some nudity and arguably obscene posturing, but its offence was perhaps more due to what it did to Shakespeare's image, the image created and endorsed in the wartime *Henry V*.

The punk, disrespectful attitude towards Shakespeare was short-lived, and the 1990s film adaptations display the exact opposite: what can be described as an evangelical reverence for the words of Shakespeare. The present wave of Shakespeare films will all expect a shelf-life beyond that of their contemporary cinematic productions, in that they undoubtedly will be used in classrooms all over the world and be subjected to a range of academic scrutiny. This may account for the astonishing number of recent adaptations: among the major film versions in the last half of the 1990s are Oliver Parker's *Othello* (1995), Adrian Noble's *A Midsummer Night's Dream* (1995), Trevor Nunn's *Twelfth Night* (1995), Richard Loncraine's *Richard III* (1995), Al Pacino's *Looking for Richard* (1995), Baz Luhrmann's *William Shakespeare's Romeo + Juliet* (1996) and Kenneth Branagh's *Hamlet* (1996). At the time of writing, Quentin Tarantino is considering his own film adaptation of *Macbeth*.

The subject of adaptation – especially the appropriation of Shakespeare by the cinema – is ingeniously addressed in Peter Greenaway's film *Prospero's Books*, released in 1990; although taking greater liberties with *The Tempest* than did Jarman, it received remarkably favourable reviews. In this free adaptation, Greenaway juxtaposes the static book with an exploration of the radical potentialities of cinema, juxtaposing the words of Shakespeare with the world of cinema. Paul Washington argues that Peter Greenaway's film breaks up recent postcolonial readings of the play by 'emplotting the iconic Book, the First Folio' (Washington 1996: 245). In spite of the radical form of the film, it celebrates the 'book' at the cost of recent postcolonial approaches to the play (which often accuse Shakespeare of racism). In Greenaway's film, Caliban (played by avant-garde dancer Michael Clarke) is importantly white (as Jack Birkett is in Derek Jarman's *Tempest* – Jarman did however toy with the idea of casting a black actor in the part: see Chedgzoy 1995: 202), in spite of postcolonial readings of him as the native who, after Prospero's 'noble' attempts to 'educate' him, becomes ungrateful and uppity and (predictably revealing his bestiality) attempts to rape the white man's daughter.[3]

In Greenaway's film, Caliban is first seen urinating and defecating on Prospero's books and last seen scooping the book *The Tempest* out of the water where it has been thrown by Prospero. Douglas Lanier reads Greenaway's film as concerned with the battle between text and performance, Greenaway being – like his own version of Caliban – a desecrator of books, but one who nonetheless rescues Shakespeare's text from oblivion (Lanier 1996). Through the figure of Caliban – barbarian and philistine – this film encapsulates the ways in which adaptations of Shakespeare's plays are seen to defile the 'original' texts in their evacuations of historical/literary content and, ironically, to deradicalize the text (Caliban is portrayed as white not black), ensuring the text is politically 'safe'. *Prospero's Books* – thematically concerned with the animation of books – is a textbook of how to 'successfully' adapt Shakespeare; enshrining it in high cultural values (Greenaway's computer-generated imagery recreates glorious moments of 'high' art), depoliticizing the text (by ignoring postcolonial readings of the play) and, most significantly, inserting a final apology, modestly paying homage to Shakespeare and implying that film adaptation (like Caliban's appropriation of Prospero's book), while ensuring the survival of the text, is a far cry from 'the real thing'.

A successful adaptation of Shakespeare must then convey an 'anxiety of influence', an awareness that the reproduction is both dependent on and inferior to the original. Yet, while it has been argued that Shakespeare was originally chosen for screen in order to increase the cultural capital of cinema, Shakespeare on screen from the mid-1940s onwards openly popularizes (like Caliban's appropriation in *Prospero's Books*), unashamedly admitting itself to be a desecrator of the original. It seems that to 'popularize' necessarily implies a diminishment of the source. One way in which Shakespeare is made popular and accessible through film is to impose images from contemporary popular culture onto the text, a strategy satirized in *The Last Action Hero* (1993) when a school teacher (played by Joan Plowright) shows a clip from Olivier's *Hamlet* ('some of you might have seen him in the Polaroid commercial or as Zeus in *Clash of the Titans*'), exclaiming that Hamlet was in fact one of the first action heroes. Exasperated by Hamlet's inertia ('don't talk, just do it'), her eleven-year-old pupil imaginatively transforms Olivier's Hamlet into his gun-slinging and cigar-smoking screen hero, played by Arnold Schwarzenegger. This Hamlet acts rather than talks about it; and the film wittily suggests that, if Shakespeare is to survive, he must be both reduced and animated. Accordingly, cartoon or popular film images intrude unexpectedly into Shakespeare on screen. In Laurence Olivier's *Henry V* (1944), the Chorus guides us through a passageway from the recreated Globe Theatre of 1600 – and filmed theatrical performance – to the more colourful world of cinema. The passage from the Globe to Southampton in the time of Henry V is like the passage of Dorothy from black-and-white Kansas to the colourful world of the Wizard of Oz (*The Wizard of Oz*, 1939; see Whelehan and Cartmell 1995). In *Henry V* the audience is transported from theatrical to filmic space, and the allusion to *The Wizard of Oz*, when Dorothy moves from black-and-white to colour, leads the audience to expect that something better is about to happen: in other words, Olivier implies that Shakespeare on film betters Shakespeare in the theatre. Similarly in Orson Welles' *Macbeth* (1948), Lady Macbeth bears an unmistakeable resemblance to the evil queen in Disney's *Snow White and the Seven Dwarfs* (1937), in her costume, make-up and especially in her well-deserved death, dramatically hurling herself off a cliff. The film draws from the determining language of the animated image: it is the way she is pictured rather than what she has to say that constructs Welles' misogynistic reading of the play.[4] Kenneth Branagh's first entrance in *Henry V* (1989) echoes that of Darth Vader in George Lucas's *Star Wars* (1977); this is repeated in Ian McKellan's first appearance in *Richard III* (1995), when Richard is heard heavily breathing, disguised by his Darth Vader gas mask and accompanied by Imperial stormtrooper look-alikes. The visual echo of Darth Vader instantly brings with it expectations of a bad guy who may have some good in him. Even the *mise en scène* of Richard Eyre's television adaptation of *King Lear* (1998) is evocative of the popular *Star Trek* television and film series – the violence depicted in the play is made 'alien' to a film-literate audience, and therefore less threatening or less 'real'.

In fact, we can see with a survey of films of *Hamlet* since 1948 that Shakespeare is 'animated' – that is, made appealing and familiar through a range of popular images accessible to respective audiences. Of all the Shakespeare plays, *Hamlet* has been most frequently adapted for cinema, although there are only three major 'straight' films of the play in English: Laurence Olivier's *Hamlet* (1948), Franco Zeffirelli's *Hamlet* (1990) and Kenneth Branagh's *Hamlet* (1996).

A comparison of the endings of Laurence Olivier's *Hamlet* with that of Franco Zeffirelli's *Hamlet* demonstrates how screen adaptations between the first wave of the 1940s and 1950s (dominated by Laurence Olivier and Orson Welles) and the most recent wave in the 1990s (overseen by Kenneth Branagh) increasingly popularize Shakespeare, substituting animation for the words of the text. An adaptation is undeniably an appropriation of the text, and although the plot remains the same, the telling – or the interpreting of it – radically changes from one generation to the next.

Olivier's reading was influenced directly by Ernest Jones (Olivier 1984), whose Freudian interpretation of the play (published in 1949) is reflected in the passionate kiss Gertrude gives to Hamlet in the film's opening, the dominance of the bed in the closet scene, and in the fact that the actress who played Gertrude – Eileen Herlie – was twenty-seven while Olivier – who played Hamlet – was forty at the time of filming. Yet the boldness of this reading is abandoned in the final scene. Gertrude's suspiciousness of Claudius commences when the king drops the pearl in the cup. Knowingly she drinks, in an effort to save her son: her face softens, her voice becomes more maternal as she bids good-bye to Hamlet with the words 'let me wipe thy face'. Olivier fully redeems the Queen, making her almost Saint (Veronica)-like in her final moments. For a post-war audience, bruised by the loss of so many sons, this must have touched a chord. Olivier suggests that this Gertrude returns to positive family values and sacrifices herself in the hope that her son can survive her.

Zeffirelli's film overtly pays homage to Olivier's in its set. The *mise en scène* inside the castle, the cold and dull empty spaces dominated by a seemingly never-ending staircase, is a clear echo of the 1948 movie. However, the casting of Mel Gibson as Hamlet and Glenn Close as Gertrude marks a radical departure. The film – in its publicity and opening credits – indicates that both are stars and, in fact, Zeffirelli enlarges Gertrude's part, possibly allowing her – rather than Hamlet – to be 'too much i'th sun'. While Gibson's previous roles as action hero on the edge contribute to the fast pace of the normally slow play, Close's earlier parts in Adrian Lyne's *Fatal Attraction* (1987) and Stephen Frears' *Dangerous Liaisons* (1988) construct Gertrude as both sexual threat and potential homewrecker. Gibson's Hamlet goes as far as simulating sex with his mother in the closet scene; while Gertrude, right up until the end, seems a woman torn between two lovers. Her recognition of her mistaken allegiance is after she has drunk the poison: aware of her fatal error, she gazes accusingly at Claudius and dies, after sexually suggestive jerking movements with Hamlet, positioned on top of her, his face dripping with sweat. The focus on the women (including Helena Bonham-Carter's Ophelia, who manages to defy her father's pompous authoritarianism through her defiant looks) makes this version more 'politically correct', directly aimed at a 1990s audience. While Olivier manages to stumble to the throne for his death scene, Gibson dies on the centre of the platform, cross-shaped, yet disturbingly vulnerable. At any rate, this is a much reduced and bewilderingly cut version of *Hamlet*, with almost as much in common with an action movie as with Shakespeare's *Hamlet*.

With the current backlash against media studies because of the so-called 'dumbing down' of English, the divide between 'high' and 'low' culture widens; as does the manner in which filmic representation of Shakespeare is regarded. Certainly such adaptation/reproduction can be regarded as devaluing, even destroying the original's unique existence (Benjamin 1969: 221). Such reverence for a first or ur-text and the threat of trivializing/destroying this reverence through adaptation can be seen as a threat to the book itself. The orthodox view of Shakespeare is epitomized by Allan Bloom in an ancient versus modern debate – according to Bloom, the yahoos of today threaten to destroy the achievements of the great writers of the past through neglect and ignorance. Writing in 1964, Bloom asserts that:

> The role once played by the Bible and Shakespeare in the education of the English-speaking peoples is now largely played by popular journalism or works of ephemeral authors. This does not mean that the classic authors are no longer read; they are perhaps read more and in greater variety than ever before. But they do not move; they do not seem to speak to the situation of the modern young....The proper functions of criticism are, therefore, to recover Shakespeare's teaching to be the agent of his ever-continuing education of the Anglo-Saxon world.
>
> (1964: 1–3)

Bloom reads Shakespeare as the timeless educator of the Anglo-Saxon world in the same way that the British Tory Party have claimed him as one of their own. Former Chancellor of the Exchequer, Nigel Lawson, for instance, proclaimed that if Shakespeare were alive today he would be a member of the Tory Party (Coleman 1983: n.p.); and former Prime Minister, John Major, has articulated a Bloomian belief in the moral value of Shakespeare's plays: 'People say there is too much jargon in education – so let me give you some of my own: Knowledge. Discipline. Tables. Sums. Dates. Shakespeare' (speaking at the Tory Women's Conference in June 1993; see Major 1994). Like Bloom, Major suggests that there is in Shakespeare all that is necessary to make us decent human beings. Bloom goes on to explain what we can 'learn' from a reading of *Othello* where Shakespeare announces his pessimism in 'the possibility of an interracial, interfaith society' (1964: 36) and 'appears to tell us that it is not good to introduce influences that are too foreign, regardless of the guise in which they may come' (1964: 58). Desdemona must die as 'we must come to the defence of civil society and see her defection as a result of a monstrous misconception' (1964: 62).

Bloom's argument that we must have 'faith' in the Shakespearean text is worrying as it clearly becomes sacred testimony for his own right-wing – in this case openly racist – views. In the late 1990s, Bloom's popularity alongside a

Figure 3.1 Hamlet (1990), with Mel Gibson in the lead role and Glenn Close playing
    Gertrude

campaign for 'back to basics', especially in education, is reflected in the latest film adaptation of *Hamlet*. Indeed, one Bloomian reviewer noted that the film is 'redeemed by the one decision that seems perverse, even indefensible, the decision that is never made in cinema: trusting the author' (Mars-Jones 1997: 5). The 'belief' in the author is at the core of the debate as to whether an adaptation should be 'faithful' to the original. In his introduction to the screenplay of *Hamlet*, Branagh outlines his own gradual conversion to performing 'the full text' (that is, the 1623 version), after his first taste of it on radio in 1992 (Branagh 1996: vi–vii). He describes the ensuing pursuit of his dream, finally realized in 1995 when Castle Rock agreed to finance the project.

Branagh not only uses the entire 1623 text, but includes interpolations and flashbacks, presumably attempting to 'suit the action to the word, the word to the action'. Arguably Branagh 'o'erstep[s] the modesty of nature' in showing, among others, Brian Blessed as Hamlet Senior dying in his orchard in the middle of winter (it's hard not to imagine why he didn't die of hypothermia), Judi Dench as Hecuba visually illustrating the Player King's speech, and Ken Dodd as Yorick (his distinctive teeth are ingeniously matched in the skull). With the exception of Branagh's dyed blonde hair (like Olivier's), there is little reference to the earlier films of the play.[5] The movie, filmed at Bleinheim Palace and in Shepperton Studios, is set in the nineteenth century and shows an opulent court, resembling that of Nicholas and Alexandra, in its final days. The final scene is intercut with soldiers advancing towards the palace. Branagh's Hamlet shows no 'unnatural' sexual interest in his mother (played by Julie Christie, who due to the lighting sometimes looks more like Hamlet's grandmother than mother); indeed this Hamlet doesn't rush to her when she dies and his grief only lasts a few minutes. In fact, the camera focuses on the reaction of Claudius, played by Derek Jacobi. Fortinbras, played by Rufus Sewell, dark and brooding, is Hamlet's exact opposite. While Hamlet is seen as aristocratic, intelligent and noble, Fortinbras is thuggish, emotionless, vulgar and self-seeking; his invasion of the castle carries shades of the storming of the Winter Palace. The positioning of the grey uniformed soldiers against the brightness of the court figures, especially the Christ-like, almost luminous figure of the dead Hamlet being carried from the palace, underlines the enormity of the loss – visually an echo of Goya's painting of *The Third May, 1808*. As in Goya's painting, individuality together with the uplifting value of art are destroyed by a new order, dehumanized by their uniform clothes and gestures. The ultimate destruction of King Hamlet's statue by Fortinbras' mob of identical soldiers symbolizes the sad end of an era and a civilization. This *Hamlet* concludes – in line with Allan Bloom's analysis of the university curriculum – with the depressing victory of the philistines and their desecration of the sacred texts of the past.

Like Greenaway in *Prospero's Books*, Branagh inserts a final apology, implying that film adaptation (like Caliban's appropriation of Prospero's book) is an act of philistinism and cannot hope to get close to the civilizing power of Shakespeare's text. Unlike Baz Luhrmann's *William Shakespeare's Romeo + Juliet*, which wittily updates and drastically reduces the Shakespearean source – to quote Claire Danes (who plays Juliet) the film asks the audience to 'forget Shakespeare' (Murray 1997: 1) – Branagh's movie is a memorial to Shakespeare (the image of the tomb frames the film) and one which accordingly expects to be accepted into the 'establishment' of Shakespeare on screen studies. Shakespeare certainly brings in the audiences (Jarman's *Tempest* and Greenaway's *Prospero's Books* are their most commercially successful films), but in order to gain critical and academic acclaim these movies need to preserve a view of Shakespeare's conservatism which is arguably epitomized by Olivier's *Henry V*. In order to be marketed to film audiences and those responsible for teaching Shakespeare, reverence for the text and the author are prerequisites. This may provide us with the vital clue as to why Shakespeare on screen has made it into the canon.

Notes

1 A list of some of the major contributions to the field demonstrates its growing acceptance: Davies 1988; Collick 1989; Donaldson 1990; Buchman 1991; Davies and Wells 1994; Boose and Burt 1997.
2 Witness, for example, the period 1995–6. Each of these collections contains an article on Shakespeare and film: Barker and Kamps 1996, Bulman 1996, Kerr *et al.* 1996 and Willson 1995.
3 See, for example, Brown 1985 and Salway 1991.
4 See Wells, Chapter 16 in this volume. I would like to thank Paul Wells for his astute comments on this chapter.
5 The one exception here is the BBC *Hamlet* (1980), directed by Rodney Bennett, in which Derek Jacobi plays the title role. Branagh is undeniably mirroring Claudius and Hamlet in his production – their similar appearances reflect back on Branagh's inspiration from Jacobi's stage performance as Hamlet.

4

CONSERVATIVE AUSTEN, RADICAL AUSTEN

Sense and Sensibility from text to screen

Julian North

John Lyttle, commenting on the wave of adaptations of classic novels in the 1990s, argues that costume drama is 'an essentially conservative, backward-looking genre' in which '[p]roduction values tend to smother political points'. He gives as evidence Ang Lee's *Sense and Sensibility* (1995), which, as he argues, 'emphasised a woman's vulnerable place in impolite society, yet visual intoxication and the RADA mannerisms thought appropriate to the genre displaced good intention' (Lyttle 1996: 2).

Lyttle's claim is that no matter what the ideology of the novel adapted for screen, the form of classic adaptation itself will ensure the failure of challenges to conservative orthodoxy. His point is a contentious one, but his choice of an Austen adaptation by way of illustration would seem safe enough. Largely, although not exclusively, as a result of the series of television and film adaptations of her work in the 1980s and 1990s, Austen has become something of a conservative icon in popular culture: a canonical author whose life and work signify English national heritage and all that implies of the past as an idyll of village life in a pre-industrial society, of traditional class and gender hierarchies, sexual propriety and Christian values.[1] As Fay Weldon remarks:

> When we say 'Jane Austen' everyone knows what we're talking about. Austen means class, literature, virginity and family viewing....The clip-clop of horses over cobbles suggests the past, and the past was when jobs were safe, and bouquets flowed, not brickbats....Or one could say, with a little more charity, but not much: 'Why, we love Jane Austen because she's Heritage'.
>
> (Weldon 1995: 2)

An important part of this construction of Austen has been the peculiarly insistent discourse of fidelity that has accompanied adaptations of her work. A reverence for Austen's texts, her 'world' and her wishes has long dogged criticism of these adaptations. Thus George Bluestone – despite arguing that film and novels 'belong to separate artistic genera' (Bluestone [1957] 1973: viii) and that in adapting the novel it is inevitably destroyed – predicated his discussion of the 1940 MGM *Pride and Prejudice* on the criterion of fidelity to the text, or to what he imagined the author intended. Accordingly he praised additional dialogue in the screenplay by Huxley and Murfin as 'the kind of thing which Jane Austen *might* have said' (Bluestone [1957] 1973: 131). Reviews of the Austen adaptations of the 1980s and 1990s have continued in this vein, feeding on publicity detailing the pains taken by adapters and production teams to be faithful and authentic.[2] There is a more knowing air here than was shown in Bluestone's comments – Huxley's dialogue is mocked in the 1990s as 'all-purpose Olde England quaint, abounding in cries of "lawks a daisy" and "ah, the polka mazurka"' (Bennett 1995: 2) – but the underlying assumption is still that fidelity to the original novel and historical authenticity are both possible and desirable. Roy Hattersley, for instance, ridicules 'the sentimentalists who regard *Pride and Prejudice* as part of the national heritage, which, like the Queen Mother and the Albert memorial, must be preserved intact' (Hattersley 1995: 19). He nevertheless reflects on the BBC *Pride and Prejudice* (1995) that '[i]t is not always possible to tread exactly in the immortal footsteps. But they mark the route to the best parts of the series' (Hattersley 1995: 21). The fact that the discourse generated by Austen adaptations has so insistently been one of conservation, reverting to a notional, pre-existing standard of the original and the authentic, has worked in itself to reinforce Austen's position within conservative ideology.

If we glance aside to the field of academic literary criticism, we see that Austen has also been read as a conservative there, although this time within a context of the literature and politics of the 1790s. In *Jane Austen and the War of Ideas* (1975), Marilyn Butler argued influentially that, in keeping with anti-Jacobin or counter-revolutionary fiction of the 1790s, Austen's narratives demonstrate a distrust of individualism in all its manifestations. Conduct should not be guided alone by the feelings and judgements of the individual; the self must submit to the moral and religious order of traditional society. However, while Butler's argument found some support among critics of Austen's work, it also provoked the response that the conservatism of the novels is not clear-cut and unassailed, but more or less severely compromised. Terry Lovell, for instance, insisted that Austen's conservatism was not impermeable, and pointed to the novels' 'cross-fertilisations' (Lovell 1976: 125) between the conservative ideology of the gentry class to which Austen belonged, and the progressive ideology of industrial and commercial capitalism. Feminist critics, from the late 1970s onwards, extended this kind of critique. Sandra Gilbert and Susan Gubar, for example, read Austen's adherence to conservative ideology as a 'cover story' (Gilbert and Gubar 1979: 154) for the 'implicitly rebellious vision' (ibid.: 153) of a writer acutely conscious of the confinements of patriarchy. Mary Poovey saw Austen as fundamentally a conservative, who nevertheless recognizes the limitations of the institutions of patriarchal society and struggles to effect

compromises between her desire to control, and her attraction to the disruptive energies of some of her female characters (Poovey 1984: 181–94). In various forms, the debate between critics arguing for a conservative Austen and those who read her texts as more or less subversive and more or less feminist has continued through the 1980s and early 1990s.[3]

The fiercely contested Austen of academic criticism seems a long way from Weldon's Jane of cobbled streets and family viewing, but there are points of contact. Despite all attempts to counter the conservative Austen in academic criticism, she remains a remarkably tenacious presence within, as well as outside, the academy. Conversely, the media construction of Austen counters reverence with iconoclasm/ The BBC *Pride and Prejudice* (1995), for instance, was heralded with the headline 'Sex Romp Jane Austen' (Birtwhistle and Conklin 1995: vi) in one of the tabloids, following the calculatedly irreverent publicity for the series, including rumours of nude scenes in what was billed as the sexiest Austen adaptation yet.[4] Bingley and Darcy, said the writer Andrew Davies, were 'young animals, young chaps galloping and sweating. Chaps with thighs' (Banks-Smith 1995: 8). Austen has been marketed as, at once, sexually restrained and sexually explicit, safely in the past and less safely in the present.[5]

Certainly within academic debate – and to some degree in the media – there is evidence of impatience with the conservative Austen, but to what extent has this impatience manifested itself within the adaptations themselves? In the following discussion I will explore this issue by focusing in detail on one Austen novel, *Sense and Sensibility*, and the 1995 screen adaptation of that novel. My purpose here is, with Lyttle's comment in mind, to look at the ways in which the subversive potential of *Sense and Sensibility*, and briefly of other Austen novels, is exploited or blocked in the adaptation of her work. My method has been to use literary critical readings of the novel as a basis for a reading of the film, although I am aware that, in the light of recent work on adaptation, this approach perhaps needs some defence. Brian McFarlane rightly points to the diversity of influences on a film adaptation and insists that the literary source is just one among many contexts within which the film may be interpreted. Other influences will clearly derive, for instance, from conditions within the film industry, and from the cultural and social climate at the time of the making of the film (McFarlane 1996: 21–2). It should not be problematic to choose to focus on one rather than another aspect of the intertextuality of an adaptation – indeed McFarlane admits to having marginalized industrial and cultural contexts in his own analysis of 'the process of transposition from novel to film' (McFarlane 1996: vii). However, in practice focusing on the literary source may run the risk of appearing to privilege it over other, non-literary contexts for the film, and over the screen adaptation itself. These are tendencies associated by McFarlane with fidelity criticism, which assumes the text carries 'a single, correct "meaning"' (McFarlane 1996: 8) which a successful film must adhere to if it is to be successful. I realize that my approach may appear to imply a hier-archy of text over film, and perhaps of academic over popular culture, but this is far from my intention. Without resorting to a simplistic fidelity criticism, I hope to show that literary criticism can establish a field of possible interpretations of the text as a legitimate basis for the analysis of the interchange between text and film.

As we have seen, Austen's novels have been read by several academic critics as dramatizing a contest between conservative and radical ideologies. *Sense and Sensibility*, with its somewhat schematic oppositions and comparatively overt didacticism, has proved particularly open to such an interpretation. Marilyn Butler, for instance, argues that, for the contemporary reader of this novel, Elinor's sense and Marianne's sensibility represented rival ideologies reflecting political debate in the 1790s (Butler [1975] 1987: 182–96). Butler finds that sense is identified in the novel with intellectual objectivity, a pessimistic view of human nature, a belief in the value of nurture over nature and in prescribed, Christian standards of conduct. Sensibility, on the other hand, is characterized by subjectivity and intuition, a trust in the innate moral sense of mankind, and in the virtues of impulsive behaviour. As Butler sees it, the values of sense are firmly asserted over those of sensibility, in a manner which is typical of conservative, anti-Jacobin fiction of the period. The ascendancy of sense ensures that sensibility, identified with a 'sentimental (or revolutionary) idealism' (Butler [1975] 1987: 194), is ultimately condemned as selfish individualism. Thus the difference between Elinor and Marianne, Butler states, 'is one of ideology.... It is the role of Marianne Dashwood, who begins with the wrong ideology, to learn the right one' (Butler [1975] 1987: 192).

In this interpretation of the novel the contest between conservative and radical ideologies results in the challenge to orthodoxy being firmly put down. However, Butler briefly concedes that the ideological scheme of the novel is disrupted by the reader's sympathy for Marianne and comparative lack of sympathy for Elinor (Butler [1975] 1987: 196). Other critics have rightly refused to brush these disruptions aside, as Butler does, on the grounds that they are aesthetic imperfections in the text. The more convincing readings of the novel have been those which recognize the extent to which the contest of sense and sensibility is not resolved.

Mary Poovey sees *Sense and Sensibility* as demonstrating Austen's divided loyalties: to moral and specifically Christian principles on the one hand, and to imagination, romance and the 'anarchic desires' of her female characters on the other (Poovey 1984: 183–94). The attractiveness of Marianne and Willoughby in comparison with Elinor, Edward and Brandon, and Elinor's rush of empathy for Willoughby after his sudden arrival at Cleveland after Marianne's illness, all encourage the reader to identify with the values of sensibility. The dominance of sense, and of conservative orthodoxy, is thereby challenged, despite Austen's apparent didactic aim. Poovey notes how Austen uses narrative indirection in scenes of romance, in order to counter the identification with sensibility – 'to keep the reader on the outside of such "dangerous" material' (Poovey 1984: 187). However, the ' "dangerous" material' remains.

Angela Leighton also focuses on the dangers of sensibility, by seeking to uncover 'the voices which her [Austen's] notoriously conservative and limiting language would conceal' (Leighton 1983: 130), especially the voice of Marianne. As Marianne is progressively silenced in the novel, Leighton argues, so paradoxically she is heard all the more loudly in the 'gaps or inconsistencies or ironies' (op. cit.) of the text: 'The more her protestations of grief must be concealed and contained by an enforced Silence of public propriety and passivity, the more eloquently violent does that Silence become' (Leighton 1983: 135). It is never louder than at the end of the novel, in her marriage to Brandon (ibid.: 139).

The degree to which sensibility wields a subversive power in the narrative is clearly debatable. However, the contest between a conservative ideology of sense – entailing a belief in self-command and submission to authority – and a radical ideology of sensibility – a creed of self-expression and individualism – is a central dynamic of the novel. This dynamic is altered in significant ways in the 1995 adaptation, most strikingly in the displacement of sense by sensibility.

Much of the humour of the film adaptation, as of the novel, derives from an ironic critique of sensibility from the perspective of sense. Marianne's passionate excesses of grief and love, her habit of rushing out of doors as soon as the weather looks threatening, her love of dead leaves, are all treated in this way in the film by means of Elinor's deflating remarks or in visual irony.[6] However, at significant moments in the action, the film omits irony and allows the voice of sensibility to dominate. After Willoughby's departure from Barton, Marianne's grief-stricken, but formulaic sensibility is thoroughly ironized in the novel: she 'would have thought herself very inexcusable had she been able to sleep at all the first night after parting from Willoughby' (Austen 1979: 110). Her tears, headaches and hours at the piano, alternately singing the couple's favourite songs and crying, are presented as selfish and insensitive to the feelings of her family (op. cit.). In the film, not only Marianne, but Mrs Dashwood and then Margaret retire to their rooms in floods of tears, watched by Elinor who controls her feelings, sits on the stairs and drinks a cup of tea. This picks up on something of the novel's critique of sensibility from the point of view of sense. However, the scene then cuts to an exterior shot of Barton Cottage and then Barton Park in the rain, followed by Marianne staring out from a window seat at Barton Park. These shots are all accompanied by mournful music. Setting and score collude in Marianne's sensibility, rather than undermining it. This effect is repeated later in the film when Marianne walks in the rain through the grounds of Cleveland and precipitates a life-threatening fever. In the novel there is little sympathy for her actions. Her illness is represented as wilfully self-induced. She takes several walks in the wet grass and refuses all remedies for her cold (Austen 1979: 302). The film, by contrast, presents the illness as an accidental result of Marianne's genuine grief. There is just one fatal walk, undertaken impulsively, immediately on arrival at Cleveland, with the purpose of going to see Willoughby's house. Marianne is carried in from the garden already insensible. Again the setting and score, with rain, lowering skies and swelling strings, participate in Marianne's mood. The audience is encouraged to take the point of view of sensibility rather than of sense.

The film's score makes a particularly important contribution here. The novel's ironization of Marianne's piano playing as part of her emotional self-indulgence is picked up at the beginning of the film when she responds to her father's death by thumping out funereal tunes. However, throughout the film, the score reprises themes from Marianne's piano playing, and the music accompanying the film's opening and closing credits picks up, respectively, a melancholy piece and a love song played by Marianne.[7] The action is thus both punctuated and framed by the music of sensibility, sanctioning emotional release and self-expression, rather than self-command.

In both novel and film, Elinor's irony operates to undermine her sister's sensibility, curbing her excesses of feeling with the voice of reason, her rebelliousness with the voice of authority. However, the film also reverses this dynamic. A key scene here is in the sisters' discussion of their feelings towards Edward. Marianne is disappointed at the apparent lack of passion in both Edward and Elinor, but Elinor refuses to be drawn and will only admit 'that I think very highly of him – that I greatly esteem, that I like him' (Austen 1979: 55). In the novel the reader is directed towards approval of Elinor's reticence, over Marianne's inability to disguise her feelings. Insight is granted into Elinor's inner life where it is not into Marianne's, and the reader consequently learns the unspoken strength of Elinor's love for Edward. Elinor also gains the edge over Marianne in this exchange by using irony against her sister, who, in keeping with her incapacity for disguise, takes her completely literally. Edward, says Marianne, is 'every thing that is worthy and amiable':

> 'I am sure', replied Elinor with a smile, 'that his dearest friends could not be dissatisfied with such a commendation as that. I do not perceive how you could express yourself more warmly.'
> Marianne was rejoiced to find her sister so easily pleased.
> (Austen 1979: 53–4)

Marianne shows no such naivety in the film, where it is Elinor who appears vulnerable and ridiculous, in bed with curlpapers in her hair and clearly shaken by her sister's interrogation. This time it is Elinor who becomes the victim of Marianne's irony:

MARIANNE (*IMITATING ELINOR*): I do not attempt to deny that I think highly of him – greatly esteem him! *Like* him!
(Thompson [1995] 1996: 25)[8]

What is presented as Elinor's self-command in the novel is revealed by Marianne as her self-delusion in the film.

Thus the film adaptation gives dominance to sensibility where the novel does not; but can we conclude, on these grounds, that this adaptation for the screen has produced a more radical Austen? The political meanings that the sense/sensibility opposition had, according to Butler and others, within the context of debates between radical and conservative factions in the 1790s, will clearly have altered for a film adaptation of the 1990s. Yet to some extent this adaptation would seem to have retained the radical, political connotations of sensibility, by enhancing and updating the feminist implications of the novel within a contemporary feminist context. This becomes apparent if we look at the way in which the character of Margaret functions in the film.

Margaret, the youngest sister, is a shadowy presence in the novel, mentioned only fleetingly and with a very minor role in the action. Her purpose there would seem to be simply to emphasize the potential dangers of sensibility for an impressionable young girl, for 'as she had already imbibed a good deal of Marianne's romance, without having much of her sense, she did not, at thirteen, bid fair to equal her sisters at a more advanced period of life' (Austen 1979: 42). The temptation in a film adaptation must have been to cut Margaret altogether, but Thompson chose not merely to retain her, but to develop her role to become one of the most significant in the film.

Margaret is introduced in the film as an absence, hiding from her family in a tree-house or under the library table – 'But where is Miss Margaret?', as Fanny says, 'I am beginning to doubt of her existence!' (Thompson [1995] 1996: 12). Her absence not only alludes wittily to her comparative invisibility in the novel, but also to the repressions of those around her. Once she resurfaces, Margaret is repeatedly used in the film to articulate the feelings which are denied by the voice of sense. It is Margaret who breaks down social reserve and brings Elinor and Edward together and, when Elinor later tries to conceal the name of her lover from the inquisitive Mrs Jennings, it is Margaret who blurts out his initial. In the film, as in the novel, this is an act which brings pain to Elinor. However, the pain is tempered in the film, as it is not in the novel, by additional dialogue in which Margaret defends her frankness. Marianne, unusually taking the part of social decorum, reproves her younger sister:

MARIANNE: You do not speak of such things before strangers –
MARGARET: But everyone *else* was –
MARIANNE: Mrs Jennings is not everyone.
MARGARET: I like her! She talks about things. We never talk about things.
MRS DASHWOOD: Hush, please, now that is enough, Margaret. If you cannot think of anything appropriate to say, you will please restrict your remarks to the weather.

(Thompson [1995] 1996: 41–2)

Margaret has exposed that which Elinor, and everyone around her, attempt to conceal in the name of female propriety. Her frankness, although condemned here by Marianne, is the natural extension of the openness of Marianne's own creed of sensibility, used with the added freedom of a child to reveal the oppressive nature of social conventions of correct female conduct.

Margaret's very first exchange with Elinor establishes her ability to expose social injustice towards women:

MARGARET (V/O): Why are they [John and Fanny Dashwood] coming to live at Norland? They already have a house in London.
ELINOR: Because houses go from father to son, dearest – not from father to daughter. It is the law.

(Thompson [1995] 1996: 7)

Margaret questions a situation that Elinor, the voice of conservative orthodoxy, tries to explain away. Only later will Margaret's question resurface as a protest in Elinor, when she is out riding with Edward and responds to his complaint that he lacks a profession:

ELINOR: You talk of feeling idle and useless – imagine how that is compounded when one has no choice and no hope whatsoever of any occupation.
EDWARD *nods and smiles at the irony of it.*
EDWARD: Our circumstances are therefore precisely the same.
ELINOR: Except that you will inherit your fortune.
He looks slightly shocked but enjoying her boldness.
ELINOR (Cont.): We cannot even earn ours.
EDWARD: Perhaps Margaret is right.
ELINOR: Right?
EDWARD: Piracy is our only option.

(Thompson [1995] 1996: 19–20)[9]

Here Elinor alludes again to her predicament, and that of her mother and sisters – all disinherited by the law of primogeniture, and forced to live largely on the charity of male relatives. This time, however, she does not try to explain it away, but adopts Margaret's blunt indignation. In the novel the situation of the Dashwood women everywhere implies the socio-economic disadvantages of women in general, but nowhere are they so explicitly stated, and certainly not by Elinor, the model of reticence, submissiveness and propriety. Edward's allusion to Margaret's boyish interests in sea voyages and piracy defuses Elinor's feminist protest with humour. However, these interests also suggest not only Margaret's, but Marianne's and Elinor's desire to escape conventional gender roles and the confines of their society. Thompson's introduction of exotic travel and piracy into the film also hints at some impatience with Austen's self-imposed limits of subject matter – '3 or 4 Families in a Country Village'[10] – and with the conservative ideology those limits imply.

Thus sensibility would still seem to wield a subversive power within this adaptation of the novel. Indeed, insofar as it identifies the ideology of sensibility with the unspoken feminist protest of the novel, and then voices that protest, the film takes on a more radical edge than the novel. However, it is significant that Thompson makes the main agent of this protest a child. Of course a child's voice will not necessarily carry less weight than an adult's in a text or film, but this is the case here. Despite Thompson's additions, Margaret is still a relatively marginal presence in the film – a comic aside who disappears from the action as soon as it moves from Devonshire to London. Her views are sympathetically presented, but are also vulnerable to adult laughter. At the end of the film, while the assembled company writhe in embarrassed silence, she alone can muster the strength to discourse on the weather. This is an ironic reversal – the adults collapse in an emotional heap and the child emerges as the model of propriety. However, it also marks the beginning of Margaret's transition to adulthood and signals the necessity for women of leaving their rebelliousness behind with childish things. Thompson's use of Margaret suggests that it would be misguided to make a simplistic equation between sensibility and radical politics in the film. Indeed, on the whole the film's promotion of sensibility actively dulls the radical edges of Austen's novel.

A notable feature of the film is the way in which it breaks down oppositions which, although by no means absolute in the novel, are relatively firmly maintained there. In the novel, the sense/sensibility opposition, as embodied in Elinor and Marianne, is preserved partly by the different narrative techniques employed in presenting the two sisters. Marianne's true feelings are typically displayed in dialogue and action, where Elinor's are fully revealed only in her inner meditations – to which the reader is a privileged witness. Thus throughout the novel, at the level of narrative point of view, the reader perceives a distinction between a woman who exposes her feelings at any cost and one who conceals them lest they damage those around her. The dramatization of Elinor's inner life in the film, where her feelings are either implied or reported in the novel, has the effect of eroding this distinction. We see her, where we do not in the novel, crying in grief for her father and when she believes Marianne may die. In both scenes in the film it is clear that Elinor believes herself to be unobserved, although Edward catches her on the first occasion. However, towards the end of the film, we also see her lose control and burst into hysterical sobs in front of her family and Edward when she learns that he is not, after all, married to Lucy Steele. This is Elinor become Marianne, as is confirmed by a reprise of the music which has accompanied romantic climaxes between Marianne and Willoughby and Marianne and Brandon, and which will accompany both sisters and their husbands at the wedding scene.[11] In the novel, too, Elinor 'burst into tears of joy, which at first she thought would never cease' (Austen 1979: 350) but there she remembers to run out of the room and close the door first.

In the novel it is Marianne who gradually capitulates to Elinor's point of view. In the film Elinor has already come half-way to meet her. The result is that sensibility loses its dangerous potential, as rebelliousness is assimilated to conformism and sources of ideological conflict in the novel are smoothed over. This gives rise to some problems, as is apparent in the omission from the film of Willoughby's surprise visit to Cleveland, during which he attempts to justify himself to Elinor. This is a troubling crux in the novel because it shows Elinor as, despite herself, susceptible to Willoughby's charms, and thereby to the creed of sensibility (Austen 1979: 326). The dominance of the ideology of sense is thus, albeit momentarily, shaken. Given the breakdown elsewhere of the sense/sensibility opposition in the film, it is difficult to see how the scene could have carried the disruptive force that it does in the novel, and this may go some way to explaining the otherwise puzzling decision to cut one of Austen's most dramatic episodes.

If the distinction between sense and sensibility is eroded in the film's representation of Elinor and Marianne, it is even more clearly so in the case of their male counterparts. The three suitors, Edward, Willoughby and Brandon, are not without common ground in the novel. All three, for instance, have shown the capacity for making more or less serious errors as a result of sexual impulsiveness. A relatively clear distinction is preserved in the novel, nevertheless, between Willoughby (as a champion of individualism) and Edward and Brandon (as supporters of social conformity and self-denial). This is not the case in the film. This is partly a matter of the associations brought to the roles of Edward and Brandon by Hugh Grant and Alan Rickman, both of whom had previously been cast as romantic leads, most notably in *Four Weddings and a Funeral* and *Truly, Madly, Deeply*.[12] In the novel, Willoughby is the only romantic hero – and even here his status as such is undermined by irony. The film gives us three romantic heroes for the price of one and does away with much of this irony, for instance replacing the acerbic anti-climax of Willoughby's fate in the novel – 'He lived to exert, and frequently to enjoy himself' (Austen 1979: 367) – with a shot of him gazing at the nuptials of Marianne and Brandon, the image of the Byronic outcast.

In both novel and film, Edward and Brandon provide an implicit and explicit critique of the values by which Willoughby lives, but by recasting them as romantic heroes the film softens and eventually dissipates this critique. This is particularly striking in the case of Brandon, who is remade in Willoughby's image. Brandon is introduced unobtrusively in the novel by Sir John as one of his acquaintances, 'neither very young nor very gay' (Austen 1979: 66). In the film he makes a dramatic entrance, riding up to Barton Park and entering the house as if drawn from nowhere by the Siren voice of Marianne, singing at the piano. He then falls in love with her at first sight. The scene is mirrored by the romantic entrance of Willoughby, who appears suddenly in a rain storm, again on horseback, to rescue the injured Marianne. The theme from Marianne's song at Barton Park also accompanies her courtship with Willoughby.[13] Later, Brandon literally takes over Willoughby's role in the novel, by providing Elinor with the justification of Willoughby's behaviour that Austen had Willoughby himself deliver on his night visit to Cleveland. Then, in a scene added by

Thompson, Brandon carries the unconscious Marianne in from the rain after her fateful walk at Cleveland. Again, this time even more clearly, the image echoes the earlier scene where Willoughby carries Marianne into Barton cottage after she has sprained her ankle. The music is the same used for Willoughby and Marianne at the Barton Cottage picnic.

By recasting Brandon in this way, in the mould of the romantic hero of sensibility, the film again tends to dispel the conflicts which exist in the novel. This is most apparent when we look at the capitulation of Marianne to the creed of sense, sealed symbolically by her marriage to Brandon. Critics of the novel, as we have seen, have been troubled by Marianne's fate. Her reformation might even seem brutally forced upon her by Elinor and Edward, for whom she is little short of a sacrificial lamb:

> They each felt his [Brandon's] sorrows, and their own obligations, and Marianne, by general consent, was to be the reward of all.
>
> With such a confederacy against her – with a knowledge so intimate of his goodness – with a conviction of his fond attachment to herself, which at last, though long after it was observable to everybody else – burst on her – what could she do?
>
> (Austen 1979: 366)

In the film adaptation, the problematic nature of Marianne's fate is neatly avoided. Brandon has been the hero of sensibility all along, and Marianne gets her Willoughby after all.

Paradoxically, the prioritizing of sensibility in this adaptation of *Sense and Sensibility* would seem to promise a more radical version of the text, but ends by giving us a more conservative one. What might be read as the repressed feminist protest of the novel surfaces in the film through the character of Margaret, but her status as a child and a relatively marginal character serves to dissipate the potential power of this protest. The fact that the novel's distinctions between sense and sensibility are broken down in the film, smoothes over ideological conflicts within the novel, and defuses the subversive potential that sensibility has, particularly in the novel's later stages.

Other recent film and television adaptations of Austen's novels show similar conflicts between the desire to enhance and to deny the radical edge of Austen's texts.[14] *Clueless* (1995) – which transposes *Emma* to Beverly Hills in the 1990s – at once parodies and exploits the conventions of romantic comedy as they operate in film and fiction. The ending, for instance, plays with the audience's expectation of a wedding between Cher (the Emma figure) and Josh (the Mr Knightly figure). The marriage is signalled, then denied, with a wedding between Miss Geist and Mr Hall, the Mr and Mrs Weston figures, instead. However, the wedding is then delivered symbolically after all in the final close-up shot of a kiss between Josh and Cher, holding the bridal bouquet. There are other, similarly compromised attempts at disrupting romantic finales in adaptations of Austen's work. In the BBC *Persuasion* (1995), the closing image is of Anne on board a ship, beside her new husband, an invention which recalls Mrs Croft's bold behaviour in accompanying her husband to sea, and which suggests, as the novel does not, a less than conventional Mrs Wentworth. However, the earlier addition of a close-up kiss between Anne and Wentworth, in the midst of a street carnival in Bath, and the backdrop of a flaming sunset in the final scene, lend a new sense of romantic closure to this least comfortably concluded of Austen's novels. The handfuls of coins tossed in the air at the marriage of Marianne and Brandon in the Columbia *Sense and Sensibility* remind the audience of the material base of romantic delusion, a theme present throughout both novel and film. Yet here, as in so many other Austen adaptations (notably the 1995 BBC *Pride and Prejudice*), the wedding scene functions principally as a visually sumptuous romantic climax, smoothing over troubling aspects in the narrative. The closing chapters of the novels, by contrast, do not dramatize, but summarily report the marriages of their heroes and heroines and are concerned, rather, with uncomfortable moral reckonings and glimpses into the future, happy and otherwise.

Michael Ryan and Douglas Kellner have argued that one of the symptoms of the conservative backlash in American society in the 1970s and 1980s was a return to the 'resolution-oriented narrative of the classic Hollywood cinema' (Ryan and Kellner [1988] 1990: 9). The gestures against traditional romantic finales in recent Austen adaptations may suggest a reaction against this state of affairs in the 1990s, but, if so, it is without much conviction. Ryan and Kellner find cause for hope in relation to Hollywood cinema in the 1970s and 1980s in their belief that 'it is in the very nature of conservative reaction to be indicative of the power of forces which threaten conservative values and institutions' (Ryan and Kellner [1988] 1990: xi), so that 'by attempting to pacify, channel, and neutralize the forces that would invert the social system of inequality were they not controlled, ideology testifies to the power of those forces, of the very thing it seeks to deny' (Ryan and Kellner [1988] 1990: 14).

One might equally argue that the power of conservative ideology is enhanced by its display of the capacity to deny such forces, whether or not that denial fully takes place. In relation to recent Austen adaptations, this would certainly seem to be the case. Austen has been radicalized on screen to the extent that, borrowing Angela Leighton's terms, some of her silences have been made to speak. However, the conservative Austen is still an indomitable presence. The film heroines can voice feminist views and the heroes be portrayed as new men (witness Hugh Grant's Edward), but the fact that the texts offer a way back to traditional, romantic roles is seized upon as eagerly as it was in the 1940 *Pride and Prejudice*. The Columbia *Sense and Sensibility* and other recent adaptations of Austen's novels capitalize on the subversiveness of her work, but more so on the fact that its subversiveness may be so safely contained.

Notes

1 These adaptations include *Pride and Prejudice* (BBC, 1980); *Sense and Sensibility* (BBC, 1980); *Mansfield Park* (BBC, 1986); *Northanger Abbey* (BBC, 1987); *Persuasion* (BBC, 1995); *Pride and Prejudice* (BBC, 1995); *Sense and Sensibility* (Columbia Pictures, 1995); *Emma* (Miramax, 1996), and *Emma* (BBC, 1996).
2 See, for example, Birtwhistle and Conklin 1995.
3 For a useful survey of this debate, see Clark 1994: 1–25.
4 Mr Darcy was seen in the bath. According to Andrew Davies, speaking at the Jane Austen Day at De Montfort University in Leicester (November 1995), Darcy was also intended to be seen swimming naked, but Colin Firth was unwilling to take off his clothes.
5 See also the British press advertisements for *Emma* (Miramax, 1996), selling the film as both classic and racily up-to-date: 'A new comedy from Jane Austen's timeless classic', 'Everything you don't expect from a classic: humour, energy and a fast pace' (*Harper's Bazaar*).
6 See, for example, the running joke at the expense of Marianne's misplaced optimism about the weather:

> MRS DASHWOOD: Marianne was sure it would not rain.
> ELINOR: Which invariably means it *will*.
> > (Thompson [1995] 1996: 52)

and Marianne to Margaret:

> Is there any felicity in the world superior to this?
> > (ibid.: 50)

juxtaposed with a shot of rain clouds and a rising wind.
7 The music is by Patrick Doyle.
8 The speech as screened contained slight variations: 'I do not attempt to deny that I think highly of him – that I greatly esteem him! That I *like* him!'
9 As screened there are slight variations: '...when one has no hope and no choice of any occupation whatever.'
10 Jane Austen, letter to Anna Austen, 9 September 1814 (Le Faye 1995: 275).
11 The relevant scenes are Marianne saying goodbye to Willoughby at the Barton Cottage picnic and being carried in from the rain by Brandon at Cleveland.
12 A parallel might be drawn here with the casting of Laurence Olivier as Darcy in *Pride and Prejudice* (MGM, 1940), after his appearance as Heathcliff in *Wuthering Heights* (Samuel Goldwyn, 1939). See George Bluestone's description of Olivier's performance in *Pride and Prejudice*: ' Behind the stiff formality of Darcy's face and dress, there smoulders the anguish of Emily Brontë's stable boy' (Bluestone [1957] 1973: 136).
13 See the scene in which she outlines Willoughby's silhouette.
14 Ros Ballaster argues that the BBC *Pride and Prejudice* and *Persuasion*, and the Columbia Pictures *Sense and Sensibility* all escape from the domestic interiors of the novels 'with a concomitant shift from the domestic to the public politics of the period', and all show 'a new interest in the eroticized athletic male body as the object of the camera's gaze', but that the viewer nevertheless comes to identify with the male protagonists, at the expense of the female, whose 'mobile intelligence' still has to be adequately represented in an Austen adaptation (Ballaster 1996: 10–13).

5

FROM *EMMA* TO *CLUELESS*

Taste, pleasure and the scene of history

Esther Sonnet

In 1995, *Clueless* – Amy Heckerling's high school/shopping mall movie – was a box office and video rental 'sleeper' hit, making $54 million for Paramount and later providing the 'original' source for an ABC TV spin-off sitcom series more specifically targeted at a teen audience.[1] Pocket Books and Paramount Pictures capitalized on the tremendous success of the film with a book version, written by H.B. Gilmour, author of *Clarissa Explains It All: Boys, Ask Me if I Care*, as well as the novelization of *Pretty in Pink* (dir.: John Hughes, 1985) and fifteen other teen fictions. As a portrait of contemporary youth culture, *Clueless* has its literary and filmic antecedents in the critically despised 'teenpic' genre that emerged in the mid-1950s as a result of the fragmentation of mass cinema audiences into age-specific consumer groups.[2] In the film, Cher/Emma Woodhouse (Alicia Silverstone) is a wealthy mobile phone-toting sixteen-year-old, with a moneyed but largely absent lawyer father. Her life revolves around fashion and designer culture which includes a computerised wardrobe that allows her to model clothes . on screen and then on Polaroid ('I don't trust mirrors') before committing herself to her day's sartorial choice. In language, attitude and social behaviour, Cher's life is humorously depicted as an intellectually vacant and trivialized exis-tence enjoyed only by an economically over-privileged and socially exclusive Beverly Hills style elite. However, what separates *Clueless* from teenage-centred movies – such as Heckerling's earlier *Fast Times at Ridgemont High* (1982) or John Hughes' *Sixteen Candles* (1982), *Ferris Bueller's Day Off* (1986) and *Some Kind of Wonderful* (1987) – is its claim to be a 'loosely based' film version of Jane Austen's *Emma* (first published in 1816). The plot centres on Cher's benev-olent attempts to transform a new girl, Tai/Harriet Smith (Brittany Murphy), from grungy Bronx skateboarder into Calvin Klein-clad fashion queen. The 'makeover', however, backfires when Tai, now more snobbishly popular within the Rodeo Drive school clique, fails to fit in with Cher's plans for a match between the socially superior Elton/Mr Elton (Jeremy Sisto) and Tai. Cher's loss of social pre-eminence forces her into some recognition of her limitations. The emotional mess created by first Elton's rejection of the infatuated Tai and then the refusal by James Dean- or Luke Perry-clone Christian/Frank Churchill (Justin Walker) of Cher's offer of her highly prized virginity provokes a reconsideration of her arrogant assumptions, leads to an awakening of new moral values and, finally, brings Cher to a recognition of her true romantic feelings for her older and wiser step-brother Josh/Mr Knightley (Paul Rudd).

But what effect does the literary parallel have on 'reading' a film whose plea-sures are evidently produced out of the 'low' cultural intertexts of *Beverley Hills 90210* and the teenpic films such as those of trash-meister Roger Corman? Does the transposition of Austen's nineteenth-century literary English comedy-of-manners into a contemporary American high school film necessarily have to invoke the usual critical response: that such 'adaptation' only indicates the 'dumbing down' of high culture, of low culture masquerading as high art? The critical climate in cultural studies is now dominated by constructions of post-modern culture as one in which differentiation between high art/low culture, art/entertainment and knowledge/pleasure is held to be increasingly irrelevant. In this respect, one could cite the fact that *Clueless* provided the opportunity for journalists and Internet contributors from both Britain and the USA to engage in the exercise traditionally accorded to the literary film adaptation: of charting the movie's equivalence in terms of characters, scenes and plot, and of identi-fying omissions or divergences from the original source narrative.[3] Some reviewers were content simply to list the obvious parallels, while others have websites dedicated to extended academic articles exploring such Lit. Crit. orthodoxies as 'Character Transformation in *Emma* and *Clueless*' or '*Emma* and *Clueless*: A Hundred and Eighty Years of the Carefree Imagination'.[4] I would argue that instead of effacing the 'difference' between the two texts, as a 'modern-day *Emma*' *Clueless* does not *collapse* high/low culture binaries, but invokes them in an increasingly complex circulation of meanings around distinc-tions of contemporary taste and aesthetic value. To support this, it is important to remember that *Clueless* appeared at the same time as a welter of what may be termed 'literal' film adaptations of Austen novels. Though Douglas McGrath's film version of *Emma* (starring Gwyneth Paltrow, Juliet Stevenson, Alan Cummings, Ewan McGregor and Jeremy Northam) appeared six months after Heckerling's film, screen versions of *Persuasion* and *Sense and Sensibility* had already prefigured its concerns. By taking both the literal and the loosely based adaptation conjointly as instances of postmodern cinema, the films raise perti-nent questions around the contemporary organisation of high/low cultural distinctions. More directly, they indicate processes of reading film which are differentiated by pleasure, gender, spectatorship and taste. First I shall use Fredric Jameson's theory of the nostalgia film (Jameson 1983, 1984 and 1991) to identify the specific ideological operations of the 'literal' literary film adapta-tion, before, second, locating the function of 'the literary' in the updated remake *Clueless*.

Jameson's conception of film in '*le mode rétro*' rests on a critical distinction between 'historical films' and those he identifies as definitively postmodern in their display of 'historical pastiche'. The latter – exemplified by a diverse range of film texts that includes *Star Wars* (1977), *Raiders of the Lost Ark* (1981) and

Body Heat (1981) – are, he contends, 'beyond history'. The historical pastiche film, which may not even consciously locate its diegesis within a recognisably 'historical' past but rather within a resolutely contemporary one, is nonetheless defined by Jameson as an 'alarming and pathological symptom of a society which has become incapable of dealing with time and history' (Jameson 1983: 117). Postmodern historical pastiche is evidence of a deeply disturbing failure of cultural consciousness that he finds in a contemporary loss of the function of 'historicity':

> Historicity is, in fact, neither a representation of the past nor a repre-
> sentation of the future (although its various forms use such
> representations): it can first and foremost be defined as a perception of
> the present as history; that is, as a relationship to the present which
> defamiliarizes it and allows us that critical distance from immediacy
> which is at length characterised as a historical perspective.
>
> (Jameson in Brooker and Brooker, 1997: 25)

For a Marxist who cannot forsake a politics of representation in which 'histor-ical perspective' is the marker of 'critical distance', aesthetic replays – pastiches, remakes, adaptations – of past historical forms are constructed on 'intertextu-ality' as a 'deliberate, built-in feature of the aesthetic effect, and as the operator of a new connotation of "pastness" and pseudo-historical depth, in which the history of aesthetic styles displaces "real" history' (Jameson 1984: 67). I want to set aside the objection that Jameson's concept of pastiche leaves no means by which to distinguish *Emma* from *Clueless* – both being intertextual 'aesthetic replays' – but to note instead that, within this context, the recent proliferation of film adaptations of nineteenth-century novels (Jane Austen, George Eliot, E.M. Forster, Thomas Hardy, Henry James, Edith Wharton, Nathaniel Hawthorne) serves only to confirm a contemporary aesthetic dominated not by 'historicity' but by its *failure*. With a 'classic' literary text as lost origin, cinematic costume-dramas seem destined to corroborate the postmodern shibboleth of the 'waning' of historical thinking and domination of nostalgia in late twentieth-century Western post-industrial cultures. But there is a paradox here: if 'historicity' has failed, why are there so many contemporary examples of a film genre which, it seems, attest instead to a widespread *fascination* with the 'real' of 'history'? That is, why bother to represent the past at all if it is a 'dead' cultural category? Further, many commentators (including Creed 1987, Denzin 1988 and Garrett 1995) have countered that Jameson's terms are so crudely drawn that his notion of pastiche cannot address the real complexities of current 'historical' films. Thus, if the chief source of Jameson's anxiety derives from his insistence that 'pastiche' is solely a matter of *textual* features (which are unproblematically given to determine a 'historical' film's 'depthless' semantic horizon), it is impor-tant to move beyond lamenting the loss of some ill-formulated version of 'real' history and consider instead what *function* they perform for audiences in their invocation. All texts bear relations to their contexts of production and these relations are profoundly historical: my concern is for the ways in which 'the past' is mobilized so that the meanings presented by the literary film adaptation for its contemporary audience are *rehistoricized*. In other words, the repetition of films in the category 'historical literary adaptation' makes sense only if broader cultural contexts of their reception locate their 'failing' of historicity on a different terrain – on that of the *pleasures of its performance*. To do this, a more culturally located – and thus more historically sensitive – analysis might better reverse the usual model of film text–spectator relations by de-privileging the film text in favour of extratextual and intertextual 'knowledges' brought to bear on the film's reception. By considering the 'meaning' of film as being in part produced through 'knowledges' formed through what Pierre Bourdieu has analysed as the larger social construction of 'taste', it is possible to see how the shared relation to Jane Austen's *Emma* functions in *Emma* and *Clueless* to invoke distinct cultural discourses which specifically and a priori define the cinematic pleasures offered. Further, it should then be possible to grasp that these are postmodern pleasures, both differentially and simultaneously defined, which are indicative of contemporary formations of 'taste cultures'.

As both are films that claim some affiliation to Jane Austen's novel, the first issue for consideration is how they are differentiated according to their relations to a high cultural *literary* text. For French sociologist Pierre Bourdieu (1984), all forms of cultural production (clothes, films, books, furniture, art, music) are intricately enmeshed in 'systems of distinction' through which social and economic class inequalities are produced and perpetuated. Individual ownership of 'cultural capital' is accrued through formal education and social class culture so that 'engagement with certain cultural commodities...distinguish the participating subject from other members of social formations' (Uricchio and Pearson 1993: 9):

> In cultural consumption, the main opposition, by overall capital value, is between practices designated by their rarity as distinguished, those of the fractions richest in both economic and cultural capital, and the practices socially identified as vulgar because they are both easy and common, those of the fractions poorest in these respects. In the intermediate position the practices are perceived as pretentious, because of the manifest discrepancy between ambition and possibilities.
>
> (Bourdieu 1984: 176)

Cinema is itself enmeshed in organizing value distinctions, which draw upon a similar vocabulary of 'taste hierarchy'. As William Uricchio and Roberta Pearson's study of Vitagraph Pictures' 'quality films' produced between 1907 and 1913 ably demonstrates, the history of popular cinema has from its inception been involved in 'reframing' high culture. For Uricchio and Pearson, prestigious 'films deluxe' – literary adaptations of Shakespeare and Dante, historical recreations of Napoleon and Washington, as well as biblical epics – are complex events which belie a straightforward Arnoldian interpretation of their social function, in which elite literary texts are used to provide moral edification for a barely literate and dangerously uneducated mass. The historical conditions of early cinema's low cultural nickelodeon audiences make it clear why the 'quality picture' might be invoked at this time as counter to the unregulated pleasures of the mass audience for 'cheap amusements' – as part of attempts to make cinema 'respectable' for the new middle-class audiences. But the still-current tendency to view high cultural 'literary taste' and 'art' as instruments for a top-down form of social pacification fails to account for the *historically shifting* conjunctions between high and low culture. Uricchio and Pearson's work is useful for illustrating that relations between 'classic' literature and cinema are always the result of 'constant negotiations and contestations within any social order' (Uricchio and Pearson 1993: 8). This Gramscian formulation avoids conceiving of relations between 'high' and 'low' as an unproblematic flow of dominant values between classes, from producers to consumers, and instrumentally from film to audience. Inflecting this further within Bourdieu's schema, however, refines the notion that 'taste' and 'cultural distinction' are used by 'classifying subjects who classify the properties and practices of others, or their own' by 'appropriating practices and properties that are already classi-fied (as vulgar or distinguished, high or low, heavy or light etc. – in other words, in the last analysis, as popular or bourgeois) according to their probable distribution among groups that are themselves classified' (Bourdieu 1984: 482). That is, *Emma* is a prime example within a film genre open to a variety of taste groups whose readings are determined by the level of cultural capital that they command. Further, the film itself can be understood as an occasion for the performance of cultural power through the exercise of cultural 'distinctions'.

Through its faithful screenplay and dialogue produced 'in consultation' with academic literary scholars, historical locations selected in accordance with archi-tectural specialists from the National Trust and attention to accurate period costume/interior décor with advice from V & A museum experts, the contem-porary historical film adaptation is embedded in an extratextual network of pre-existent fields of 'distinction' which are aggregated to it. In this sense, film readings are produced out of the mobilization of cultural capital by which spec-tators both 'classify' and are therefore 'classified'. This would account for a two-way process that typifies the broader cultural construction of historical literary film adaptations.

The first of them is the use of 'experts' to authenticate the film, which works to minimize perceived distance between literary original and filmic re-presentation, thus accruing to it the 'value' distinctions necessary for what Bourdieu terms the proper 'aesthetic attitude' required by 'legitimate culture': refinement, literary sensibility and artistic discrimination. The second is the intense media interest in how the 'experts' (such as the Jane Austen Society) feel about a treasured literary classic being adapted for a mass medium and 'whether Jane would like it'. Here, the potential *paucity* of the film version with regard to the original novel or the historical veracity of its translation is measured to reveal Bourdieu's 'manifest discrepancy between ambition and possibilities'.

Between them, the discourses of authenticity construct the historical literary film adaptation as a site for deploying 'knowledges' at a level at which 'practices [are] designated by their rarity as distinguished'. However, it is usual to view the aesthetic 'disposition' that Bourdieu identifies as the hegemonic value of bourgeois 'legitimate culture' as a purely *intellectual* exercise of discrimination. Critically distanced and detached, it is symbolically powerful for its 'refusal of any sort of involvement, any "vulgar" surrender to easy seduction and collective enthusiasm' (Bourdieu 1984: 35). However, given that the 'literariness' of the film adaptation clearly works to efface its existence as a mass-media experience, this would miss an important point that *Emma* (1996), *Howards End* (1992) or *Age of Innocence* (1993) are not themselves high literary events. What is needed is an account of the operation of 'distinction' that also fully respects the adaptation as *popular cinema*. Expressly, I want to explore the notion that it is the convergence of the exercise of class-determined extratextual 'taste' with the specifically filmic conditions of popular cinema that identify an intrinsic and distinguishing mode of cinematic spectatorship – a definitive mode not of intellectual detachment but of *visual pleasure*.

As in other instances of the genre, the film adaptation of *Emma* is significant for its *overmarking* of 'history'; but using Bourdieu to identify how operations of 'taste' inform the pleasures of the historical literary film adaptation also pulls into focus what Jameson's analysis of the nostalgia film effaces: that those pleasures of cultural consumption simultaneously perform *contemporary* social and economic power relations. Of particular consideration here are the means by which late twentieth-century concerns around sexuality and gender are enacted. For it is evident that the pleasure of *Emma* is in part ensured by the 'rightness' of a social order in which heterosexual femininity and masculinity are given. This does not run counter to the pleasures of the exercise of cultural 'distinctions' already put forward but is, rather, an important dimension of them. This is to suggest that cultural capital as it is manifested through 'taste' *also* organizes the field of sexuality in contemporary historical literary film adaptations. To elucidate this, Bourdieu's broad schema can be supplemented with Michel Foucault's thesis that sexuality is not a 'natural', 'timeless' or even 'essential' quality of human existence, but that these qualities are discursive effects of specific social, historical and cultural *construction* (Foucault 1978). For Foucault, the production of Western sexual pleasure is inextricable from forms of discipline: taboo, prohibition and interdiction do not 'repress' an otherwise fully formed sexuality (as in a Freudian model of libido) but are the very mechanisms through which sexuality is produced. The prevailing conception of dominant cinema as a cultural form fundamentally imbricated in patriarchal structures of visual pleasure, and often more narrowly with representations of sexuality, suggests that the spectators of the 'literary film' genre might be offered specific pleasures which nonetheless conform to the same principle: to *an intentionally solicited experience of repression.*

In this context, Martin A. Hipsky's reading of 'Anglophilic' Merchant–Ivory adaptations – *Room With a View* (1986), *Howards End* and *Shadowlands* (1993) – is germane. The 'elements of setting, architecture, landscape, furniture, interior design, costumes – pretend to exist as markers of a kind of filmic social realism':

> Meticulously reproduced, these elaborate layers of setting are what take us back to the era depicted. And yet in these movies the setting is over-powering – is in fact *superfluous* to plot, history, and character portrayal. We are given an overdose of what I would call 'circumambi-ence'; we do not need it to transport us back into the period depicted. Instead, circumambience functions as escapist fantasy, a spectacular excess of signification that is unironically meant to provide great sensual pleasure.
>
> (Hipsky 1989: 102)

As many film theorists (who have followed Laura Mulvey's argument that, in Hollywood cinema, visual pleasure is deeply implicated in structuring libidinal drives and in the constitution of patriarchal sexual identities) would contend, film spectatorship is always a matter of visual pleasure – regardless of genre or narrative (Mulvey 1975). The historical costume adaptation, then, offers a distinctive organization of visual pleasure in which 'spectacular excess' of 'circumambience' functions to incite visual pleasure through sensory overload. For Hipsky, this sets it apart from the dominant visual pleasures of the 'carnal heterosexuality' of Hollywood blockbuster movies such as *Basic Instinct* (1992) and *Sliver* (1993) or, I would add, from the kinetic spectacles of action, sci-fi or thriller films. The absence of mainstream eroticism, which narrows sexuality and sensuality to soft-core sex acts, instead imbues clothing, landscape, piano-playing, letter-writing and conversation with a dispersed and diffuse form of sexuality that represents for Hipsky a 'refreshing transgression' from genitally driven representations. For my argument, this further confirms the spectator in Bourdieu's space of 'distinction' in differentiating a qualitatively 'superior' mode of 'genteel' spectatorship from that demanded by most mainstream film narratives. It is the libidinal corollary to the exercise of 'taste' through cultural capital: it invites spectators to partake in a simulated analogue of the very struc-tures of 'refined sensibility' upon which the genre predicates its 'historical' diegetic world. But the Marcusian 'de-sublimated' libidinal economy suggested here is nonetheless countermanded by an overarching structure of class-bound social repression: 'what these films' main characters generally seek is a perfect balance between the expression of libidinal energies and the powerful counter-forces of middle-class Tradition, Convention, Reason, Discipline and Order' (Hipsky 1989: 104). However, Foucault's theory can recast this Freudian model of libido as an otherwise 'healthy' and 'natural' force or drive, which is malformed through social – thus individual – repression. For Freud, repression is the psychical denial of sexuality and fear of its explicit depiction: it is a painful process which produces reaction-formations in forms of hysterical and/or neurotic symptomologies, but beneath repression lies a more adapted and adjusted psychical arrangement. However, few have ever considered the *pleasure* that repression might entail. What needs to be recognized is that, in the histor- ical literary drama, the intensification of visual pleasure in 'circumambience' is not the *symptom* of sexual repression, the sign of its 'will to power'. Rather, this pleasure is made available only in the intentional *performance* of repression. Again, this indicates a form of spectatorship specific to the genre which, as a site of pleasure now freed from the 'vulgar' trappings of carnal sexuality, fabricates 'repression' through an over-investment in 'the look', in gestures, fleeting glances, failed speech, clamped emotions and frustrated intentions.

It is clear that such an economy of repressed pleasure works to deliver moments of intense erotic charge – most famously in the 'Darcy effect' of the BBC's serialization of *Pride and Prejudice* (1995) – but spread throughout the genre. However, this indicates the *gendered* nature of spectatorial pleasures offered here, and shifts attention to the historical literary film adaptation as a female-addressed 'women's genre'. The emergence of Darcy (Colin Firth) from a lake in diaphanous wet shirt led to an explosion of articles in national newspa- pers, magazines and television shows attempting to answer the question: 'Why did the emotionally repressed Mr Darcy send the nation's women into a swoon?' (Aitkenhead 1995). Apart from fulfilling the romance genre's require- ment that the masculine hero must be unable to express his emotions and should transform 'from icy, arrogant bastard to warm, caring individual' (ibid.), a general feature of contemporary film adaptations of Austen novels is a visual eroticization of the male body, effected largely through the cut and styling of costume. While the spectacularization of the male body in recent films has been well documented for muscular figures such as Jean-Claude van Damme, Arnold Schwarzenegger and Bruce Willis within male-addressed genres, analyses have often been underpinned by a concern for the homoerotic nature of representa- tions of the male body (Neale 1983; Dyer 1993; Tasker 1993). That they have largely excluded questions of *women's* relationship to men as erotic spectacle is, I would suggest, of primary importance to modes of female spectatorial plea- sure. The 'Darcy effect' suggests that the contemporary historical literary adaptation has become a site of licence for female visual/sexual pleasure. It is significant, however, that it is a remote past which both permits and confines expression of specifically female desires to a form of masculinity that has been the ideological staple of popular cultural genres from Gainsborough costume- pictures to historical romance sagas and the formula fictions of Mills and Boon: English, 'aristocratic', white, heterosexual, Christian, asexual and romantic.

To return, then, to Hipsky's use of the concept of 'escapist' fantasy to account for the libidinal pleasures of the genre, it makes little sense to approach the historical literary adaptation as a film form predicated on an absolute *loss* of contemporaneity. Instead, rather than regard 'circumambience' simply as a mechanism for inducing a suspension of the prevailing sexual economy, it is better to pursue it as a symbolic space firmly embedded in contemporary cultural concerns. The circulation of meaning between current constructions of white, heterosexual female subjectivity, the historical film adaptation and spectatorship is a complex one. It evidently underpins the question Barbara Creed raises of the nostalgia film: 'Exactly what is it that modern audiences wish to feel nostalgic about?' More pointedly, she asks: 'Does this nostalgia take a different form for men and women?' (Creed 1987: 45). For Creed – and for Doane and Hodges (1987) and Friedberg (1993) – the answer is clear enough: nostalgia 'can hide the discontinuities between the present and the past; it falsifies, turning the past into a safe, familiar place' (Friedberg 1993: 188). So much can be argued from the general view that nostalgia is a necessarily retrogressive narrative form, but the implications of 'pastness' are more complex when posed in the gendered terms suggested by Creed. Friedberg pinpoints what is at issue here by arguing that nostalgia is an '*algia*, a painful return, but it also offers up pleasures, albeit bittersweet ones. The compulsion to repeat is based in the desire to return' (Friedberg 1993: 189). The proliferation of historical costume dramas in the 'post-feminist' 1990s can thus be read not simply as the *absence* of contemporary concerns but a rather more disturbing 'longing' for a 'return' to a specifically pre-feminist past, and to the sureties of a social order grounded in a stability of gender-fixed positions. Both male and female spectators are offered the pleasures of a spectacle of history immune from contemporary uncertainties around gender identity, personal and political struggles for economic independence, and personal autonomy in marriage, relationships or parenting. In place of these, obedience to class hierarchy through formal courtship, female dependency and economic powerlessness, the power relations of kinship exercised through marriage, and the social consequences of infractions of codes of etiquette, construct a past in which tightly defined gender roles are the bedrock of domestic, political and social order. Unlike, say, Sally Potter's adaptation of Virginia Woolf's *Orlando* (1994), which insists on the mutability of gender (Garrett 1995), or Jane Campion's *The Piano* (1994), which offers to re-envision the terms of historical female subjectivity (Bruzzi 1996), the scene of history in *Emma* works to naturalize and to confirm fixed, stable and 'natural' sexual identities which, for the duration of the film at least, offer a 'return to outworn values', thus 'erasing the effects of all intervening history' (Freidberg 1993: 188).

Reading the postmodern historical literary adaptation as symptom of a popular cultural antifeminist articulation of nostalgia for an unchallenged patriarchal order may in itself be enough to account for its emergence. But at a deeper level it also signifies what Lyotard has characterised as the 'attempts of the patriarchal order to disguise the fact that "there is no signifier"' (Creed 1987: 46) and of which Baudrillard has argued: 'When the real is no longer what it used to be, nostalgia assumes its full meaning. There is a proliferation of myths of origin and signs of reality...a panic-stricken production of the real and the referential' (Baudrillard 1983: 354). The film's overall representational strategy of 'historical authenticity', a regime of representation governed by verisimilitude, thus takes on a different function in this context: to fabricate a symbolic *mise en scène* to stage the 'real' of the patriarchal order. This puts a new slant on the loss of historicity felt by Jameson. As Creed pertinently asks: '...isn't it possible that the "missing past" which lies at the heart of these films is that which once validated the paternal signifier?' (Creed 1987: 46). Moving from this to *Clueless*, it is clear that Heckerling's adaptation sets itself precisely against the seriousness of the class- and gender-determined visual pleasures of the 'literal' adaptation. By presenting itself as a 'modern-day' *Emma*, *Clueless* claims some consideration for its relationship to the novel, even if the film is explicitly framed by the *licence* it takes with regard to the book. Moreover, the 'commercial' *Clueless* appears alongside its more 'cultured' movie-sibling and this, I suggest, raises further issues around the relational organization of contemporary 'taste' and the deployment of cultural capital.

If Austen's literary text works to stabilise the semantic horizon of the spectatorial pleasures afforded by its popular cinematic adaptation, *Clueless* proposes a quite different relation to its textual 'origin'. It does not signal itself as 'past', and therefore does not cue in the 'gentrification' effect I have argued typifies those 'literary' adaptations that make up 'highbrow' popular cinema. Instead, the resolutely contemporary setting of *Clueless* plays as much *against* its source as it does with it. The film is filled with literary and other high cultural references that attest to a 'double-coded' audience address. One of the pleasures offered by *Clueless* is its frequent invocation of spectatorial possession of the 'capital value' of high cultural knowledges. When another teenager attributes the quotation 'To thine own self be true' to Hamlet, Cher triumphantly identifies that it actually comes from Polonius – she knows because she has seen the Mel Gibson movie. Similarly, Cher's scheme to match two teachers (in the self-interested hope of better grades) leads her to leave an anonymous copy of one of Shakespeare's love sonnets in Miss Geist's locker. Her best friend Dion is enraptured: 'That's so beautiful. Did you write that?', to which Cher replies incredulously: 'No – it's a way famous quote' – 'Where from?' – 'Cliff's Notes'. Dickens' *A Tale of Two Cities* is playfully misquoted as: 'It is a far, far better thing doing stuff for other people'. The jokes are sophisticated plays on the discrepancy between those that have the cultural capital to 'read' the film through prior knowledge of literary culture and those that do not. From the point of view of those that do, *Clueless* generates real humour from an audacious undervaluing of the social value of culture. Nubile young women are 'Botticelli chicks', a woman who looks good from afar but a mess close-up is known as a 'Monet', Friedrich Nietzsche and William Burroughs are used as style statements to differentiate boys in their 'post-adolescent idealistic phase' from those in 'contempo–casual land', and sculptures by Claes Oldenberg are used decoratively without any real respect for their 'legitimate' worth. Though hardly as formalized as in Bahktin's formulation of carnivalesque as a site of popular subversion, *Clueless* can be read comparatively as a deliberate destabilization and healthy refusal of the 'class-appointed' spectator positioning that its 'literal' counterpart in *Emma* solicits. However, what can be termed the film's *cultural catachresis* (a deliberate misplacing of categories of cultural knowledge) is most revealing here because it clearly understands the currency of high cultural knowledge but actively contests its value for a generation grounded in a 'total material availability' (Appleyard 1995) afforded by postmodern commodity culture.

For Cher, the shopping mall is both the public space that offers the pleasures of female *flaneurie*[5] and an intimate space, a 'sanctuary where I could gather my thoughts and regain my strength'. Similarly, Tai's 'makeover' conforms to the post-*Pretty Woman* format of personal/female transformation – the most poignant cinematic trope for the acquisition of new personal identity via the symbolic imaginary of the constructed 'self' of 'taste'. In its exhibition of conspicuous consumption and display of fashion and lifestyle taste-codes, *Clueless* invokes a contemporary culture defined by consumption, shopping and fashion, and asserts the global currency of Christian Dior, Donna Karan and Estée Lauder for a global capitalist elite. The 'double-coding' of the film, then, offers another audience the pleasure of asserting the 'value' and 'distinction' of style and commodities against seemingly irrelevant and outdated high cultural capital. In its allusions to the failure of this capital to command any value whatsoever, *Clueless* is highly symptomatic of profound shifts in the real organization of 'late' or 'postmodern' economic and cultural capital. In late twentieth-century postmodernity, *cultural* (and not only material) wealth is measured through consumption, and style *is* high culture: the new globally distributed middle and upper classes utilize 'bodily presentation and lifestyles as indicators of social status' (Featherstone 1991: 110). But Bourdieu's point is that formal economic categories and cultural capital do not necessarily entail one another. With style and consumption choices indicative of the ownership of high cultural capital, the prospect of being able to 'read' class and status (real economic power) from those choices becomes increasingly unstable. As Featherstone notes, shifts in the global organization of postmodern capital have marked effect at the level of culture:

> If postmodern points to something it is the eclipse of a particular coherent sense of culture and associated way of life which was dominant in the Western upper and middle classes which set the tone for the culture as a whole...the notion of a common culture as a goal; as based on an educational formative project, as something unified, a totality of knowledge (the classic in literature, music and the arts) which had to be struggled through to improve the person. Along with it went the notion of a cultured or cultivated person...since the 1960s

the process of cultural de-classification has seen the decline and relativisation of this ideal.

(Featherstone 1991: 110–1)

Set against the ideologically oppressive class sureties of *Emma*, *Clueless* repositions the meaning of literary value within contemporary codes of social signification which subsume it. In this, it mobilizes extratextual 'taste' formations and 'knowledges' that contest those that support the 'literal' film adaptation of Jane Austen's novel. I would argue from this that, for *Clueless*, Creed's 'missing past' is that which once validated the deep-rooted organic connection between high culture and a ruling economic elite, a validation that literary culture once seemed to guarantee.

In this sense, for all its frothy humour and celebration of 'depthless' surface identity, *Clueless* registers real anxieties around the increasingly hegemonic values of a taste elite that actively contest older, traditional class-based hierarchies. This is mirrored in the increasingly complex analysis cultural critics might make of the film. It resists easy assimilation into high/low categories of interpretative value that the internal schema of 'distinction' between the two film adaptations might at first imply. Despite this, though, my analysis effaces the undeniable entrenchment in symbolic power held by *Emma* over *Clueless* in the construction of cinematic 'taste' hierarchies.

Notes

Acknowledgement to Peter Stanfield for productive discussion and evaluation while writing.

1 The television series (which did not star Alicia Silverstone, but was written, produced and directed by Amy Heckerling) was originally scheduled at 9.00–9.30 PM (ETZ) as part of a 16–21 demographic for TGIF – Friday Nights on ABC – then shifted to UPN at 8.00 PM in September 1997 where it was ranked as forty-sixth most popular show.
2 For a fuller history of the Hollywood teenpic genre, see Doherty 1988.
3 For example:
   http://www.geocities.com/Hollywood/Theatre/1229/emmaclueless.html
   http://family.starwave.com/reviews/conners/archive/co082695.html
   http://uts.cc.utexas.edu/~churchh/clueless.html
4 Jordie Margison, 'Character Transformation in *Emma* and *Clueless*' at http://www.pemberley.com/janeinfo/maclulss.html; Jodi Servatius, '*Emma* and *Clueless*: A Hundred and Eighty Years of the Carefree Imagination' at http://imctwo.csuhay ward.edu/faculty_dev/Jodi/Paper.html
5 Much literature on contemporary consumption supports the view that shopping and the public performance of the *flaneuse* indicates that women are more aesthetically skilled in the art of consuming 'taste'. See Falk and Campbell 1997.

6

IMAGINING THE PURITAN BODY

The 1995 cinematic version of Nathaniel Hawthorne's *The Scarlet Letter*

Roger Bromley

This chapter will explore the ways in which Puritanism was organized around a set of principles which elevated mind, reason and order, over the body, emotion and nature which were equated with chaos. The latter trio were also closely identified with the figure of woman, particularly the woman's body as the primary source of sin: hence the extensive attempts that were made to curb any sense of women's agentive activity. The 1995 film version of the novel *The Scarlet Letter* reverses the characteristic privileging hierarchy of Puritanism, but in making space for women as agents it succeeds only in inverting its organizing principles in the form of contemporary hedonism. In the process, the central dynamic of the text's conflict is reduced to the level of an individual struggle in which, ultimately and fairly easily, the sovereign self triumphs over the oppressive constraints of society. The problem to be resolved is confined to the body of a particular woman, not the larger question of the challenge of the body (of woman) to Puritanism. It is a liberal version in which society is simply a medium through which the individual seeks expression, rather than the complex individual/community dialectic which is the source of the novel's problematic. Even if in the novel, as Leverenz has argued, 'the narrator has established a broad array of sympathies joining feminism, nature, youth, the body, and imaginative life' (Leverenz, in Murfin 1991: 267), these features do not manage to displace their oppressive opposites with the ease registered in the film.

The novel and its context

The Scarlet Letter is about *governance* – the action of governing and the state of being governed. One seventeenth-century use of the term referred to 'wise self-command' which is very appropriate to this particular text. Governance for the Puritan was very much concerned with the body as the primary object of intervention – not just the physical body but, more importantly, the desiring body: bodies of desire. The 'city on the hill' of Puritan discourse was an ordering space, the continuous Order which is 'the regimen that bodies pass through;

the reduction of randomness, impulse, forgetfulness; the domestication of an animal, as Nietzsche claimed, to the point where it can make, and hold to, a promise' (Wellbery, in Falk 1994: xv).

'Domestication', with its particular gendered inflection, is an essential part of Puritan discursive ordering, and is contrasted with the 'wild' and 'wilderness', the literal and metaphorical space of bodies and pleasures. Puritan fundamentalism was a literalism, a reduction of the contingent and the affective to the rational, the uniform and the univocal. The concept of the body takes priority over the concept of the subject. In a sense this led to the need for continuous regulation and surveillance, as, in David Wellbery's terms, bodies are multiple, as well as being layered systems, and finite and contingent products. The link between the body and self-formation was carefully policed – bodies could not know themselves, but were directly involved in a political field: 'power relations have an immediate hold upon it [the body], invest it, mark it, train it, torture it, force it to carry out tasks, to perform ceremonies, to emit signs' (Foucault [1984] 1991: 173). *The Scarlet Letter*, as will be seen, is about the conflict over the signs emitted/omitted.

As Pasi Falk has pointed out, for Lacan subject-formation takes place at the intersection of the body and the signifier, whereas Derrida and Kristeva focus on the intersections of body, self and culture (Falk 1994: 6). *The Scarlet Letter* encompasses both aspects insofar as one of its principal themes is the relation between the body of (the) woman, Hester Prynne, and the signifier 'A', which the patriarchal order seeks to reduce to a literal, denotative, singular and absolute signification. The text as a whole is concerned with controlling the boundaries of the body, the self and culture. The location of the community on the edge of the shore and at the borders of the 'wilderness' makes this boundary-setting agenda very clear – the sea and the forest are both arenas associated with the female body and with the possibilities of desire. Body, self and culture have to be articulated with the closures and codes of the social order, predicated upon a Calvinist concept of sin. The book is structured around the conflict between culture (rational, ordered, male) and nature (inchoate, evil and irrational, female), with society's very survival in the wilderness depending on the outcome of the struggle, according to those responsible for governance. The text is composed of endless binaries confounded by dispersals of meaning, complexification and elaboration.

Part of the complexification is produced by the tension between what, in Bakhtin's terms, might be called a 'residual' medieval body marked by openness and flexible boundaries, and a modern body in which 'all of the orifices of the body are closed' (Bakhtin 1968: 320). The possibility of interiority is shut off. In a sense, the Puritan anatomy, closed and rigid, gave rise to a monochromatic culture in which consumption (mouth), sexuality and the excremental are all closely monitored (with its original sense of admonishment). It is a punitive society because it is so insecure and, in a sense, over-determined. Expressivity, interiority and the symbolic – forms of individuality – are seen as threatening to the 'monologic' of the community.

Hawthorne is, of course, writing of Puritanism in a period of Romantic thought, where the inner, the expressive and the 'individual' were all pressing for attention. The 'expressive' position is defined by Charles Taylor in the following way: 'Fulfilling my nature means espousing the inner élan, the voice or impulse. And this makes what was hidden manifest for both myself and others' (Taylor 1989: 374). The hidden/manifest dialectic is at the root of the Puritan social formation. The 1995 film version of the novel exceeds this model of expressivity by over-simplifying the self/society distinction and adding a dimension of hedonism. As many critics have pointed out, the period Hawthorne treats in the novel is as much drawn from a complex nineteenth-century culture as it is from an earlier period. Roland Joffé's film offers a *mélange* of contemporary concerns but makes no attempt to articulate the complex layering of the novel. For example, as Leverenz has pointed out: 'As a solitary, victimized woman Hester can rethink all social relations, but as a mother she has to nurture conventional womanhood, in herself as well as her daughter' (Leverenz, in Murfin 1991: 269). The film's 'rethinking of all social relations' is not just a distortion of the novel, it fails to address the complex situation of women in contemporary society, as though the conflict expressed by Leverenz – Hester's maternity – is no longer relevant. The Louise Woodward case, with its vilification of the dead child's mother, suggests that the issue has not yet gone away.

Puritan society, understandably in some respects given its provenance and vulnerability, was based upon frugality and a negative perspective on the body and corporeality. It was a renunciative culture, anticonfessional. The disciplinary techniques of Puritanism – the Word, the court room, the prison and the scaffold – were developed in a world in which 'individual or collective subjects...are faced with a field of possibilities in which several ways of behaving, several reactions and diverse comportments may be realized' (Foucault 1982: 221). Governance and power required the maintenance of an order based upon the continuum of individual and collective codes, the enclosing of the field of possibilities, and the reduction of the several and diverse to the singular and the same. Bodies of difference were anathema.

In *The Consuming Body*, Pasi Falk has traced the sovereignty of reason as a discourse of Puritanism which was predicated upon the limiting of corporeality (desires and needs). In this process, he argues, the soul was redefined as rational and calculating will which 'transformed the body into a medium for action based on rational will and especially action furthering personal interests' (Falk 1994: 50). Increasingly, therefore, this reason/body duality came to see sin as connected with the body of desire. Confinement of the body was an essential task of the regime. As Falk shows, the bourgeois Puritan reason/body binary was centred around the nature and culture duality.

The Scarlet Letter is, therefore, much more than a simple individual/society conflict, and can be seen as an exploration of a founding moment in bourgeois social formation (it is set during the first phase of the Puritan revolution in England, 1642 to 1649). The political process is one in which a community of dissenting, excluded 'others' founded their power and authorized themselves by offering ontological security in return for a monopoly of the means of legitimated physical and symbolic violence. This monopoly was sustained by the construction of a territory and set of boundaries which conferred a sovereign self-identity – an imperial self – on its subjects by structural intolerance of all that was 'other' (a 'chosen' people, and elect, takes its meanings from the 'not chosen') and by the maintenance of an authoritative discourse – sacred, scriptural, timeless and fundamentalist in its closure of interpretation – which was predicated upon a civilized/barbarian absolute binary. If the novel *is* an allegory, it is of state formation and its founding contradiction – the pathological act of violence out of which the 'civil' constitution grew. The passage from a 'natural' to a 'civil' state is a complex and unstable form of *political* subjection. It is above all, as the novel shows, a *gendered* subjection. For all its apparent immersion in 'feminist' discourses and multiculturalism, the 1995 version of the film ultimately succumbs to a set of patriarchal and racist values which, although generated out of Hollywood, would not have been out of place in seventeenth-century New England.

Perhaps in compelling Hester Prynne to wear a scarlet letter, the community elders were seeking to confine and reduce the flows of blood to a single literal meaning, *their* meaning: by so doing woman is brought symbolically *within* the law. An observation by Héritíer-Augé is helpful in this respect:

> What man values in man, then, is no doubt his ability to bleed, to risk his life, to take that of others by his own free will; the woman 'sees' her blood flowing from her body...and she produces life without necessarily wanting to do so or being able to prevent it. In her body she periodically experiences, for a time that has a beginning and an end, changes of which she is not the mistress, and which she cannot prevent. It is in this relation to blood that we may perhaps find the fundamental impetus for all the symbolic elaboration, at the outset, on the relations between the sexes.
>
> (Héritíer-Augé 1989: 298)

This is quoted in Arthur Frank's essay 'For a sociology of the body: An analytical review' (1991), which I have found the most comprehensive and valuable account of the body for my purposes. At one point, Frank says: 'The dominating body's response to its sense of its own contingency, its dissociated self-relatedness, and its dyadic other-relatedness are all configured by lack' (Frank 1991: 79). This configuration of lack is at the centre of the Puritan patriarchal discourse in the novel, as is the differentiated experience of blood which produces a different response to contingency, as Frank argues. 'Symbolic elaboration' and 'flows' are inimical to the postural fixities of masculinized Puritan discourse. The novel traces the course from the monological *custom-house* (Bourdieu's *habitus*) and market-place (Puritanism was an economic project also) to the 'ever-glowing point' of the dialogical ending: 'On a field, sable, the letter A, gules'. The heraldic figuration carries the black of Puritanism *as well as* the red of blood, of contingency, of the possibility of difference. This returns us to the opening of the novel where the rose-bush, juxtaposed with the weight and blackness of the prison, exists on the threshold of the narrative and on the threshold of the symbolic.

As the whole novel turns on interpretation and the literal/symbolic antagonism, representation is a crucial issue. The central conflict is between 'how one chooses to represent one's own body [and]...how society provides for bodies to be presented' (Frank 1991: 45). The Salem community provides the scriptural text, the dwelling-house, the meeting-house, the market-place, the prison and the scaffold for the presentation of the body. By metaphorically removing Hester's 'blood' and transforming it to the letter on her breast (a dangerous site), the community externalizes its fear of the internal flow: 'Desire can only operate on objects by turning them into signs' (Frank 1991: 64). In the end, Hester appropriates the signifier, transfigures it and uses it to represent her own body 'of her own free will'. *The Scarlet Letter*'s 'Conclusion' conveys this in a form which 'resumes' the whole text by acknowledging that '*there was more than one account* of what had been witnessed on the scaffold' (Hawthorne [1850] 1986: 270; my italics). The final section reminds us of the narrative complexity and diversity, the subtle process of exchange between encoding and decoding, and the means by which a community *stories* itself and seeks to establish a hegemony of code and ideology.

The community of the novel is a society on the threshold; the novel is about the struggle over forms of representation, means of encoding. Above all, it stages the Puritan attempt to render the correlation between signifier and signified unidirectional and confined. The process of signification and elaboration breaks down the attempt by the Puritans to appropriate nature, birth and reproduction as masculine experience. The resulting *body politic* has to remain a constant source of vigilance – its legitimation and domination perpetually open to 'more than one account'. For all its energy and endeavour, and given the complexity of both men and women (shown as 'masculinized' and unmerciful), the governance of Salem includes, but cannot ever finally contain, oppositional spaces. The encoding 'state' constitutes itself as the Symbolic Order, in the name of the Father, and through the *letter* of the law – but is always unsettled by those ever-present 'absences' which may cause it to reconstitute itself: the absolute/dynamic dyad. The monadic transaction can never ignore/refuse the *trans*, the crossing, the transgression of arbitrary territorial boundaries, internal or external. Above all, what the Puritans sought, and what Hester Prynne and Pearl refuse by their contingency, is *predictability*, manifested in their failure to conform with the disciplined body. As Frank argues: 'with regard to desire, the disciplined body understands itself as *lacking*. What it lacks is itself; the regimentation does not remedy this lack, but it can forestall total disintegration' (Frank 1991: 55).

The appropriately named Chillingworth, Hester's estranged husband, *embodies* this lack; his revenge on Dimmesdale is a revenge on the lack which is himself. In the wilderness, he has 'gone native', the posture and regimen disintegrate. Resuming his place in the 'civilized' society he can only remedy his lack by domination of another, by a process not of creating himself but of destroying another self/himself. The productive, reproductive and contingent are all seen as dangerous: 'the danger is being alive itself'. In the whole community, Chillingworth is the most dissociated from himself. When he is introduced in the novel he is wearing 'a strange disarray of civilized and savage costume' (Hawthorne [1850] 1986: 87). He occupies the 'dangerous space in-between' – the space of heterogeneity. The 'Indian' at his side is the nomadic and the heterodox.

That the community is a field of possibility and potentially dialogical is shown by the fact that Hester is not killed. The logic of 'monologic' suggests the 'persistence of female sacrifice' (Theweleit 1987: 370), but the community holds back, gives itself space for choice and 'reformation' despite its deep fears of the fluidity and contingency of the 'woman taken in adultery'. Perhaps the community 'unconsciously' is protecting itself, its own lack, aware that the unknown father of the child, Pearl, is *within* the society and has potentially enacted the desire of every one of them. It is, in other words, a knowing society which refuses to make manifest what it knows. In this way, it can both sustain its ideological assault and its moral certainties, while at the same time avoiding the risk of disintegration by 'installing dark territories, sources of terror and anxiety, in and on people's own bodies and the bodies of those they desired' (Theweleit 1987: 415). This helps to create 'fear and uncertainty, of people's feeling that there were many places within themselves that no one could enter – neither they themselves, nor anyone else. Those were the territories occupied by the gods, the police, laws, Medusas, and other monsters' (Theweleit 1987: 415).

In other words, Hester could not be sacrificed because the community needed her *body* – outcast – to sustain their own ideology and to shore up the territories occupied by God, the Bible, the Law and the prison. The body of Hester re-presents the dark territory, the sources of terror and anxiety. As Shari Benstock has shown: 'Woman's body serves as the space where social, religious and cultural values are inscribed (quite literally in Hester's case); moreover it produces the very terms of that inscription: Pearl *is* the scarlet letter in human form' (Benstock, in Murfin 1991: 289). (This is something the film misses entirely in its double representation of Pearl, as child and as adult narrator.) Silenced, Hester becomes the medium through which the community speaks its contradictions and ambivalences: both *lack* and the body of desire. Ultimately, she is performative: 'the body seeking to break out of the codes in which it cannot express itself and find self-expression in a code of its own invention'

(Frank 1991: 85). Whatever else it stands for, as I shall argue later, the letter 'A' stands for 'autonomy'; the phrase 'as if of her own free will' which is first used when she issues from the prison, is repeated in the conclusion. The chosen/choosing conflict runs right through the text.

As Benstock has argued, 'the patriarchal construction of femininity, based on masculine fantasies of the female body, is the sign under which sexual difference parades itself in our culture' (Benstock, in Murfin 1991: 291), yet the film, in liberating the woman's body from those fantasies and giving Hester some authority over her own identity, allows no scope for an exploration of the 'patriarchal fears of female sexuality' nor for that 'other' femininity that cannot be controlled:

> this other feminine, which is not visible to the eye of man, is the place where representation is obscured and where interpretation fails. Refusing to expose itself to public view or to mouth the words it has been culturally assigned, this 'other' femininity unsettles orders of patriarchal logic, rendering as nonsense the stories by which culture explains itself to itself.
>
> (Benstock, in Murfin 1991: 291)

This links up with my comments below about 'disclosed presence', but the problem with the film is that in representing disclosure as something freely chosen by Hester, as though cultural assignment is not deeply prescriptive and inscribed, patriarchal logics are simply discounted rather than unsettled; there is no 'other' femininity (except that sustained by Mistress Hibbins), as 'what you see is what you get': in its explicitness the film leaves no scope for other representations or interpretations.

On the other hand, the second chapter in the novel, 'The Market Place', epitomizes many of the features of Puritan culture of the mid-seventeenth-century period. It is very much a *public* culture, with an emphasis on the seen and the manifest underpinned by an empirical, fundamentalist mentality which allowed no scope for interpretation, the indeterminate, or the figural. It presupposes an absolute correlation between seeing and knowing. This chapter places Hester in the 'public gaze' and there are numerous references to a scopic regime of 'disclosure', perspectivalist in the sense that:

> the gaze of the painter *arrests the flux* of phenomena, contemplates the visual field from a vantage-point *outside the mobility of duration*, in an eternal moment of *disclosed presence*.
>
> (Bryson 1983: 94; my italics)

Although Bryson is speaking of the 'founding perception' of the Cartesian perspectivalist tradition, the phrases I have italicized could well be applied to Puritanism insofar as it sought to arrest flux, to stand outside the mobility of duration by positing an 'eternal' city on a hill, and it allowed no 'absence' or concealed interiority but insisted on disclosed presence. However, as Benstock points out, 'Hester Prynne stands before the crowd not "fully revealed" as the text claims, but fully concealed, her sexual body hidden by the cultural text that inscripts her' (Benstock, in Murfin 1991: 300). By revealing the sexual body, or rather a contemporary version of it (more of a 'sexy' body), the film dispenses with the cultural inscriptions which form the basis of the text and converts the novel into a Hollywood romance. In the book, 'The Market Place' chapter is a disclosure, a moment of the unreturnable gaze where the observed does not look back at her spectator: it is a reifying action of looking. The Puritan eye is an absolute eye, the eye of God. It is a framing device. Surprisingly, the film version does not make much of this scopic regime in which everything has to be brought into the public focus, made representable: brought into cultural *legibility* through a literal 'optic' purified of all ambiguity – 'the heavy weight of thousand unrelenting eyes, all fastened upon her, and concentred at her bosom' (Hawthorne [1850] 1986: 84). This compulsory visibility is part of the optical paradigm of power, defined by Allen Feldman as: 'Within a system that is dependent on the alternations between embodiment and disembodiment, visibility and invisibility, power is defined in terms of increasing distance and disengagement from the body' (Feldman 1991: 127).

Despite the objectifying gaze of the crowd, Hester Prynne is able to make of the scaffold a point of view from which she is able to trace her past trajectory. This section (Hawthorne [1850] 1986: 85) consists of a series of visual terms ('saw', 'beheld', 'look', 'bleared optics') used metaphorically to see (in the mind's eye) beyond the Puritan look and the Puritan location to a complex, heterogeneous, metropolitan vision of Europe. Thus is she able, even when transfixed by the absolute and reifying *masculinized* gaze of the local, to fashion another account, another version than the closed-down reality confronting her. The baroque, elaborate letter on her breast embodies this 'other' vision, a world of paradox and contradiction confronting a society of regulation with the possibility of risk and contingency.

The following chapter, 'The Recognition', where Chillingworth and Hester face each other in silence, operates upon a similar set of visual codes. His invasive and penetrative look is included in the public gaze, but another dimension has been revealed by their tacit agreement not to uncover their relationship:

> When he found the eyes of Hester Prynne *fastened on his own*, and saw that she appeared to recognize him, he slowly and calmly raised his finger, made a gesture with it in the air, and laid it on his lips.
>
> (Hawthorne [1850] 1986: 88; my italics)

The society of the 'disclosed presence' is *unsettled* by the riddle of the child's father, and the mystery of Chillingworth's identity. From the opening sequence of a public and manifest event – Hester is 'punished *in the sight of* rulers and people' (Hawthorne [1850] 1986: 88; my italics) – the text and the community is plunged into enigma, the hidden, dissimulation; all 'out of sight' of 'man' and, by implication, perhaps God. Hester is only able to return the gaze of the stranger but she is relieved to be distanced from him by the presence of the crowd: 'She fled for refuge, as it were, to the public exposure' (Hawthorne [1850] 1986: 90). There is no simple 'public bad/private good' dichotomy, as the 'private' is a source of pain and anxiety.

Beyond the 'sages of rigid aspect', the Reverend Arthur Dimmesdale, a young and learned clergyman (the father of Hester's child) is called upon to speak of the 'mystery of a woman's soul, so sacred even in its pollution'. The sacred/pollution dyad is at the heart of the text and has been discussed above. Dimmesdale addresses Hester and urges her to reveal the name of the child's father, but when she steadfastly refuses to speak (crucial to a community of the 'Word', of *revealed* truth) he is unable to complete his discourse. When Hester vanishes from the public gaze and returns to prison, she has left a community with the unseen, the unknown and the unspoken – all inimical to its 'eternal moment of disclosed presence', its culture of *immediacy*: a public moral space lodged in the 'Word'. As Feldman has argued in another context, confession is crucial to the generation of 'truth':

> The past act of transgression and knowledge of the past are defined by the interrogators as an absence hidden by the presence of the body with its own depths and recesses. Confession is the inversion of this relation between the absent past and the body's present. The body is unfolded in order to expose the past in discourse.
>
> (Feldman 1991: 136)

This absence/presence dialectic runs throughout the text and, in a sense, Pearl is the present outcome of Hester's bodily unfolding, conceived in that absent past.

The 1995 cinematic version of the novel

To my knowledge, there have been eight film versions of *The Scarlet Letter* and one mini TV series since 1904. Five of the films were silent versions (1904, 1907, 1911, 1917, 1926 – the latter starring Lillian Gish as Hester Prynne), the 1934 and 1995 adaptations were American, and the remaining one was Wim Wenders' *Der Scharlachrote Buchstabe* (March 1973). The TV series was a PBS version in 1979. The 1995 Roland Joffé film was rated 'R' for sex and violence. Wenders has virtually disowned his version which was a complete critical and commercial failure. For the purposes of this essay I have been concentrating upon Joffé's 1995 film which, as the opening credits state, was 'freely adapted from the novel by Nathaniel Hawthorne'. As we shall see, 'freely' is very much the operative word.

71

The 1995 Roland Joffé version is very much a hybrid text which conflates parts of the novel with Arthur Miller's *The Crucible*, Maryse Condé's *I, Tituba, Black Witch of Salem* and what can only be called a pastiche of feminism: about half of the film covers material constructed prior to the opening of the novel. With a number of stars (Demi Moore, Gary Oldman, Robert Duvall and Joan Plowright), it seems designed to provoke contemporary fundamentalism by conferring on Hester and Dimmesdale an ongoing sexual relationship and an *autonomy* which are both at the core of bourgeois ideology, but take no account of the Puritan context of an authoritarian theocracy. The film celebrates their 'true romance' in a way that takes no account of the ways in which historical, or contemporary investments in the 'origin' narrative of liberal capitalism are constructed through discourses of power. Historicity and the political are repressed, all structuring determinations other than those of individual agency are evacuated. A historical and canonical text is used to sanction, or supplement, that liberal individualism of the 'end of history'.

At the same time the film does try to 'thicken' the context of the Puritan settlement in the light of an understanding not available to Hawthorne. The opening sequences represent the very strong presence of nature, the wilderness, and people it with the Native Americans whose culture and territory were threatened by the Puritans. The chants, dance and fires highlight the ceremonies of those 'othered' by the Puritan. The scale and numbers suggest another kind of narrative, post-quinquennial in some respects. The problem is that this narrative is sentimentalized by using Dimmesdale as the link figure between the two communities, empowered by his fluency in the local language, translating the Bible into Algonquin. The fact that Chillingworth also speaks the language gives the text a certain (over-simplified) symmetry, as well as suggesting that the Native American presence is really a pretext for siting a 'conversion' narrative (the Puritan community accommodates 'praying Indians', and Dimmesdale has his Tonto, Johnny Sassamon) within the struggle of a white male hegemony. The Algonquins achieve their meaning as the 'savages' at the root of Chillingworth's destabilized personality and his alternative medicines, and as translated into society by the agency of the white minister.

I mention these things by way of suggesting that the film introduces a number of 1990s preoccupations in an over-schematic, formulaic and gestural way. In this world, the stars matter more than the stares. The original narrative is filleted for material which will serve as a vehicle for a blockbuster. This is not necessarily a problem, as successful popular films have been made as adaptations from canonical texts (Hardy and Austen are the most obvious examples). A director like Ang Lee, for example, could have produced a film in which the central moral conflicts and power relationships derived from a sense that sin, adultery and penitence were *culturally* meaningful, and that gendered power relationships were at the heart of real deprivations and repressions. Adapting the novel for the 1990s it is incumbent upon a director to trace ethical and cultural analogues, if they wish to do more than produce a period piece. One thinks of

Figure 6.1 The Scarlet Letter (1995), starring Demi Moore as Hester Prynne

Loncraine's *Richard III*, Luhrmann's *Romeo + Juliet*, or Michael Bogdanov's 1998 BBC television version of *Macbeth*, set on the Ladywood Estate in Birmingham.

Although attempting to devise a proto-feminist text, the whole narrative process is in a sense predicated upon its romance ending. The decision to cast Dimmesdale as a heroic active figure (over-)played by Gary Oldman, converted the revenge motif into a form of melodrama, and reduced the central Chillingworth/Dimmesdale relationship into a struggle over a woman. What it is essential to remember is that in the novel, Hester – although pilloried and outcast – remains in and of the Puritan community in terms of her spiritual and cultural values. She accepts her fate but transfigures it by her integrity and 'witness'; Pearl is the free spirit, the creature of choice and freedom. In the 1995 film Hester becomes Pearl in a sense, a caricature feminist, while Pearl is reduced to becoming little more than a static toddler. There is no sense of what Kristeva called the 'semiotic chora' that Hester and Pearl inhabit at moments in the novel, and that is foregrounded in Chapters 16 to 19, as discussed below.

Although Hester finally embraces the community's values and remains in the settlement, her actions are not simply the 'accommodation' described by Sacvan Bercovitch, nor do we as readers unequivocally 'enact the same ideology of liberal consensus that his novel celebrates and represents' (Bercovitch, in Murfin 1991: 357). Bercovitch takes no account of the extensive forest inter-lude, covered by Chapters 16 to 19, in which Hester introduces Pearl to Dimmesdale, after she has thrown herself into Dimmesdale's arms and then removed the scarlet letter from her bosom and thrown it 'to a distance among the withered leaves' (Hawthorne [1850] 1986: 219). Momentarily, she and Dimmesdale feel released, exhilarated and revitalized, bright and radiant and 'breathing the wild, free atmosphere of an unredeemed, unchristianized, lawless region' (Hawthorne [1850] 1986: 219). In other words, Hester may ultimately compromise but the memory of the 'forest walk' cannot be utterly erased, so her acceptance is conditional and unillusioned, symbolically passing to Pearl in these chapters the liberation denied to herself. For all the celebration of nature and of Hester's 'sex, her youth, and the whole richness of her beauty' (Hawthorne [1850] 1986: 220), the text carefully places limits upon this inter-lude. When Hester discards the letter 'A' it falls among 'the withered leaves', showing that nature itself is subject to time, and it rests 'on the hither verge of the stream', tantalisingly close to – 'a hand's breadth' away from – but signifi-cantly not *in* the water.

In a sense, the 1995 filmic interpretation of the novel takes its cue from this section of the novel – the woman liberated from the formal bonds and signs of a patriarchal society – but it is inattentive to the withering of the leaves, the passing of the light, and to the fact that the letter remains (with)in, if not of, what turns out to be the conflicted space of freedom. The film uses Pearl as a voice-over narrator relaying her mother's story in retrospect, although we never see the mature Pearl and are uncertain as to where she is located. The main burden of Hester's narrative is the quest for independence, and she is portrayed as actively transgressive of the rules and order of the community. Her intention of seeking a house of her own is the first sign of this independence. In the novel, Hester's only 'transgression' is her forbidden love for Dimmesdale, and her independence grows organically from her ethical position. In the film the independence seems more a question of posturing or attitude; it predates her 'sin'. The novel shows independence as a condition generated by her refusal to reveal something which she regards as private to a society whose very survival depended on 'disclosed presence' and a culture of the public gaze. Independence is achieved through conflict, her autonomy is not a creed but a praxis. Nor is it an expression of romantic individualism for, as Nina Baym has demonstrated, 'almost nothing that she does in *The Scarlet Letter* can be labeled as an example of romantic individualism' (1981: 53).

Hester enters the 'filmic' community as 'headstrong' and performs a number of actions which mark her out as independent; she has a bathing machine, she bids for indentured labour and a slave (Mituba) at auction, drives her own carriage and goes into the forest on her own. In the forest she is seen as a creature of nature, enhanced by sound, image and touch. The stress is on her sensuality, brought into focus when she sees Dimmesdale swimming naked in the river. The scene that follows epitomizes Hester's 'conditional' feminism. Her carriage gets stuck in the mud and she is rescued by Dimmesdale/Rochester/ Alec D'Urberville, who guides her through the forest as she follows his horse – skilfully ridden at great speed over very difficult terrain. This establishing cliché marks the most prominent of Hester's four core relationships: with Dimmesdale, with Chillingworth, with the female 'commune' of Harriet Hibbins, and with the Puritan authorities. For all her independence, Hester is dependent throughout on Dimmesdale as rescuer, scholar, pastor, lover and, ultimately, companion. In contrast to the novel, Dimmesdale is the active figure; even when weakened by Chillingworth, Dimmesdale's vulnerability exercises a certain power over Hester. After their initial clandestine meeting, Hester keeps on being 'introduced' to Dimmesdale and their 'forbidden' romance takes shape.

In this film version, Mistress Hibbins (played by Joan Plowright) is the older woman of the novel and is the centre of a group of 'outcast' women, condemned as witches living between the Puritan community and the wilderness. Initially, this seems like an extremely interesting conception, an alternative community cherishing the memory of alcohol, dance and bawdy songs in a new world where the whipping post has replaced the maypole. Hester is commended by Harriet for her knowledge of 'simples' and is welcomed as a kindred spirit. For Hester, however, the community is simply a resource, a site of opportunist 'feminism', whereas the women who dwell on the edges have, under Harriet's leadership, gradually converted their unchosen situation into a condition of choice and relative autonomy. Harriet knowingly represents herself in a stylized form to suit the Puritan settlement: 'the wilds at night are my natural territory, especially at full moon!' The representation of Harriet is one of the strengths of the film, especially as she knowingly embodies 'the myth of an unrestrained feminine libido that operates *independently* of cultural codes [which] is a male fantasy-fear' (Benstock, in Murfin 1991: 298). Potentially, this is a very creative adaptation of a minor presence in the novel, but is little more, in the end, than an enabling device, a 'feminist' gesture, which is very much in the background of the central romance – the heroic but vulnerable male and the superficially independent female ('Reader, I sailed away with him'). The Native Americans perform a similar function to the outcast women – a resource in which a form of liberty (hedonism) 'does not take easy to bridle and bit': 'No man should', Hester says. The Native Americans are 'liberals' *avant la lettre*, a site and source of individualism. The film works throughout with this over-simplified individual/society conflict – missing the dialectic of independence (of the 'elect') and dependence at the heart of Puritanism. It is a dehistoricized adaptation.

In the novel, Hester refuses to name Dimmesdale as part of her own penitence and integrity, whereas in this film she says that if he speaks it denies her right to stand up to the society's hypocrisy. It is the difference between an explicit and an implicit approach. Hester, in the film, is charged with heresy for arguing that the laws of men are but the imagination of mortals and for claiming to speak directly to the deity. The challenge to patriarchy is, quite properly, foregrounded in a 1990s adaptation, and the scenes in which the men object to the women's meetings 'because no ordering men' are present, condemn their discourse as idle chattering and sentence Hester to prison for her 'adulterous' pregnancy, are all made possible by the insights and analysis of feminist discourse. Her confinement in prison also provides an opportunity to extend this dimension, with Harriet Hibbins visiting regularly and acting as midwife. Later, when Harriet is brought to trial as a witch, she is irreverent and defiant, and Hester Prynne speaks up for her saying that here is no witchcraft, and that Satan is not present among the women but, if anywhere, is among the men.

These are all valid interpretative additions to the novel, vitiated as I have said by its upbeat post-feminist ending which makes the emphasis on women's struggle seem gratuitous. Another interesting variation from the novel is the role of Hester's black slave, Mituba (Tituba from *The Crucible*), although her characterization as the mute shadow of her mistress is based upon a number of racist stereotypes, including that of the faithful, naive black retainer. In one of the first scenes in which she is present, Mituba (concealed) watches her mistress's body in a way that transfers the voyeuristic gaze to the mute, female slave as surrogate for the forbidden Puritan male look of desire. Similarly, when Dimmesdale and Hester make passionate love among the grain and the seed (another symbolic link with nature marked by a lack of subtlety), Mituba sensually mimics her mistress's desire by undressing herself alone, entering the bathing tub and masturbating. All this is in the presence of a small bird, seen as an analogue of freedom, but later denounced by the Puritans as one of the guises of Satan. Mituba is the go-between for Hester and Dimmesdale, but

confronted by Chillingworth and brought before the magistrates, she reproduces her mistress's adultery in mime, and indicates that the Devil (in the form
of a bird) made her strip naked. Having betrayed her mistress, Mituba commits
suicide; an action which Hester condemns as murder by the community.

Maryse Condé's novel, *I, Tituba, Black Witch of Salem* ([1986] 1994), is
based on the life of the only black victim of the Salem witch trials. Unlike the 1995
film, with its 'scattergun' attempts to draw parallels with the contemporary, the
novel does produce a critique of the racism and sexism of late twentieth-century
American society. Tituba has no place in *The Scarlet Letter*, nor does John
Indian (Johnny Sassamon) who was her lover. For perhaps obvious reasons,
Condé anachronistically has Tituba and Hester Prynne meeting in prison in her
novel. They meet, however, as equals, not as mistress and slave. Hester is given
a clear 'feminist' identity: brought up in a family that believed in sexual equality
and encouraged her to read the classics. This is the Hester which the film
partially draws upon – what is missing is her desire for revenge against
Dimmesdale: 'And while I am rotting here the man who put this child in my
womb is free to come and go as he pleases' (Hawthorne [1850] 1986: 97).
Hester also says that she would like to write a book where she would 'describe a
model society governed and run by women! We would give our names to our
children, we would raise them alone…'(Hawthorne [1850] 1986: 101). (In the
film, Dimmesdale baptizes and names the child in prison.) The film derives its
community of 'witches' from the Condé novel too, but probably via *The Crucible*.
The Condé novel also has a moment when Hester and Tituba lie down together
– 'Was Hester showing me another kind of bodily pleasure?' – which perhaps
explains Mituba's 'spying' on the body of Hester. Unlike the Condé novel,
women's bodies in the 1995 film are still very much subject to the prurient and
voyeuristic gaze of the camera, the Puritan proxy, and the nakedness is titillating
not liberating. Women's bodily pleasure is still 'ordered' by men.

The film also develops quite extensively the few references to Native
Americans in the original novel, giving body and voice to the fears of wilderness
and otherness in the Puritan settlement. As has been said, there is also a conversion narrative inserted into the plot and a conflict set up between a 'savage' and
a Christian Native American. One of the settlers, Mary, has been forcibly 'taken
by a savage' and there is a sense that, when Brewster Stonehall forces himself
upon Hester and when Chillingworth kills and scalps him (mistaking him for
Dimmesdale), their behaviour is an aberration, a result of wilderness impulses –
thus displacing excess beyond the boundaries of the Puritan self.

At one point, even the Native Americans are worried by Chillingworth's
excess. His ship has been attacked by a band of Tarantines and most of his
companions massacred. Freed from Puritan society, Chillingworth 'goes native'
(another racist formulation), learns alternative cures, becomes fluent in the
language and is seized by powerful spirits.

The governor's wife in recommending clemency for Hester says, perceptively, 'put the prison in her, not her in prison', which neatly summarizes much

of the Puritan culture. Hester contests their claims and argues that she believes that she has sinned in their eyes, but doubts whether God shares their views; her badge of shame is rightfully theirs not hers. (Unfortunately Demi Moore wears the scarlet letter like the 'S' of Superwoman.)

As has been indicated, there are several problems with the 1995 adaptation: it tries to pack in too many contradictory features, verges on the melodramatic and the absurd at times, lacks focus and direction, and is not helped by weak central performances. The later sequences are rushed and contain many of the faults described here. The killing of Brewster Stonehall is blamed on the 'praying Indians', who are expelled from the colony. Hester is arrested again and joins the group of 'dissident' women in jail. The women are taken to the scaffold, bound and gagged, to be hanged. Dimmesdale intervenes and offers himself to be hanged. In a farcical moment, the whole group are rescued, in cavalry fashion, by a band of 'praying Indians'. The director has the grace to omit the bugle call, but as a moment of intertextuality it beggars belief (maybe this is why one of the Native American bands are called Tarantines!). It is as if Hollywood is only capable of working generically within two founding individualist paradigms – the romance and the Western – both of which are gratuitously imposed upon the novel as part of the process of evacuating history in order to justify the ideology of 'the imperial self'.

To conceal things from England, the anxious governor agrees to remove the letter and make a public apology. As it happens, Hester discards it herself and gives it to Pearl, confirming the independence which has marked her position throughout. In the novel, the letter remains and is transfigured in and through Hester's ethical stand and community witness. In the film, she leaves the colony with Pearl and Dimmesdale for the Carolinas; Pearl's voice-over comment: 'My parents shared a love like no other – who is to say what is a sin in God's eyes', dissolves all the complexities and ambivalences of the novel, the foundational politics of the Puritan experiment, and the literal/symbolic dialectic, reducing the novel in the process to a secular romance, a bourgeois love story oblivious to the codes and gendered power of an 'originating' social formation. Society is something it is seemingly easy to disaffiliate from, whereas for Hawthorne (and for an 'exile' colony) the needs of the social order cannot readily be dispensed with. The society and the history ultimately evacuated from the film are core components of the novel. Hester's point of view is not, despite the film's insistence, sovereign; her 'take' on the Puritan colony distorts the fact that not only women, but men, were victims of Puritan ideology.

From the very outset of the film, Hester is seen to conceive of society in an anachronistic modern way 'as a set of attitudes and powers which exert a coercive power and from which she is wholly distinct' (Anderson 1971: 70). Even the community of outcast women are simply another pretext for expressing Hester's outrage at the irrational, self-righteous and unjust society. In the novel, as I have said, Hester is not distinct from the colony but in it, if not entirely of it.

The violence initially enacted upon and suffered by the Puritan body was then translated and re-enacted upon other *altered* bodies. The novel is about gendered power and the ways in which sites of legitimation and authorization seek to suppress historicity through linear, teleological, eschatological or progressive temporalities – no *alternative* narrative can be imagined beyond the Puritan body.

In Fredric Jameson's terms, *The Scarlet Letter* narrative has to be related to the conception of a political unconscious:

> The idea is…that if interpretation in terms of expressive causality or of allegorical master narratives remains a constant temptation, this is because such master narratives have inscribed themselves in the texts as well as in our thinking about them; such allegorical narrative signifieds are a persistent dimension of literary and cultural texts precisely because they reflect a fundamental dimension of our collective thinking and our collective fantasies about history and reality.
>
> (Jameson 1981: 34)

Hawthorne's text precisely addresses this 'allegorical narrative signified' by writing in 1850 of a moment two centuries earlier, aware of the roots that Puritan discourse sent down into 'the contingent circumstances' of his own historical time and shaped *its* cultural script. The Joffé version detaches itself from anything but the contingent circumstances of its own time, resisting in the process 'the reading and the writing of the text of history within [its]self' (Jameson 1981: 34). It is, in a limited and contemporary sense, 'politically' conscious, but it actively works against any conception of the political *unconscious*.

My problem with this adaptation is not that it desecrates a canonical text, or even is 'unfaithful' to it, but that it produces meanings which give credence to the ideology of the 'imperial self' and ignore the fact that, in a political culture, the self that narrates speaks from a position of *having been narrated and edited by others* – by political institutions, by concepts of historical causality and by 'allegorical master narratives'. Perhaps the letter 'A' stands not for adulteress nor for angel, but for autonomy – a highly conditional autonomy which allows no ultimate scope for a redemptive, or heroic, resolution. As Joanne Feit Diehl claims, the letter 'A' also represents, 'the desire for contact and reunion with the forbidden, which must be approached through a language that will protect the very distance the author seeks to traverse' (in Murfin 1991: 250). The film is never able to develop the cinematic equivalent of this language, nor is there any sense that the 'forbidden' is an active, living and, for the patriarchal order, menacing presence in the society. The relationship between the semiotic of the letter and legitimation is never closed, but nor is it ever fully open in any but an illusory sense. The Puritans knew that they lived, literally and metaphorically, on the edge of social order and that, theocracy notwithstanding, their society was an incomplete project *of their own devising*, continuously in need of renewal and re-making, hence the fear of autonomy, fragmentation and any form of border crossing: 'leaky boundaries'.

The Scarlet Letter then is not just a seventeenth-century plot, nor a nine-teenth-century novel, but a text of *modernity*, the consequences of which we still live.

7

FOUR *LITTLE WOMEN*

Three films and a novel

Pat Kirkham and Sarah Warren

This chapter focuses on the novel *Little Women* ([1868–9] 1987)[1] by Louisa May Alcott and film adaptations of it from 1933, 1949 and 1994, with special reference to the cult of domesticity and 'true' femininity, feminism, romance, costume- and set-design, characters, casting, and contextualization.

A story of the transition of four sisters (Meg, Jo, Beth and Amy March) from girlhood to womanhood at the time of the American Civil War (1861–5), *Little Women* was written specifically for young girls. It quickly became one of the most popular novels ever published in the English language (Saxton 1977: 4) and is regarded as a 'classic' – one mainly read by women and girls (Showalter 1991: 42; 1995: 19). There were two silent film adaptations (both now 'lost'), one in Britain (1917) and one in the USA (1919).[2] The first 'talkie' *Little Women*, with Oscar-winning screenplay by Sarah Mason and Victor Heerman, was released in 1933 (dir. George Cukor, RKO; b/w) and a remake, with screenplay by Sally Benson and Andrew Salt, in 1949 (dir. Mervyn LeRoy, MGM; Technicolor). It was nearly fifty years before another film version. The book remained popular in the immediate post-war years, and many women who grew up then, but were too young to have seen the films on theatrical release, remember the book as central to their negotiations of 'appropriate' femininities. Some were encouraged to read it by mothers who loved the book and the films. The elder co-author of this article (born 1945) was one such, yet such were changes in attitudes towards women and domesticity and the increasing attraction of film, television and video over books, that she was unable to persuade her eldest daughter and co-author (born 1975) to read it. It took the 1994 film, seen when already a feminist and no longer a 'little woman', to capture the daughter's heart and imagination in the way that the book had done her mother's and grandmother's.

By the 1960s the novel's sentimentality and espousal of Christian virtues aroused ambivalent responses in readers who considered themselves 'modern'. Writer Brigid Brophy was so hidebound by the modernist abhorrence of sentimentality that she was unable to come to terms with the fact that *Little Women* moved her (Brophy 1965). From the 1970s, Alcott and her work became a focus of feminist scholarship, producing new Alcott fans and revalidating youthful readings. The 1994 film (dir. Gillian Armstrong, Columbia Pictures; Technicolor) is, in part, the product of this understanding of Alcott and the novel as feminist or proto-feminist. Despite considerable support by influential women in the business, it proved difficult to convince a major studio of the box-office potential of a film with a feminist angle about the daily life of four adolescent girls living at home with their mother 130 years ago (Davis 1995: 66).

Alcott details the trials and tribulations of girlhoods spent learning (or, in the case of Jo, resisting) versions of femininity rooted in the mid-nineteenth-century cult of domesticity. For middle-class women 'true womanhood' involved creating a moral framework for the family, maintaining appropriate levels of gentility and respectability, and managing the home (Sparke 1995: 59; Welter 1966: 151–74). This gendered ideology existed before mid-century, but by then the separate spheres of male/public/utilitarian and female/home/trivial were so polarized that the division was regarded as 'natural' (Sparke 1995: 59). Even those who held radical positions on women's rights regarded women as sacred guardians of the home (Matthews 1987: 21) and the personification of Christian virtue (Stevenson 1995: 31). The attainment of 'true womanhood' permeates Alcott's novel, but the films tone down the sisters' spiritual battles against their imperfect natures. Although Alcott's Mrs March (Marmee) personifies 'true womanhood' (with Beth a junior version), the book covertly and overtly subverts the cult of domesticity, not least in making Jo the most engaging character while Beth dies (Fetterley 1979: 379–83). The films are all faithful to the novel in having Beth die, thus signalling ambiguities about living out the cult of domesticity.

The films end with Jo accepting a marriage proposal but Alcott's narrative takes the family saga to six years after that event, to Marmee's sixtieth birthday, at which Jo and her own two children are present. By earlier including short scenes of Jo performing domestic tasks and holding her sisters' children, the films allude to her acceptance of the cult of domesticity, but they freeze-frame Jo before she makes the transition to wife and mother, and gives up writing to enable her to run a school with her husband. The life of 'Mother Bhaer' (Alcott [1868–9] 1987: 585) is regarded by some as a surrender to the patriarchal values of 'self-denial, renunciation and mutilation' (Fetterley 1979: 382) and the films all avoid depicting the ending of the novel.

Another problem in terms of adaptation is that the book's final coupling is not the expected one between the central pair, but between the 'heroine' and a male character introduced late in the story who does not conform to generic expectations of the romantic hero. Alcott states in the book that some might think there is too much romance (Alcott [1868–9] 1987: 287), but took delight in thwarting readers' wishes for Jo to marry Laurie (Showalter 1991: 54) – the rich boy-next-door whom Alcott made dark, handsome and sexual (Hollander 1980: 35). None of the films cast Laurie as anything like Alcott's black-eyed, dark-skinned, half-Italian lover of music and beauty. When Alcott did pair Jo, it was to an unattractive, absent-minded, asexual, intellectual twenty years her senior. Aware it would disappoint readers, she gave 'perversity' as the reason for the 'funny match' (Showalter 1991: 54). Bhaer is certainly a letdown, even for the most high-minded young women, and (not surprisingly) all three films made changes to the character and to his relationship with Jo. Another significant difference *vis à vis* characterization is that the films tone down the less pleasant characteristics of Jo, Meg and Amy, to which Alcott devotes many pages.

The notion that money cannot buy happiness or self-esteem runs through all the texts, which depict an idealized poverty: recently fallen on hard times but nobly borne, requiring few sacrifices and cushioned by rich relations and neighbours. The ways in which the genteel poverty described by Alcott is represented on screen differ as greatly as the films themselves. Wittily dubbed *Little Sufferers* (1933), *Little Shoppers* (1949) and *Little Feminists* (1994) (Hollander 1995: 11–21), each broadly reflects the period in which it was made.

Little Women (1933)

Of the films, the 1933 adaptation most self-consciously set out to be faithful to Alcott's story. The film was RKO's attempt to cash in on the box-office success of movies such as *Daddy Long Legs* (1931) and *The First Year* (1932) ('a spotlessly clean little tale'; *New York Sun*, 1932), at a time when film-goers were tired of gangster movies and Westerns (*Los Angeles Times*, 1934). In 59 per cent of studio mail related to the film, the desire was expressed that 'the little women...be presented just as they were in the book' (*News*, 1933), and there was fairly close adherence to the dialogue as well as the plot of the novel in the sections adapted. Fan mail was also important in the choice of stars: Katharine Hepburn, Joan Bennett, Frances Dee and Paul Lukas were all demanded by large numbers of fans (*News*, 1933).

This film places more emphasis than the later ones on the 'burdens' borne by the sisters as they struggle against morally weakening qualities such as jealousy, anger and self-regard. Their pilgrim's progress is a feature of the novel,[3] and the screenplay uses Alcott's terminology in a letter from the girls' father which encourages them to 'fight their bosom enemies bravely and conquer themselves so beautifully' that he will be fonder and prouder of them on his return. Amy confronts her selfishness, Meg her envy and Jo vows to be less rough and wild, and to be content to be at home; Beth simply looks sad. The scene underscores Alcott's fusion of the sisters' moral journeys and the espousal of 'true womanhood'. The family rendering of the hymn *Abide With Me* (not specified by Alcott) quickly establishes a Christian framework but, thereafter, the film focuses on the girls growing up and on romance, which is how it was advertised (Dickens 1971: 51).

Written during the Great Depression that followed the Wall Street Crash of 1929, the screenplay made much of what Alcott referred to as 'the departed days of plenty' (Alcott [1868–9] 1987: 26) before Mr March lost his fortune

(Alcott [1868–9] 1987: 45). Both film and novel emphasize 'courage in the face of want' (Hollander 1995: 11). Unlike the other films and the book, however, this text opens with scenes of personal and material hardships during the Civil War that must have had strong resonances for audiences suffering hardship during the Depression. References to the war added to the modernity of Alcott's original story, but had a historicizing function in the films. The 1933 film, like the others, uses 'period' sets and costume, and offers viewers the comforts and security of an imaginary past. But nostalgic notes are also there in Alcott's own descriptions of pleasures considered 'traditional' in 1868–9, such as home theatricals, the 'household custom' (Alcott [1868–9] 1987: 15) of singing together before retiring to bed, Christmas presents and carols – all of which are made visual in the film. The emphasis on a happy Christmas in 1933, even a Christmas with less abundance than usual, works as a nostalgic device and offers a respite from the hardships of contemporary life. Family solidarity also can be interpreted as harking back to an earlier (mythic) period at the same time as representing a desirable bulwark against the tough times of the 1930s.

The opening scenes add to the 'realism' of the text by binding it to a specific historic period, whereas the other films open with less specific Christmas-cardy snow scenes (dispensed with here in the title scene). This is the only film to introduce the March women in relation to their 'occupations' – Marmee/Spring Byington at the Soldier's Aid Society, Meg/Frances Dee as a nanny, Jo/Katharine Hepburn as a 'companion', Amy/Joan Bennett at school and Beth/Jean Parker helping at home – all trying to make ends meet. A scene of three sisters returning home from their outside activities further roots this domestic-centred drama in modern worldly concerns. It is only after these scenes that the film picks up where the book begins – with four sisters chatting by the fireside. No matter how focused the film remains on the home thereafter, viewers are in no doubt that there is a wider world outside. Despite the 'realism', little of the biting poverty of the 1860s or 1930s is depicted. The ways the film deals with poverty and longing for better times suggest there is no simple relationship between the film and the Depression; the relationship between the two also needs to be understood in terms of the 'escapism' of romance, humour and visual pleasures offered by this costume drama,[4] and the representation on screen of one of literature's most popular independent-minded women.

In the novel, abject poverty is represented by a fatherless immigrant family, but Alcott does not linger unduly on the recipients of the Marchs' 'good works'. The poor family is even more marginalized in the 1933 film, but its representation of poverty is more convincing than in the 1949 remake, where the younger children appear to have been specially scrubbed to be filmed with Elizabeth Taylor. (In the 1994 film, which like that of 1933 aims at authenticity, the focus remains as much on the responses of the middle-class Marches as on the poor themselves.)

With the exception of the scene in which Jo goes to a party with a patch on the back of her dress, there is little effort to indicate poverty through dress. Less 'showy' than those he created for the 1949 remake, Walter Plunkett's costumes serve to prettify both the wearers and the poverty they were supposed to be enduring. Studio publicists made much of Plunkett's search for historical accuracy (see Press Book A) but there is little sense from the dress, particularly that of Amy and Meg, that being poor is even irksome to the process of looking attractive. These 'little women' look wonderful in pristine frocks and hair styles with more contemporary appeal than historical accuracy (the case in all the films). It is not clear how the costume was read by contemporary audiences, but women viewers were used to fashion being an important part of film pleasures (Herzog 1990: 134–59). The beauty and alluring nature of many of the gowns and the fashion product-promotion which took place around this movie (*International Herald Tribune*, 1933) suggest that there were many pleasures for women viewers related to dress.

Alcott describes the March house as 'an old brown house' covered in vines and surrounded by flowers in summer but 'rather bare and shabby' in winter (Alcott [1868–9] 1987: 57). The 1933 film never shows the exterior in its entirety, visually implying, in the spirit of the novel, that what goes on inside it is more important. (The later films use the house, glowing with warmth from within, to make a similar point.) Within the home, the 1933 film did little to represent poverty. To many contemporary viewers the interior – full of furniture and objects – must have seemed desirable. Together with the Laurence house, it is there to be admired, even longed for. Alcott writes about objects in ways that solicit desire while at the same time criticizing such desires (Bedell 1983: Introduction), and the 1933 film uses Amy's fashionable costumes and Meg caressing the silk on Beth's piano to suggest the ambiguities inherent in the novel.

Laurie/Douglass Montgomery's fair-haired good looks and energy make him a match for Jo/Hepburn, even if he is not as alluring as in the novel. A certain asexuality is countered by the sexual frissons created when he chases Jo/Hepburn through the woods. In the book it is a race suggested by Laurie, who wins it. The alteration to him chasing *after* her, makes a feminist point which is reinforced by her reaching home first. She shuts the garden gate, indicating that she is in control. The sexualized interlude is over and the film makes visual a recurrent theme of the novel – Jo's refusal to accept the implications of growing up female.

Alcott's forty-year-old stout German with bad table manners and without 'a really handsome feature in his face except his beautiful teeth' (Alcott [1868–9] 1987: 404) was portrayed in the film by handsome Hungarian Paul Lukas. The most serious of the film Bhaers, he is given spectacles as the mark of the scholar – Alcott notes he sometimes used them (Alcott [1868–9] 1987: 429) – but they do not stop him from looking dashing in evening dress. All three films use music to mark Bhaer as romantic and sensitive. Indeed, he is given the musical talents Alcott allocated to Laurie. The screenplay added scenes of him playing the piano and singing romantic songs to a swooning Jo to pull the text nearer to Hollywood romance. The music is powerful and Jo/Hepburn wears a 'special' dress that signals romance (Kirkham 1995: 195–214).They form a handsome couple and viewers know that he adores her; in a moment of blissful voyeurism, they watch him watch her as she watches the stage through opera glasses. As if to stress their equality, towards the close of the film Jo/Hepburn and Bhaer/Lukas literally bump into each other and resume their romance. (By contrast, the later films show Jo running down a lane after him in a scene which condenses several in the Alcott text.) There is a suggestion, as a slightly bossy Jo/Hepburn almost drags Bhaer/Lukas into the family home, that she will be the more dominant.

Today the film is remembered for Hepburn's portrayal of Jo. Independent of mind and with strong views on women's rights, she grew up as a tomboy in a New England 'progressive' household (Dickens 1971: 2–3). Cukor declared her born to play the part, and she gave a bravura performance (Higham 1975: 48). The dialectic between star persona and character is strong. Hepburn's Jo is rest-less, talkative, spirited, intelligent, gawky and wishes she was a boy. The film has her express that wish, dress in male clothes for family theatricals (in scenes which reference pantomime and play on gender ambiguities), and 'swordfight' with Laurie using pokers. She is shown sliding down banisters, snowballing, shovelling snow, skating, running and writing – activities which distinguish her from sisters who have learned appropriate femininity better than she. A scene (not in the novel) in which Jo/Hepburn vaults the garden fence in hooped skirts, symbolizes her determination to overcome the barriers between the domestic and public worlds; between the world of women – who cannot be professional writers – and the world of men. In the 1949 remake Jo/June Allyson falls at the first attempt, but her determination to surmount the obstacle is signalled by immediately trying again.

Alcott refused an 'ugly duckling' narrative; her Jo was not physically attrac-tive at the beginning of the book and nor was she at the end. The 1933 film capitalized on, rather than denied Hepburn's attractiveness; she is presented as visually 'modern' and at her most Garboesque in an elegant evening dress, further referencing beauty and contemporaneity (Bourget 1991: 81). Despite this discrepancy, or perhaps *because* of it, because of the performance itself and because throughout her life she displayed an independence similar to Jo's, to many people Katharine Hepburn was/is Jo. The film and the performance have come to be regarded as 'classics', and Hepburn's characterization informed later ones.

Little Women (1949)

The poverty of the past is even more sanitized in the star-packed 1949 film, which audaciously uses costumes, sets and dialogue to saturate viewers with objects of desire. Rooted in the Hollywood musical as much as 'classic' dramatic adaptation, the later film emphasizes abundance – a key element of the musical (Dyer 1977: 2–13). Made in Technicolor, it is very different from the 1933 black-and-white film of which it is technically a remake. Despite an almost identical screenplay (offering considerable intertextuality) this neglected film has been dismissed as syrupy (Halliwell 1991: 655) and 'semi-hysterical' (Brown 1994: 68). Utilizing a more lyrical and light arrangement of the melodic musical score written for the 1933 film[5] and drawing on the best visual talents of Hollywood (including art director Cedric Gibbons), it plays on the senses. Luminescent colour, lyrical camera-work and music, and luscious costume and sets linger in the memory. The references to Hollywood musicals, especially of the MGM stable, are consolidated through the recasting of members of the film family in *Meet Me in St Louis* (1944)[6] (Hollander 1995: 21) and the direction of Mervyn LeRoy who, a decade earlier, had been acclaimed for *The Wizard of Oz* (1939). In a flamboyant touch of intertextuality, LeRoy gives *Little Women* a rainbow ending, suggesting an idyllic land lies 'Over the Rainbow'. The film, which received an Academy Award for cinematography, was a major reference point for the cinematography of the 1994 film.

Released only four years after the end of World War Two, during a period which re-emphasized a femininity that was feared lost or eroded by the 'masculinization' of women during the war (Kirkham 1996: 152–74), this film places most emphasis on the home. Over 70 per cent of scenes are set inside the

Figure 7.1 Little Women (1949). The March family gathered at the piano

87

March home and garden, as opposed to approximately half in the other texts (Warren 1997: Appendix). A recurring image is the family home. The viewers are voyeurs as they look in on the family from the outside – the windows glowing with light from the interior. Warm colours, tints and tones suggest a rosy 'present' for the film, and comfort in a sepia past. Unapologetic in terms of nostalgia, the film opens with jolly shouts of 'Merry Christmas' – that mythic ever-happy season.

Despite the late nineteenth-century setting, references to the past are layered with references to the present, mainly through costume, body shape, make-up and hair styles. Here Alcott's genteel poverty meets high fashion. Dior's 'New Look', *the* style of 1947 which radically re-shaped women's appearance (Maynard 1995: 43–59), informs the costume. If Dior wished 'New Look' women to look like flowers (Dior 1958: 21), Plunkett ensured that they were in full bloom. As in the 1933 film, costume signals plenty and prettiness, some-times against the grain of the dialogue, but does so more consistently and with greater emphasis on display. Meg and Amy provide a constant fashion parade. Hollander notes that *Little Shoppers* 'celebrates the fresh post-war pleasure of acquiring sleek new possessions' (Hollander 1995: 21), a pleasure most clearly expressed through dress. There was a huge amount of fashion promotion around this movie (Press Book B), in which even Marmee gets to wear attrac-tive clothes. Hollander cites two shopping expeditions as marking out 'the national feminine pastime for the next decade' (Hollander 1995: 21). Only one appears on screen, but viewers see that it takes precedence over reading Mr March's letter. When the sisters finally read his exhortations to 'fight their bosom enemies and conquer themselves' there are no vows of self-improvement as in the 1933 version. This is not a film about want, but about want*ing* – about having what had been missed during wartime austerity. It can be read as a film in which women want and get what they want, in terms of home and husband, and (in the case of Jo) a career too.

Readers and viewers who identify with sisters other than Jo have been encouraged to come out of the closet (James 1994: 3). Blonde Amy was described by Alcott as the most beautiful of the sisters and RKO cast Joan Bennett, a conventionally beautiful actor with abundant blonde curls in the role. But for many Elizabeth Taylor remains 'the ideal pampered Amy' (op cit.). Only seventeen years old, but hailed as 'one of the screen's greatest beauties' (Press Book B), she glows on the screen. This and her perky acting style ensure this Amy is no mere foil to Jo, as she is in the 1994 film. Taylor's beauty and sensuality make her a worthy mate for Laurie, played by a dashingly handsome Peter Lawford, who had recently appeared with her in *Julia Misbehaves* (dir. Everett Riskin, 1948) (Press Book B).

Material was added to make Laurie appear more manly – viewers learn that he had joined the Union army under age and had been wounded in battle (Showalter 1991: 61) – and a 'dashing new star' (Press Book B), Italian heart-throb Rossano Brazzi, was cast as Bhaer. Alcott exoticized Laurie as part-Italian, and the film uses the same device in relation to Bhaer/Brazzi. He brings sexuality to scenes which present Bhaer as scholarly, quietly subverting the dialogue and enhancing the scene (taken from the 1933 screenplay) in which he sings to Jo/June Allyson. In this version he removes his spectacles, indicating a changed point of view as he falls in love.

Alcott has Meg run a close second to Amy in terms of attractiveness and all the films follow Alcott in casting conventionally pretty women. Eighteen-year-old Janet Leigh added much to the spectacular pleasures of the film and her saucy portrayal ensured that the 1949 Meg is the least dull. Alcott has Meg poor after marriage, as does the 1933 film, but here her smart clothes work against such a representation, depicting married Meg as affluent and chic. In a major shift from the novel, Meg becomes a smart woman-about-town: at a time when increasing numbers of women in the USA were driving cars, Meg gets to drive her own buggy. Throughout the film, as in the other texts, Meg represents respectability and acts out appropriate femininities. She is rewarded not with a struggle to make ends meet, but with the products and pleasures of a full economy (as in post-war USA). In contrast to the novel and the other two films, the 1949 version suggests that even for a woman as conventional as Meg there is life outside the home. In this it is more radical than the other texts, including the more overtly feminist film of 1994.

The ambiguities inherent in Alcott's finely drawn observations on learning the rules about and skills related to 'true womanhood' and the cult of domesticity are captured in this film, which uses humour and visuals to great effect. To some extent all the films follow Alcott's depictions of Jo refusing appropriate femininities or being incompetent at them, and of their uncritical acceptance by Meg and Amy. This text, however, pushes the petty snobberies, etiquette and accoutrements of fashionable femininity to extremes. Much of the critique by humour centres on Amy/Taylor, a character so 'over the top' in terms of dress and attitudes that it can only be read as parodic. All the films use Alcott's brilliantly economical motif – representing the pressures on women to achieve perfection – and depict Amy sleeping with a clothes-peg on her nose to reconstruct it. Amy/Taylor is filmed in heavy make-up in bed, with strawberry blonde hair almost as pink as her night-cap ribbons. As in the book, much is made of Amy's vanity, snobbery, selfishness and materialism. Taylor/Amy feeds the poor in designer hat and chiffon scarf. This signals the lady bountiful she becomes and lampoons her lack of generosity in that, faced with starving children, she keeps every third piece of orange for herself. At this point she is close to Patsy Stone in the TV series *Absolutely Fabulous* (1992–6): a parody of a selfish, materially-obsessed woman who gives out mixed messages about the lifestyle she represents, but not about femininity itself (Kirkham and Skeggs 1997: 296). In the novel the young Amy 'matures' and 'reforms'; Amy/Taylor remains the original material girl. Despite its transgressions against the original novel, the 1949 *Little Women* captures something of the spirit of Alcott's critique of the constructed nature of femininity and adds other dimensions of its own. For this alone it deserves more critical attention.

Little Women (1994)

The 1994 film adaptation is the only one directed by a woman. It reveals a respect for feminist ideas, the history of feminism, Alcott and her work, and cannot be understood without reference to the feminist movement of the last thirty years, particularly feminist scholarship in literature and history. Feminist views inflect the screenplay and 'historical' additions based on the 'progressive' beliefs of Alcott and her family make this adaptation substantially different from the originary text and from the other films.[7] Much has been made of the feminist aims of those responsible for bringing it to the screen, including director Gillian Armstrong (who also directed *My Brilliant Career*, released in 1978), Lisa Henson of Sony Pictures, scriptwriter Robin Swicord, producer Denise Di Novi and actress Winona Ryder (Schaeffer 1994: 37, McKenna 1995: 20 and Davis 1995: 66). Much has also been made of its 'political correctness' in terms of gender, 'race', education, vegetarianism, alternative medicine and other social issues (McKenna 1995: 20, 36) – though not, noticeably, class. Swicord considered writing a screenplay as early as 1983 (Davis 1995: 66), but production only became a possibility after the success of movies with active female protagonists and feminist messages, such as *Thelma and Louise* and *Terminator 2* (both 1991). Also crucial to the making of this film was the increasing popularity of adaptations of 'classic' texts, including several adaptations of Jane Austen, *Bram Stoker's Dracula* (1992), *The Age of Innocence* (1993) and *Mary Shelley's Frankenstein* (1994).

The film portrays the joys of familial and domestic life, but with less subversion than the Alcott text. As in every version, the March family is effectively a single-parent family (the father is 'absent' in every respect) but, surprisingly for a film which aims at relevance to contemporary life, this feature of 1990s life and the ways in which it affects women is not highlighted. It seems significant that the film was made at a time of far greater accommodation within contemporary feminism of women staying at home and raising families as their primary concern than was the case twenty years ago. The production and reception of the film also relate to the 'return' to 'Victorian' and Christian values of home and family, as exemplified in Thatcherite Britain and American politics from the late 1970s. There is some debate as to the degree to which they inform the movie (Lurie 1995: 5), but such values can be read in its cosy and comfortable mood, as well as the emphasis on home and domesticity. The experience of relative poverty after affluence is another aspect of the film which touches chords with contemporary viewers who have experienced, directly or indirectly, 'downsizing' and unemployment. In this there are similarities between the 1933 and 1994 movies.

90

Figure 7.2 Little Women (1994). Marmee and her daughters read a letter from their father

Although intended to pay homage to Alcott, this film departs from her text more than the others. It alters Alcott's language and story in order to make the film more acceptable to contemporary audiences, but more importantly includes, as a seamless part of the whole, additional material related to the 'advanced' views of Alcott and her parents on women's rights and other issues. In an attempt to better capture something of Alcott's own beliefs, as opposed to those of her fictional characters, the 1994 film sets aside parts of Alcott's fiction and adds fictionalized social history, albeit based on her own life. The addition of (fictionalized) aspects of Alcott's life and beliefs overemphasizes the autobiographical nature of her novel, while the retention of the idealized family of the novel evades the fact that the Alcott household was far from harmonious. Recent feminist scholarship has shown that, although Alcott suggested a simple parallel between her family and the March family, *Little Women* is not the auto-biographical story it was once purported to be (Keyser 1988: 211, Halttunen 1984: 233). The film's use of Jo/Ryder as narrator (the only text to do so) adds to the autobiographical mode, as does a device taken from the 1933 and 1949 screenplays (but without basis in fact or in Alcott's novel), namely having Jo's book published. In 1933 the book was not named, in 1949 it was *My Beth*, but in 1994 it became *Little Women*. Jo/Ryder's holding of the book *Little Women* further emphasizes the autobiographical at the end of a film which slips between the harmonious and mutually supportive March family on screen and the highly complex dysfunctional and visually absent Alcott family. Despite being moved in many ways by this film, one wonders if a better tribute to Alcott would have been either to tamper less with her most commercially successful work or to have made a film about her life, work, family and the 'progressive' circles in which she moved.

The additional material extends the tribute beyond the Alcotts to all who struggled to further the radical causes mentioned, adding considerable poignancy for viewers proud of those histories. However, the insertions are not always dramatically or cinematically interesting. Much of the text relating to contemporary (1868–9) feminist issues takes place as monologues by Susan Sarandon, whose Marmee is transformed from the epitome of the cult of domesticity to ideal feminist mother and confident spokesperson for the emancipation of women. Sarandon, implanted in cinematic memory as a gun-toting free-wheeling heroine of *Thelma and Louise* and known for her own radical views, was an inspired choice, but some of the speeches remain wooden. Alcott's Marmee also sermonized (about 'true womanhood'), but some find her more human than this 'mother-machine' (Lipman 1995: 42) and 'dispenser of progresssive platitudes' (Ansen 1994: 57). But all is not dull polemic. Humour is used to offset a speech about girls' need for exercise and the restrictions of corsets (Meg's suitor is shocked and Meg upset that her mother is so lacking in decorum as to mention the unmentionable), and points about racism in education and the use of slave- and child-labour in silk production are skilfully covered in a scene where Meg's more wealthy friends gossip about the radical attitudes held by her family. These are all worthy feminist points – and ones espoused by Alcott – but they are *not* espoused in her *Little Women*.

The most convincing additions arise in the course of conversation or debate where the history clearly relates to issues at the heart of Alcott's text. One example is when Jo/Ryder asks Bhaer/Gabriel Byrne if he has heard of transcendentalism,[8] and the conversation touches on the problems of growing up in a household where one was expected to do daily battle with one's imperfections. The best is the scene in which Bhaer/Byrne and his male friends, joined by Jo/Ryder, discuss the affairs of the day over a glass of wine (used to convey that the 'advanced' Marches were teetotallers). Men dominate the discussion, but when Jo makes her point it is short and very sweet. She argues *for* the vote but *against* supporters of the cult of domesticity who believed that women should be rewarded with the vote because of their Christian virtues. The point that black men could vote already having been made, Jo/Ryder states: 'I find it poor logic to say that because women are good, women should vote. Men do not vote because they are good but because they are male. Women should vote not because they are angels and men are animals but because we are human beings and citizens of this country'. The point is the more effective for being posed against others. Jo/Ryder expresses one of several feminist positions on suffrage in the 1860s, but it is the one that best accords with contemporary views. The strengths of this scene compensate for the stiffness of other 'interventions' – but the fact remains that Alcott herself does not have Jo articulate this position in the novel.

At the same time as embedding progressive politics more centrally in the text, the film fetishizes the home in much the same way as the 1949 one – through sepia tones and lyrical camera-work. The Alcott family home in Concord, Massachusetts, and Alcott's descriptions of the March home and Meg's simple but desirable cottage (Alcott [1868–9] 1987: 191–2), inform the cinematic March home which several critics noted is in the currently fashionable Ralph Lauren/Laura Ashley/Ethan Allen mode of interior design (Thomas 1994: 1 and Hollander 1995: 21). Popular interest in 'period' homes and furnishings has never been greater, and the sets offer many interior-design pleasures – a much neglected area of pleasure for working-class as well as middle-class women (Skeggs 1997: 89). The house, like Amy/Mathis and Bhaer/Byrne's trip to Europe, is an object of desire. It also locates the March/Alcott family as 'advanced' because it is of the type admired by design reformers and adherents of the 'Simple Life' expounded by Emerson and others in the Alcott circle (Robertson 1987: 336–57).

In contrast to desirable sets, locations and actors, there is little to desire in much of the costume. As if to consciously counteract the critical denigration of costume films as 'inauthentic', the costume serves mainly to indicate hard times and the reforming zeal of the March/Alcott family. The emphasis is on wear, tear and drabness in the name of authenticity (though the hairstyles in particular are far from 'authentic'). Of all the films, this is the only one to achieve anything near fidelity to Alcott's text in terms of costume. All the texts have the older Amy in highly fashionable clothes, but only this film includes the scenes in which Alcott unpicks the many pleasures of dress, dressing-up and constructing 'the feminine'. Foreshadowing recent feminist interest in the topic (Doane 1982: 74–87, Gaines 1990: 23–7 and Bruzzi 1997: 128–32), Alcott has Meg feel as if she had been to a masquerade (Alcott [1868–9] 1987: 115) in 'the first makeover in women's fiction' (Showalter 1997: 86), and the 1994 adaptation makes visual Meg/Alvarado's transformation by friends. The cinematography is as seductive as the clothes but, as in the novel, Laurie's censorious remarks interrupt the pleasures of voyeurism, of seeing a young woman enjoying herself and her sexuality. The 'excess' (low neckline and drinking) seems trivial by contemporary standards, but there are parallels with contemporary definitions of femininity which exclude hedonistic or vulgar behaviour. Despite Laurie's disapproval, many readers and viewers retain more than a 'sneaking fondness' for Meg's visit to Vanity Fair (Showalter 1995: 86).

Bruzzi has categorized films into those which 'look through' and those which 'look at' clothes (Bruzzi 1997: 36). Like *Howard's End* (1992), *Little Women* (1994) 'looks through' clothes in an effort 'to signal the accuracy of the costume and to submit them to the greater framework of historical and literary authenticity' (Bruzzi 1997: 36). The overtly glamorous dance dresses and Amy's European clothes, like many of the clothes in the earlier versions but particularly those of Leigh and Taylor in the 1949 film, also 'create an alternative discourse, one that usually counters or complicates the ostensible strategy of the over-riding narrative' – thus placing them in the 'look at' category (Bruzzi 1997: 36). The costume also straddles two other categories established in relation to contemporary women film-makers working within the costume film genre. Gillian Armstrong's *My Brilliant Career* is cited as an example of the 'liberal' model, which 'seeks to map out, via the lives of emblematic or iconic personalities, a collective women's cultural and political history' in which clothes 'are merely signifiers to carry information about country, class and period' (Bruzzi 1993: 232–42 and 1997: 36). The dress in Armstrong's *Little Women* largely functions thus but, at times, it is part of 'a contrapuntal, sexualised discourse' which forms the basis of Bruzzi's 'sexual' model of film-making (Bruzzi 1993: 232–42 and 1997: 36). These differing significations draw attention to the ambiguities within the originary text. None of the approaches to film costume detailed by Bruzzi is more feminist than another *per se*, and the duality of approach seen in each of the three films of *Little Women* befits adaptations of this ambiguous novel.

The literary and cinematic outcome of transformations from poor girl to belle is romantic coupling, and in all three films Meg is seen as desirable and desired at the dance. Tensions between visuals and text are less frequent in the 1994 film, but in one scene an attractive Marmee/Sarandon tells Meg/Alvarado and Jo/Ryder that looks are not important. A discussion about it being acceptable for men to behave in the ways that women cannot marks the scene as feminist, but there is no attempt to suggest the position – expounded in contemporary texts such as *Absolutely Fabulous* – that women as well as men should have the right to behave in a vulgar and hedonistic manner (Kirkham and Skeggs 1998: 291). Curious also in a story about the independence of 'little women' is the attribution to Marmee/Sarandon, rather than to Jo as in the book, of the idea to turn the house bequeathed to Jo into a school. It seems the 1994 film is reluctant to have the sisters stray from the 'true feminism' of the mother who, also only in this text, is responsible for saving Beth's life after her first illness. At times the 1994 film is even more mother-fixated than the book.

Unlike the other texts, the 1994 Jo is not a girl constantly wishing to be a boy. The message that girls can act as boys do is reinforced by the evangelizing of Marmee/Sarandon and her ideas on rearing daughters. Only Jo was active in the other texts; here all three younger daughters romp in the snow with Marmee/Sarandon's approval. A scene about the sisters' Pickwick Club, which links the literary world of the Marches to Dickens – whose influence can be seen in Alcott's writings (Showalter 1991: 51) – shows them in male dress, although gendered apparel is not specified in the novel. Such devices ensure the character of Jo is different from that of the other texts, where she is a misfit for being active and a tomboy. One critic commented that Jo/Ryder was 'sexier and more vulnerable than the tomboy Jos we're used to' (Ansen 1994: 57) and another that 'a vital ingredient' of the novel had been missed by not making Jo 'wild and difficult and clumsy' (Lipman 1995: 42).[9]

Androgyny and contemporary dress-modes are referenced as much as the tomboy in the male swashbuckling role Jo/Ryder plays with a knowing sense of masquerade in the home theatricals. In terms of cross-dressing, this is the most extreme of the films: she not only has a moustache (as in the earlier films) but also a beard and hides her hair under a hat. The novel has Jo come to desire the 'true femininity' which had so irked her. In the 1933 film Jo/Hepburn is seen ironing. Ryder disapproved of this (Seigel and Seigel 1997: 17) but the 1994 film staged a similar coming to terms with the cult of domesticity when the character she plays is shown baking and holding her sisters' children. Interestingly, the film too often regarded as merely reflecting the post-war re-emphasis on women in the home, resolutely ignores the issue. The 1949 Jo (Allyson) is the least domesticated of all, suggesting that a feminist re-evaluation of it is long overdue.

The 1994 film shows more of the conflicts of sisterly existence than the others. It is the only one to show Jo/Ryder's physical attack on Amy/Kirsten Dunst who, in a fit of jealously and vindictiveness, burned Jo's manuscript. The film places less blame than Alcott on Jo in a subsequent scene in which Amy nearly drowns. In general, the film pays less attention to the character 'faults' of the sisters, who are more sanitized than in the book or the 1949 film. The young Amy/Dunst is not the 'selfish brat' (Hollander 1980: 32) of the novel and the older Amy/Mathis is less materialistic and pretentious. A change of actress helps viewers accept what remains a considerable transformation from perky and knowing child to the most pallid and passive of all older Amys[10] – surprisingly so, given the aversion within mainstream feminism to women's passivity. Alcott has Amy 'work' on character defects which here are presented as childhood foibles. Unlike the other two films, which show Amy returning home in the highly fashionable dress noted in the novel (Alcott [1868–9] 1987: 539), this one costumes her in mourning dress. The rationale is that she would still have been in mourning for her sister, but had Alcott wanted to specify mourning clothes rather than Meg's envy of her sister's fashionable dress, surely she would have spelled it out? That the 1994 Amy is nicer, aids audience acceptance of her eventual coupling with Laurie/Christian Bale (the character established as suitable for Jo), as do scenes which link the young Amy with Laurie. His role in saving her life is in the book but not the other films. In the book, he and Jo take Amy to Aunt March's, whereas the 1994 film has Amy alone in the carriage with Laurie. Completely new is a scene of Laurie/Bale's promise to the precocious, pretty twelve-year-old to kiss her before she dies – and her swoony kissing of his sleeve when he hugs her.

As in the earlier movies, both men in Jo's life are attractive. Bale's boyish charms add to his portrayal of an enthusiastic and teasingly companionate Laurie. He portrays the anguish of spurned passion better than any other Laurie and his blonder youth contrasts well with the older dark Byrne, who is never seen in spectacles and is considered by almost every reviewer to be the sexiest Bhaer of all. Such is the power of Byrne's sex appeal that – although the couple kiss only twice (and not particularly passionately) – one critic feared 'for Jo in the worldly professor's clutches' (Adams 1994: 39). Many women viewers (and not a few men) wish they could be in those clutches – any lack of fidelity to the novel is forgiven in the pleasures of Jo finally pairing with the type of man Alcott refused to give her.

To differing degrees, each film might be labelled *Little Feminists* because each addresses issues related to feminism. The 1933 and 1994 films are more easily categorized as *Little Sufferers*, though there is less self-sacrifice and more self-reliance in the most recent film. The 1949 version is the only one sufficiently devoted to objects-of-desire to be considered as *Little Shoppers*, but all three films arouse desires for selected material trappings of prosperity.

The differences between the films – and between them and the originary text – can also be seen in the endings which all refer, in one way or another, to the cult of domesticity. Alcott ends her story with Marmee surrounded by her children and grandchildren, her 'face full of motherly love, gratitude and humility', commenting that she can never wish her 'girls...greater happiness than this' (Alcott [1868–9] 1987: 592). In the 1933 film Hepburn/Jo pulls Lukas/Bhaer into the family home. His struggle with his umbrella which sticks in the doorway adds a comic note and suggests that competence, usually a male preserve in movies (Kirkham and Thumim 1995: 26), here resides in the female. Her 'Welcome home!' is taken from the penultimate chapter of the book, when Jo and Bhaer turn 'from the night and storm and loneliness to the household light and warmth and peace waiting to receive them' in the March home. The 1949 film avoids comedy and competence, depicting Jo and Bhaer as equal, but Marmee is added to the scene, welcoming them into the domesticity that the March home has represented. The camera shifts heavenwards and LeRoy adds the rainbow, symbolizing the heaven that is home and referencing the cult of domesticity central to Alcott's novel. Although critiqued during the previous two hours, the film – like the other texts – ends by upholding the status quo in terms of gender politics and domesticity. So too does the 1994 film, the main difference at the end being that the couple are not seen to enter the family home. They kiss outdoors – a space allocated to romance in all the texts, thus reinforcing the romance of this ending. The 1994 film deliberately leaves viewers contemplating Jo/Ryder and Bhaer/Byrne as an ideal couple in their own space – although the very last shot includes her family home in the distance, thus establishing not only a connection (albeit a looser one) to that home and to domesticity, but intertextual references to the other versions.

Notes

1 The book referred to here as *Little Women* consists of the eponymous novel (published in 1868) and its sequel (*Good Wives*, 1869). They were published separately until the end of the 1870s, when the two volumes were combined into one. This has remained the case, particularly in the USA.

2 Dir. G.B. Samuelson and Alexander Butler (Samuelson Film Manufacturing Company, GB, 1917; b/w) and dir. Harley Knowles (Paramount Artcraft, USA, 1919; b/w).

3 Alcott used John Bunyan's *The Pilgrim's Progress* (1678–84) as a structuring device for part of the novel (Halttunen 1984: 243).

4 For a broader discussion of 'escapism' and costume drama, see Harper 1994.

5 The 1933 music score is by Max Steiner, the 1949 one by Adolph Deutsch (after Max Steiner) and the 1994 one by Thomas Newman.

6 Leon Ames, Mary Astor and Margaret O'Brien play father, mother and child.

7 Other recent examples of the 'life' of the author being used in an adaptation include *Prospero's Books* (1990), *Sense and Sensibility* (1995), *Trainspotting* (1996) (in which author Irvine Welsh gets a cameo role) and the BBC's *Oranges are not the Only Fruit* (1990) (where Winterson also wrote the screenplay and was closely involved in the production).

8 Alcott's father was a prominent transcendentalist (Rose 1981: 197–206).

9 Ryder's performance was also referred to as: 'Properly youthful, delicate enough for a pre-Freudian period piece...the right degree of barely contained spunk to play proto-feminist Jo March' (Anderson 1994: 82) and 'vivacious, headstrong and delicious' (Adams 1994: 39). It was noted that at least she did not 'upstage' fellow actors as did Hepburn (Adams 1994: 39).

10 'It's impossible Amy would grow up into a bland bloodless Samantha Mathis unless, in the four years interim, she'd suffered some unmentioned trauma' (Brown 1994: 68).

8

WILL HOLLYWOOD NEVER
LEARN?

David Cronenberg's *Naked Lunch*

Nicholas Zurbrugg

My nephew…was not an author.…Very few of those employed in
writing motion-picture dialogue are. The executives of the studios
just haul in anyone they meet and make them sign contracts.
Most of the mysterious disappearances you read about are due to
this cause. Only the other day they found a plumber who had
been missing for years. All the time he had been writing dialogue
for the Mishkin Brothers. Once having reached Los Angeles,
nobody is safe.

(Wodehouse [1935] 1954: 236–7)

If you go to Hollywood.…And if you really believe in the art of
the film…you ought to forget about any other kind of writing.
A preoccupation with words for their own sake is fatal to good
film making. It's not what films are for.…The best scenes I ever
wrote were practically monosyllabic. And the best short scene I
ever wrote…was one in which the girl said 'uh huh' three times
with three different intonations, and that's all there was to it.

(Chandler, in Gardiner and Walker 1984: 138)

For God's sake Bill, play ball with this conspiracy.

(*Naked Lunch*, 1993)

Like P.G. Wodehouse and Raymond Chandler, William Burroughs has long
anticipated the worst from mainstream cinematic adaptations. Writing to the
painter Brion Gysin in a letter of 24 May 1977, for example, he memorably
complains: 'What can happen to your script is not to be believed. It's like you
came back from Istanbul and there was a Dali bent watch right in the middle of
your picture. You write a part for James Coburn and you wind up with
Liberace' (Morgan 1988: 541).

One way or another, Burroughs suggests, Hollywood invariably imposes the
kind of pseudo-surreal effects that the French cultural theorist Paul Virilio

98

equates with 'the poverty of the trivial dream, which is so curiously lacking in variety and imagination that the representation of our desires becomes a load of drivel, with endless repetitions of a few limited themes'. For Virilio, the same can be said for both 'digital imagery' in particular, 'which merely imitates the special effects and tricks of old 3D cinema' (Virilio [1993] 1995: 71), and for the accelerated pace of media culture in general, which in his terms ruins 'the pause of luminous contemplation' and exhausts 'the fragile sphere of our dreams' (Virilio [1993] 1995: 70–1).

As his notes on the American multimedia performance artist Robert Wilson's 'visionary' capacity to present 'beautiful life-saving dream images' indicate, Burroughs regards dreams as both a poetic necessity, circumventing 'the crippling conventions of dramatic presentation' and 'soap opera plots', and quite literally as 'a *biological necessity*' (Burroughs 1991: 17). In this respect, Burroughs – like Virilio and Wilson – is best understood as an ecologist of the dream, striving to remedy what Walter Benjamin calls 'the shock effect of the film' by identifying multimediated forms of 'heightened presence of mind' and re-establishing 'time for contemplation and evaluation' (Benjamin [1936] 1970: 240).

Likewise, as the subtitle of *Nova Express* – demanding 'WILL HOLLYWOOD NEVER LEARN?' (Burroughs 1966: 70) – suggests, Burroughs seems to have little sympathy for the mass-cultural banality of what he thinks of as the American 'non-dream'. So far as Burroughs is concerned:

> America is not so much a nightmare as a *non-dream*. The American non-dream is precisely a move to wipe the dream out of existence. The dream is a spontaneous happening and therefore dangerous to a control system set up by the non-dreamers.
>
> (Burroughs [1969] 1974: 102)

Paradoxically perhaps, some quarter century after the French edition of *The Job* first published this warning, the independent Canadian film-maker David Cronenberg met Burroughs for the first time in New York and initiated a project to film Burroughs' supposedly 'unfilmable' anti-novel, *The Naked Lunch* (1959), for mass-market distribution, and against all odds, to endorse Burroughs' prodigal career with the seal of Hollywood approval.

Cronenberg carefully defines his plans for *Naked Lunch* (1993) as the attempt to create 'a combination of Burroughsian material but put into a structure that's not very Burroughsian'. Such an adaptation, Cronenberg contends, 'still deserves to be called *Naked Lunch*' by virtue of "accurately reflecting some of the tone of Burroughs, what his life stands for, and what his work has been" ' (Emery and Silverberg in Silverberg 1992: 65). For his part, Burroughs affirmed that Cronenberg's script offered 'a good example of the cinematic license the film-maker takes... to realize his vision on film' (Burroughs 1992b: 14–5).

Significantly though, far from considering Cronenberg's film to have anything of the interactive quality of his early 1960s cut-up experiments in the

Beat Hotel with Brion Gysin, Harold Norse and Ian Somerville, when they 'held constant meetings and conferences with exchange of ideas and comparison of cut-up writing, painting and tape-recorder experiments' (Burroughs 1983: Introduction), Burroughs clearly regarded Cronenberg's film as 'a profoundly personal interpretation' rather than any kind of collaboration, stipulating that he 'had no writing input into the script whatsoever, and only courtesy rights to request any changes, which I didn't' (Burroughs 1992b: 15).

Cronenberg, by contrast, relates how he felt 'forced to...fuse my own sensibility with Burroughs and create a third thing that neither he nor I would have done on his own' (Cronenberg 1997: 162); at once confirming Burroughs' dictum that: 'No two minds ever come together without, thereby, creating...a third mind' (Burroughs 1979: 25), and partially fulfilling Burroughs' dream of 'taking over a young body' in 'an experiment of transference which would be of benefit to both of us, perhaps of incalculable benefit, but in all fairness not without danger' (Burroughs 1974: 28–9).

What are the advantages and disadvantages of a cinematic adaptation that foregrounds 'the tone' of a writer, what their life 'stands for' and what their 'work has been'? And what are the most obvious benefits or dangers of placing literary 'material' within a structure that's 'not very' typical of its author? In Burroughs' case, such questions are best considered in terms of the significant differences in 'tone' between Cronenberg's highly personal but in many ways predominantly mainstream cinematic adaptation of *Naked Lunch*, the more dynamic collaborative register of earlier adaptations of Burroughs' writings such as Antony Balch's underground classics *Towers Open Fire* (1963) and *The Cut-Ups* (1967), and such subsequent increasingly 'overground' ventures as Howard Brookner's *Burroughs: The Movie* (1983), Gus Van Sant's *Drugstore Cowboy* (1989), and Robert Wilson, Tom Waits and Burroughs' collaborative opera, *The Black Rider* (1990).

But what does it mean to 'adapt' a novel for the screen? And what, after all, is a novel? Such questions seem best approached by comparing Burroughs' and Cronenberg's writings and observations about text/screen adaptation. Burroughs dismisses soap opera as being 'not – sort of – even *below* lowbrow' (Burroughs 1990: 47), and speculates that 'if you have a film that has, oh say, ten good minutes in it' that's 'a pretty good film', '[a] *very* good film, actually. You can't expect much more' (Burroughs 1990: 45). He generally concedes, however, that most novels lend themselves to certain 'old, old' formulas.

> Take any novel that you like, and think about making a film out of that novel. Or say in one sentence what this book is about. What is *Lord Jim* about?'...Two sentences, 'Honour lost. Honour regained.'
> (Burroughs 1990: 43)

But as he equally readily emphasizes, 'some novels won't break down like that', and even if they do, 'just because you can get a novel into one sentence doesn't mean you can make a film out of it'.

> You can get *The Great Gatsby* into a couple of sentences, but you can't make a film out of it. What is this about? 'Poor boy loses girl. Poor boy tries to get girl back, which results in tragedy.' 'Poor boy loses girl to rich man, and tries to get her back. Does get her back for a brief inter-lude, and then there is a tragic dénouement, because he's trying something that isn't going to work – he's trying to put back the clock.' But this isn't film material.
>
> (Burroughs 1990: 43)

And why isn't this 'film material'? Because – for Burroughs at least – the impact of *The Great Gatsby* arises not so much from its plot as from what Barthes defines as the 'grain' of the text, or what Chandler equates with a 'particular preoccupation with words for their own sake' (in Gardiner and Walker 1984: 138). 'It's all in the prose, in Fitzgerald's prose. That's where Gatsby exists', Burroughs concludes, and nothing but nothing, can translate this into film:

> Well, you remember the end of *The Great Gatsby*, that's one of the famous scenes in English prose, like the end of 'The Dead' by James Joyce, the famous 'snow falling faintly – like the descent of their last end, upon all the living and the dead'. There's no way that you can put that effectively into film. I mean, you can show snow, but what does that mean? It doesn't mean anything. And the same way with the end of *The Great Gatsby*. And all they could do was a voice-over.
>
> (Burroughs 1990: 43)

While Burroughs insists that film cannot do language's job more effectively, he acknowledges that words are equally powerless to emulate such cinematic effects as the *trompe-l'oeil* montages in Antony Balch's film *Bill and Tony* (1972). Here – in a 'little experiment' in 'face-projection', 'intended to be projected onto the faces of its cast' – Balch and Burroughs 'are seen first inde-pendently, then side-by-side, introducing themselves (as each other) and then speaking short texts', before dubbing each other's voices in the otherwise iden-tical 'second half' (Balch 1972: 12). Even a summary of *Bill and Tony* becomes daunting, and as Burroughs concludes: 'there's no way you could put that on the printed page' (Burroughs 1990: 43).

Contending that '[w]hen someone says, "Well, the film didn't do justice to the book", or vice versa, they're talking about things which aren't the same medium', generally observing that whenever 'Hollywood gets hold of some-thing that's a classic…the results are usually terrible' and speculating that 'films made from quite mediocre books' usually 'make the best films', Burroughs concludes that '[t]he film must stand up as a separate piece of work, quite apart from the book' (Burroughs 1990: 43–5), resting his case upon the precedent of *Chandler* v. *Hollywood.*

> Raymond Chandler was once asked, 'How do you feel about what Hollywood has done to your novels?' He reportedly answered, 'My novels? Why, Hollywood hasn't done anything to them. They're still right there, on the shelf.'
>
> (Burroughs 1992a: xv)

But as Chandler indicates, Hollywood certainly does do things to novels, not least by contorting verbal complexity into what Beckett dismisses as the 'sweet reasonableness of plane psychology à la Balzac' (Beckett 1934: 976). Or as Homer Mandrill puts it in Burroughs' *Exterminator!*, Hollywood poetics (like redneck politics) compulsively turns the clock back 'to 1899 when a silver dollar bought a steak dinner and good piece of ass' (Burroughs 1974: 106), and – one might add – when a silver dollar also bought a good, no-nonsense read, rather than what P.G. Wodehouse memorably calls 'those psychological modern novels where the hero's soul gets all tied up in knots as early as page 21 and never straightens itself out again' (Wodehouse [1935] 1954: 246).

As the author of convoluted anti-narrative which 'actually caused at least one unprepared square to vomit on the carpet' (Nuttall [1968] 1970: 108), Burroughs very reasonably warns that '[i]t is probably an understatement to say that the novel does not obviously lend itself to adaptation for the screen' (Burroughs 1992a: xiii). In turn, as the ill-fated adapter of a 'mother of epics' into which he felt he could at best 'dip', rather than read 'from start to finish', Cronenberg determined 'to be absolutely ruthless when it came to using Burroughs' material' (Silverberg 1992: 161–2):

> I started to think about what I didn't want to do with *Naked Lunch.* I didn't want it to be a movie about drugs…I wanted it to be about writing…I wanted the movie to have characters…I wanted a woman to have an important character…I wanted it to have narrative cohesiveness.
>
> (Cronenberg, in Silverberg 1992: 164–5)

At the same time, Cronenberg's 'wants' list admits a number of symbolic exceptions. Following his early sense 'that drugs were for jazz musicians' (Silverberg 1992: 164), Cronenberg sets the scene for *Naked Lunch* with 'meandering alto sax notes from Ornette Coleman, gracing the highly stylized graphic design of the opening credits' (Conomos 1992: 16). Thereafter Cronenberg evokes addiction increasingly indirectly in terms of alien invasion imagery, as 'a metaphor for control'. 'I understood the metaphorical side. That's what I responded to' (Silverberg 1992: 164).

But Burroughs' vision is as much about low-life as hi-sci-fi life, and one neglects Burroughs' more or less direct evocations of the 'junk-sick dawn' at one's peril. As the virtuosity of *Naked Lunch*'s early pages suggests, Burroughs is at once the Balzac, the Baudelaire and the Ballard of New York's underworld, confidently charting its sordid, spectral or stomach-turning detail in narrative hovering between dispassionate restraint and paranoid anxiety, and generally anticipating the alacrity with which his later 'routines' evince 'simultaneous insight and hallucination', as 'three-dimensional fact merges into dream, and dreams erupt into the real world' (Burroughs 1993: 243, 300).

While Cronenberg's evocation of addiction in terms of the mechanized, fluid-emitting Mugwump offering 'the teat on its head to addicts eager to partake of its irresistible substance' (Duncan, in Silverberg 1992: 94–6) certainly suggests the presence of alien creatures in the real world, the prospect of his plastic monsters in a vaulted, Hammer-style 'Mugwump dispensary' (Duncan, in Silverberg 1992: 96) smacks of the world of Dr Who rather than of Dr Benway. Cronenberg accurately observes that there is 'a lot of hi-sci-fi and horror imagery in Burroughs', particularly the 'Mugwumps, and all kinds of creatures' (Cronenberg, in Silverberg 1992: 166). But as a glance at *Naked Lunch* indicates, most of Burroughs' creatures are not so much exotic 'hi-sci-fi' mutants as vagrant 'terrestial dogs' (Burroughs 1966: 18). Alienated both at home and abroad, these are quintessentially flesh-and-blood aliens, whether clinically described in terms of the kind of 'real scene' in which 'you pinch up some leg flesh and make a quick stab hole with a pin', before fitting the dropper 'over, not in the hole and feed the solution slow and careful so it doesn't squirt out the sides', or whether self-consciously caricatured in such 'pin and dropper' routines as:

> She seized a safety-pin caked with blood and rust, gouged a great hole in her leg which seemed to hang open like an obscene, festering mouth waiting for unspeakable congress with the dropper which she now plunged out of sight into the gaping wound.
>
> (Burroughs [1959] 1982: 20)

Occasionally, to be sure, Burroughs' world rocks to the 'Monster Mash', as mutants like Bradley the Buyer spread terror 'throughout the industry':

> Junkies and agents disappear. Like a vampire bat he gives off a narcotic effluvium, a dank green mist that anesthetizes his victims and renders them helpless in his enveloping presence....Finally he is caught in the act of digesting the Narcotics Commissioner and destroyed with a flame thrower – the court of inquiry ruling that such means were justi-fied in that the Buyer had lost his citizenship and was, in consequence, a creature without species and a menace to the narcotics industry on all levels.
>
> (Burroughs [1959] 1982: 27)

But usually Burroughs depicts business as usual. Blandly concluding: 'Isn't life peculiar?' (Burroughs [1959] 1982: 15), he catalogues an underworld populated by such everyday grotesques as Willy the Disk, 'blind from shooting in the eyeball' (Burroughs [1959] 1982: 17); by the unwashed, such as 'Old Bart...dunking pound cake with his dirty fingers, shiny over the dirt'; by the frailty of 'spectral janitors, grey as ashes, phantom porters sweeping out dusty old halls with a slow old man's hand, coughing and spitting in the junk-sick dawn'; or by shameless 'old junkies' – 'Really disgust you to see it' (Burroughs [1959] 1982: 15).

Ironically, while Cronenberg spares his viewers graphic representation of the 'unspeakable congress' between 'dropper' and 'wound' (Cronenberg, in Silverberg 1992: 20), his most powerful symbols of addiction evince an almost Burroughsian propulsion towards 'only the most extreme material' (Burroughs 1993: 262). Indeed, as Emery and Silverberg report, initial responses to the film's evocations of 'unspeakable congress' between the latex organs of 'fifty Mugwumps suspended horizontally and attended to by a hundred "slaves"' (Silverberg 1992: 71), occasionally proved equally disturbing to both Cronenberg and cast:

> Of the hundred extras...three defected. One of the defectors, a lawyer, said, 'I just can't have my clients see me sucking on a Mugwump teat,' and fled. One visitor who thoroughly enjoyed his encounter with a Mugwump, however, was Burroughs. 'I was impressed with the Mugwump,' he says. 'He's very engaging, rather simpatico.'...This rather worried Cronenberg, who had designed the Mugwumps... to resemble old, elongated junkies that represent the evil spirit pervading the film.
>
> (Silverberg 1992: 71–2)

Both enjoying the Mugwump's immediate 'simpatico' presence, and condoning the 'masterstoke' of Cronenberg's 'substitution of...Mugwump jissom – for the rather more mundane heroin and marijuana depicted in the novel', Burroughs generously concludes: 'One of the novel's central ideas is that addiction can be metaphorical, and what could underscore this better than the film's avoidance of actual narcotics?' (Burroughs 1992a: xiv).

Naked Lunch is self-evidently anything but a purely metaphorical novel without reference to the 'actual'. As Burroughs himself emphasizes, it abounds in 'endless parenthesis' (Burroughs 1989: 128), multiplying realistic and metaphoric perspectives across his 'banquet of thirty, forty components' (Mailer 1965: 42), and hinges upon a sense of obligation towards all facts at all levels, whether metaphoric or literal, indirect or direct. Writing to Jack Kerouac on 18 September 1950, for example, Burroughs insists that '[f]acts exist on infinite levels' and that 'one level does not preclude another' (Burroughs 1993: 71), and in a letter to Kerouac of 12 February 1955 he still more explicitly determines to refine an 'absolute, direct transmission of *fact* on all levels' (Burroughs 1993: 265).

In turn, *Naked Lunch* unequivocally asserts that there is 'only one thing a writer can write about: *what is in front of his senses at the moment of writing*', and that its title 'means exactly what the words say...a frozen moment when everyone sees what is on the end of every fork' (Burroughs [1959] 1982: 218, 1). If Allen Ginsberg's sensitivity to the literal quality of Burroughs' 'actual visions' leads his poem 'On Burroughs' Work' (1954) to caricature them as being free from 'symbolic dressing' (Burroughs 1993: 40), Cronenberg's admiration for the general – rather than the local – satirical register of *Naked Lunch* leads him to overemphasize its symbolic content by treating much of the novel's most disturbing verbal content 'in a metaphorical way' (Cronenberg, in Silverberg 1992: 64).

At the same time, Cronenberg frequently modifies the particularity of the novel's detail in terms of his general insights into what Burroughs' life as a whole 'stands for' and 'what his work has been' (Cronenberg, in Silverberg 1992: 65). Acknowledging, for example, that his treatment of *Naked Lunch* is 'not as aggressive and predatory in its homosexuality' as Burroughs' novel, Cronenberg hints that his film may be closer to reality than the novel itself, insofar as it reflects Burroughs' more tentative evocations of his sexuality in 'letters, prefaces and other things': 'I was trying to see beyond, to the reality of the situation, which is much more ambivalent and ambiguous in terms of sexuality' (Silverberg 1992: 163). At such points Cronenberg's film becomes 'as much an adaptation of Ted Morgan's biography of Burroughs, *Literary Outlaw*...as it was *Naked Lunch*' (Rodley, in Silverberg 1992: 171).

But, as Burroughs remarks in *Interzone*, he is far more interested in Paul Klee's notion of art with 'a life of its own', placing the artist in 'real danger' (Burroughs 1989: 128), than in literary self-portraiture. While Cronenberg certainly evokes this kind of danger thematically, his general approach is often that of a biographical *roman-à-clef*, rather than that of a more dangerously corrosive *roman-à-Klee*. Gaining much of its iconic force from the deadpan detachment of Peter Weller, who as 'Lee' seems a dead-ringer both for a younger Burroughs and a younger Joseph Beuys, Cronenberg's *Naked Lunch* invites the viewer to play 'Spot the Bowles', to 'Spot the Ginsbergian "Martin"' and to 'Spot the Kerouacian "Hank"'. Declining to play, Burroughs bluntly observes: 'I don't recognize anyone I ever knew in those characters' (Burroughs 1992b: 15).

Far from arising from the concrete details of veiled autobiography, *Naked Lunch*'s impact surely derives primarily from its evocations of what Burroughs calls the 'poltergeist knockings and mutterings of America's putrefying unconscious' and the 'incredibly obscene, thinly disguised references and situations that slip by in Grade B Movies' (Burroughs 1993: 259). Reluctant to offer a literal translation of Burroughs' cathartic 'shitting out my educated Middlewest background' (Burroughs, in Morgan 1988: 264) for fear of being 'banned in every country in the world', Cronenberg takes *Naked Lunch* to Disneyland, mechanizing and masking its menace with all the inventions of 'a heavy-duty effects movie' (Cronenberg, in Silverberg 1992: 161, 166).

Dispensing with Burroughs' most offensive characters and delegating their dialogue to 'effects that also talk a lot', *Naked Lunch* enlivens its decimated cast with the 'Bugwriter' – a robotic 'talking sphincter' (Duncan, in Silverberg 1992: 99, 101) with all the charm of what Burroughs calls 'a Dali bent watch' (Morgan 1988: 541). As Lyden Barber observes (1992: 34), the more one sees of this pulsating incarnation of Dr Benway's routine about 'the man who taught his asshole to talk' (Burroughs [1959] 1982: 133–5), the more tiresome it becomes, and the more grateful one feels for Burroughs' inspired role as Benway in the brief adaptation of the operating scene from *Naked Lunch* (Burroughs [1959] 1982: 66–7) in Howard Brookner's *Burroughs: The Movie* (1983).

Put another way, Burroughs' most forceful accounts of his literary crises derive not so much from the iconic quality of obscene descriptive detail, as from the ironic discursive energy with which Burroughs introduces such detail. Nowhere is this more apparent than in a letter to Kerouac (7 December 1954) outlining the difficulties of writing in 'a popular vein' (Burroughs 1993: 242), recording the involuntary genesis of *Naked Lunch*'s 'interzone' section, and generally generating the vitriolic humour so frequently missing from Cronenberg's adaptation of his novel.

> I sat down seriously to write a best-seller Book of the Month Club job on Tangier. So here is what comes out first sentence: 'The only native in Interzone who is neither queer nor available is Andrew Keif's chauffeur...Aracknid is the worst driver in the Zone. On one occasion he ran down a pregnant woman in from the mountains with a load of charcoal on her back, and she miscarried a bloody, dead baby on the street, and Keif got out and sat on the curb stirring the blood with a stick while the police questioned Aracknid and finally arrested the woman.' I can just see that serialized in...*Good Housekeeping.*
> (Burroughs 1993: 241–2)

Amusingly confirming that nothing about 'Burroughs in Tangier' was ever *Good Housekeeping* material, Paul Bowles' reminiscences suggest the ways in which Burroughs' distinctive performative energies subsequently offered remarkably good film-making materials to such early collaborative adaptations of his work as Balch's *Towers Open Fire* (1963). Doubtless the same cinematic energy might also have invigorated Cronenberg's adaptation of *Naked Lunch* had the disparity between fact and fiction not led to his exclusion from the film for fear that his presence 'might jar the viewer out of the story' (Burroughs 1992b: 15).

The litter on his desk and under it, on the floor, was chaotic, but it consisted only of pages of *Naked Lunch*, at which he was constantly working. When he read aloud from it, at random (any sheet of paper he happened to grab would do) he laughed a good deal, as well he might, since it is very funny, but from reading he would suddenly (paper still in hand) go into bitter conversational attack upon whatever aspect of life had prompted the passage he had just read.

(Bowles 1959: 43)

Following Bowles' lead, and remarking how 'Burroughs' humour is peculiarly American, at once broad and sly', Mary McCarthy persuasively argues that while there are 'many points of comparison between Burroughs and Swift', what saves *Naked Lunch* 'is not a literary ancestor but humor'. More specifically, McCarthy explains:

It is the humor of a comedian, a vaudeville performer playing in 'one,' in front of the asbestos curtain of some Keith Circuit or Pantages house long converted to movies....Some of the jokes are verbal ('Stop me if you've heard this atomic secret' or Dr Benway's 'A simopath...is a citizen convinced he is an ape or other simian. It is a disorder peculiar to the army and discharge cures it'). Some are 'black' parody (Dr Benway, in his last appearance, dreamily, his voice fading out: 'Cancer, my first love')....The effect of pandemonium, all hell breaking loose, is one of Burroughs' favorites and an equivalent of the old vaudeville finale, with the acrobats, the jugglers, the magician, the hoofers...all pushing into the act.

(McCarthy [1963] 1991: 4–5)

Sadly, Cronenberg virtually pushes such humour out of 'the act' in order to save his film from degenerating into what he calls 'a very nasty kind of soft, satirical social satire of the *Britannia Hospital* variety, with no emotional content and without the beauty, grace and potency of Burroughs' literary style' (Silverberg 1992: 161). But Burroughs' style is quintessentially a 'nasty' mixture of beauty, grace and the worst extremes of *Britannia Hospital* and *Carry On* humour, and any attempt to rarify it falls on its face. Lee's deadpan rendition of 'Bobo's death', for example – a funereal soliloquy stifling the bedpan hilarity of Benway's account of the quite literally 'sticky end' of Professor Fingerbottom, whose 'falling piles blew out the Duc de Ventre's Hispano Suiza and wrapped around the rear wheel' – prompts alarm rather than amusement, and the suggestion, 'You sound as if you could use a drink' (Burroughs [1959] 1982: 165). While Burroughs resists simplistic categorization as 'a stand-up comedian' (Bockris 1981: 27), his writing is certainly that of a 'sit-down' comedian, and Cronenberg's fork-waving and lunch-contemplating 'Lee' pales before Harry Dean Stanton's far more convincing Burroughsian presence as the sardonic Bud in Michael Nesmith's quirkily urban magic-realist *Repo Man* (1984).

In this respect, Cronenberg's greatest successes are surely his humourless evocations of the long-gone scenes that Burroughs distils from 'many sources: conversations heard and overheard, movies and radio broadcasts' (Burroughs 1986: 19). From the opening shot of Lee's silhouetted fedora, we enter what Burroughs persuasively calls a 'masterful thriller' (Silverberg 1992: 14) made up of third-hand images borrowed by Cronenberg from Burroughs, and borrowed by Burroughs from 'Grade B movies' (Burroughs 1993: 259). Yet as John Conomos observes (1992: 16), against all odds such refined cinematic simulation is 'extraordinarily atmospheric'. Typifying Cronenberg's tendency to borrow images and phrases from both *Naked Lunch* and other Burroughsian novels, Lee's visit to the 'bug drug' building builds on the opening section of *Exterminator!*; an episode written in surprisingly cinematic prose, rich in anecdotal bit-parts and still richer in such evocative sound-bites as Lee's catch-phrase – 'Exterminator! You need the service?' – and the 'older' Cohen brother's rant – 'You vant I should spit right in your face!? You vant!? You vant? You vant!?' (Burroughs 1974: 4, 3). Clearly sharing Burroughs' acute 'ear for dialogue' (Burroughs 1986: 185), even if unwilling or unable to find a way of integrating Burroughsian utterance into his film, Cronenberg beefs things up with a bonus one-liner from the Chinese druggist whose abrupt four-worder brings *Naked Lunch*'s last six lines (quoted here in full) to their fragmentary conclusion.

> "They are rebuilding the City."
> Lee nodded absently…."Yes…Always…"
> Either way is a bad move to The East Wing….
> If I knew I'd be glad to tell you….
> "No good…no bueno…hustling himself…."
> "No glot…C'lom Fliday"
>
> (Burroughs [1959] 1982: 232)

Is this appropriate mainstream movie dialogue? One thinks not. And yet as Paul Bowles remarks, Burroughs' improvisations offered a remarkably theatrical spectacle: 'Surely…worth hearing, and worth watching', as he 'stumbled from one side of the room to the other, shouting in his cowboy voice' (Bowles 1959: 43). In turn, subsequent expatriate celebration of Burroughs' voice on the Paris-based English Bookshop's LP, *Call Me Burroughs* (1965), prompted the American poet Emmett Williams to write:

> The first time I heard Burroughs' voice…I thought: Mark Twain must have talked like this…and I'm sure he likes apple pie. Later when I first heard these excepts from *The Naked Lunch*…Twain…and apple pie were still in evidence, plus a large dose of Texas Charley the medicine-

show man selling tonic to a lot of rubes....His voice is terrifyingly convincing.

(Williams 1965: n.p.)

It is precisely this terrifyingly convincing voice that the British film-maker Antony Balch uses to capture the viewer's attention in the opening scene of Burroughs' first major cinematic adaptation and collaboration, *Towers Open Fire*. Described as 'an 11-minute collage of all the themes and situations in the book, accompanied by a Burroughs soundtrack narration' (Balch 1972: 10), *Towers Open Fire* rushes in where Cronenberg fears to tread (and where Cronenberg can no longer tread), documenting Burroughs shooting up, partially documenting Balch masturbating to Burroughs' incantation 'silver arrow through the night', and offering little other characterization or narrative continuity than fleeting images of Burroughs and Gysin inside or outside the Paris Beat Hotel.

Towers Open Fire opens with a static close-up of Burroughs staring blankly at the camera for fifty seconds or so, before finally blinking and almost smiling, as a burst of trance music signals a cut to the next scene in which he acts as chairman of 'The Board'. Nothing happens, one might say. Or at least, nothing happens but Burroughs' impassive reading and audition of the horrendous 'old white schmaltz' droned out by 'the District Supervisor' in *The Soft Machine*. Here, for a highly unnerving minute, the viewer quite literally has 'no place to go' other than this forced encounter with disquieting dramatization of what the next sentence in *The Soft Machine* calls: 'Most distasteful thing I ever stood still for'.

> Now kid what are you doing over there with the niggers and the apes? Why don't you straighten out and act like a white man? After all they're only human cattle – You know that yourself – Hate to see a bright young man fuck up and get off on the wrong track – Sure it happens to all of us one time or another – Why the man who went on to invent Shitola was sitting right where you're sitting now twenty-five years ago and I was saying the same things to him – Well he straightened out the way you're going to straighten out....You can't deny your blood kid – You're white white white – And you can't walk out on Trak – There's just no place to go.
>
> (Burroughs [1961] 1968: 140–1)

As becomes evident, Burroughs in the 1960s was altogether different to the Burroughs of the 1990s who claimed to be 'relieved' that Cronenberg did not ask him to 'write or co-write' the screenplay for *Naked Lunch*; who expressed surprise that writers still 'think they can *write* a film script, not realizing that film scripts are not meant to be read, but acted and photographed' (Burroughs, in Silverberg 1992: 14); and who generally argued that 'the rule of film is that movies move, with minimal talk' (Silverberg 1992: 13). Here, in black and white, Burroughs demonstrates the considerable impact of maximal 'talk' set against almost wholly motionless imagery, writing for – and reading and acting in – a cinematic adaptation built both around and upon the auratic energy of his cinematic presence.

Four years later, Balch's film *The Cut-Ups* (1967) explored still more radical text–screen collaboration and adaptation. On the one hand, as Gysin explains, Balch randomly spliced documentary footage of his collaborators:

> Antony was applying…the 'cut-up' technique where he simply took all the footage he had and handed it over to an editor, just telling her to set up four reels, and put so many feet on each one in order – one, two, three, four, and start again, the same number.
>
> (Gysin 1997: 177)

On the other hand, Gysin and Burroughs produced an independent made-to-measure soundtrack, patiently intoning such mind-numbing greetings as 'Yes – hello', before juggling with the question, 'Does this image seem to be persisting?' and other phrases 'taken directly from the Scientology classes that [Burroughs] was going to at the time' (Gysin 1997: 180). As Gysin relates, predictably neither *Towers Open Fire* nor *The Cut-Ups* enjoyed commercial success when first screened at the Academy Cinema, Oxford Street, which 'finally asked if we could please take them off the screen because they'd had such a high incidence of people forgetting very strange things in the theatre'. Surprisingly, though, even greater hostility awaited them in New York, where even the artistic underground recoiled from Burroughs' 'very heavy aura' as a writer who 'had shot his wife' and 'published the most shocking book of its time' (Gysin 1997: 182).

Neither literary adaptation nor literary adoption seemed on Burroughs' cards in the late 1960s and early 1970s, and only in 1974 did his 'aura' grow lighter, following the success of his first New York readings. Recalling that 'Burroughs had gotten very paranoid in London', Andreas Brown describes how '[y]ou could see his face change as he realized that people wanted to hear him' (Bockris 1981: 77–8). In New York, as in Tangier and Paris, Burroughs once again wowed his contemporaries with his prowess as a performer and raconteur of semi-autobiographical texts, and in his film *Burroughs: The Movie* (1983), Howard Brookner gave Burroughs *carte blanche* to adapt or perform his writings and generally reminisce about the past. Here we see a besuited Burroughs reading on stage at a desk; a begarbed Burroughs in operating theatre greens, acting out one of the Dr Benway routines from *Naked Lunch*; and an avuncular Burroughs, nostalgically guiding Grauerholz around his old St Louis haunts. Without doubt, Burroughs was back in town.

In May 1983, Burroughs' induction into the American Academy and Institute of Arts and Letters marked his formal literary rehabilitation, and in

October 1983, the first major public screening of *Burroughs: The Movie* at the New York Film Festival offered him the approval of independent cinema culture. Five years later, Hollywood itself confirmed that Burroughs was no longer *persona non grata*, as fact, fiction and Burroughs' conflicting personae as literary outlaw and grand old man of American letters coalesced in his role as Tom the Priest – based on The Priest in *Exterminator!* (Burroughs 1974: 156) – in Gus Van Sant's film *Drugstore Cowboy* (1989). Here, as in *Burroughs: The Movie*, Burroughs exemplifies the streetwise old-timer, this time guiding Bob (played by Matt Dillon) around town. And here, once again, Burroughs worked on his script, suggesting to Van Sant that his character – the 'middle-aged' junkie Bob Murphy – should become 'an old junkie', and describing 'how he would have behaved in Murphy's circumstances'. When Van Sant's 'rewrite didn't really capture it', Grauerholz 'rewrote four scenes for William...and then William put his own unique polish on it, his own imprimatur' (Grauerholz, in Miles 1992: 14).

The following year, Burroughs entered his final collaboration with the post-modern multimedia avant-garde, writing the libretto for Robert Wilson's opera *The Black Rider* (1990). Hailing Burroughs as a fellow visionary willing 'to destroy the codes in order to make a new language', Wilson welcomed the opportunity to set Burroughs' 'dreamy, cloud-like texts' against his own anti-naturalistic practice of telling stories 'visually, in scenery and in gestures' (Wilson 1992: 50–1). Wilson set Burroughs' words within multimedia narratives evincing 'an ongoing thing...a continuum...something that never, never finishes', unlike commercially viable cinematic 'one-liners' in which 'you get information in three seconds, and then that's it' (Wilson 1992: 52). This time, collaborative multimedia adaptation and integration of Burroughs' writings struck gold, and (as Burroughs reports) when *The Black Rider* opened at Hamburg's Thalia Theatre in March 1990, 'There were fifteen curtain calls, which is almost unheard of' (Burroughs 1994: 70).

Revered as a living legend on almost all fronts, Burroughs now presented the ideal subject-matter for Hollywood legend. And so it came to pass, in Cronenberg's strangely puritanical homage to the undeniable 'beauty, grace and potency' of much of 'Burroughs' literary style' (Cronenberg, in Silverberg 1992: 161): a film made too late to integrate the dynamic authorial performances in *Towers Open Fire* and *The Cut-Ups*, made too cautiously to countenance the burlesque Burroughsian 'routines' authorially hammed to perfection in *Burroughs: The Movie*, made too conventionally to opt for the 'dreamy, cloud-like' logic welcomed by Wilson in *The Black Rider*, and made too wisely to replicate the authorial self-caricature in *Drugstore Cowboy*.

Cronenberg's adaptation of *Naked Lunch* surely works best when its camera-work lugubriously glides through beautifully observed sets with exemplary deceleration, partially compensating for its sins of omission with remarkable atmospheric intensity and spectacular 'adult' special effects, generating what Burroughs calls a 'miasma of paranoia' (Burroughs 1992b: 15) entirely commensurate with the 'dead-end despair' (Burroughs 1993: 255) permeating the bleaker sections of his 'very funny book' (Burroughs 1990: 38).

As Cronenberg indicates, writing as demanding as Burroughs' fiction almost inevitably places the cinematic adapter in a no-win situation, in which they can at best 'dip' into their subject, 'a little bit here, a little bit there' (Cronenberg, in Silverberg 1992: 161). Given such circumstances, Balch, Brookner, Van Sant and Wilson suggest, the most winning way to work with living experimental authors may well be the 'double-dipping' strategy of integrating the interactive 'special effects' offered by *collaborative* intertextual adaptation.

9

ADAPTING THE HOLOCAUST

Schindler's List, intellectuals and public knowledge

Mark Rawlinson

Thomas Keneally's *Schindler's Ark* (1983) relates the actions of an ethnic German war-profiteer who preserved more than 1,000 Kraków Jews from extermination in Auschwitz-Birkenau. Among the 'Righteous Gentiles' whose altruism has been documented and honoured by Yad Vashem, the Martyrs' and Heroes' Remembrance Authority in Jerusalem, Oskar Schindler is an unusual figure: his economic and sexual opportunism make his virtue unconventional. This in part explains the form of Keneally's book: 'the novel's techniques seem suited for a character of such ambiguity and magnitude as Oskar'. But fictionalization threatened to 'debase the record', to hamper discrimination between 'reality and the myths which are likely to attach themselves to a man of Oskar's stature' (Keneally 1983: Author's note).[1] The propriety of representing the Holocaust within the structural and ideological conventions of imaginative narrative is a question that has been brought to bear with considerable force on Hollywood's version of Keneally's emplotment of testimony about Schindler. But Keneally recognized another problem of credibility, relating not to the documentary authority of the story, but to the problem of believing in it so as to understand it. It is a story about:

> the pragmatic triumph of good over evil, a triumph in eminently measurable, statistical, unsubtle terms. When you work from the other end of the beast, when you chronicle the predictable and measurable success evil generally achieves, it is easy to be wise, wry, piercing, to avoid bathos. It is easy to show the inevitability by which evil acquires all of what you could call the *real estate* of the story, even though good might finish up with a few imponderables like dignity and self-knowledge. Fatal human malice is the staple of narrators, original sin the mother-fluid of historians. But it is a risky enterprise to have to write of virtue.
>
> (1983: 1)

The way Keneally couches this problem of narration, as a tension between the inevitable and the inconceivable, suggests parallels with the historiography of the Holocaust. In the early 1960s, the prosecution strategy at the Eichmann trial lent further authority to the view that Jews had 'gone to their deaths "like sheep to the slaughter"' (Marrus 1995: 86–8). Scholarship has been dominated by studies of the perpetrators.

At the centre of this picture has been the 'machinery of destruction': the bureaucratic and technological apparatus with which the Nazis exterminated Europe's Jews (Hilberg 1985). Claude Lanzmann's film *Shoah* (1985) is structured around the painstaking 'corroboration' of the minute details of this apparatus, in its continual, *ad hoc* development, appropriating existing techniques and inventing new ones. Raul Hilberg himself interprets for Lanzmann the timetables and invoices, at pre-war tourist-group rates, for the rail transportation of Jews to the death camps in Poland. The idea of the inevitability of the destruction of persons thrown into the *univers concentrationnaire* has been crucial to the collective effort of documenting and imaging the Holocaust, not least to overcome the resistance implicit in the concept of the human being as an autonomous and free agent. Of course, the principle of inevitability – 'everyone must be snatched away from liberation' – was central to the implementation of Nazi policy: 'today was history. There had been for more than seven centuries a Jewish Cracow, and by this evening...those seven centuries would have become a rumour' (Keneally 1983: 168). Registering the abnormality of the 'terrible...but also indecipherable' world of the camps requires that we conceive the impossibility of an exit from what Primo Levi termed the 'Grey Zone' (Levi 1989: 5). This is the world of the death camps 'in which the room for choices (especially moral choices) was reduced to zero', and where the Special Squads who did the labour of extermination were largely Jewish, for 'it must be the Jews who put the Jews into the ovens, it must be shown that the Jews, the sub-race, the sub-men, bow to any and all humiliation, even to destroying themselves' (Levi 1989: 33, 35).

The way knowledge of the Holocaust has been formed since 1945 reinforces the trope of inevitability. The world's belated recognition of what occurred in the extermination camps, in part the result of Nazi secrecy, is a temporal figure for the helplessness of Europe's Jews. The sparse information reaching the Allied states in wartime was suppressed, disbelieved, or incomprehensible. While photographs and newsreel footage of the liberation of concentration camps like Belsen were exhibited in the months after victory over Germany, post-war British and American culture did not engage substantially with the Holocaust as each set about telling their story of the Second World War. One of the triggers of the by now disproportionately greater interest in the Holocaust in the United States was the Israeli state's kidnapping, trial and execution of Adolf Eichmann (1960–2), which drew world attention to the Jewish experience of the war and its aftermath (Kushner 1994: 242–9; Evron 1983).

Schindler's Ark begins 'perilously', both for its hero (who is taking substantial risks in opposing the Nazi apparatus) and, in a different sense, for its narrator (who is relating a story that runs against the grain of the fact that for millions it was too late). For it may 'stretch belief' that Schindler, who has gone out of his way to know 'earlier than most would dare to know it, what "*Sonderbehandlung*" means...pyramids of cyanosed corpses in Belzec, Sobibor, Treblinka, and...Auschwitz-Birkenau', should risk 'a multiplicity of hangings, beheadings, consignments to the huts of Auschwitz or Gröss-Rosen' in order to 'salvage certain human lives' (Keneally 1983: 18–9).[2] From his arrival in Poland in the wake of invasion as an agent of Admiral Canaris' *Abwehr* intelligence service, Schindler has been an antagonist of Himmler's SS (and is thus implicated in a rivalry which dates back to Hitler's progressive seizure of the apparatus of the German state in the 1930s). These contacts permit him to warn Itzhak Stern of the SS *Einsatzgruppen* attack on the Jewish quarter of Kazimierz, and of the edict of March 1941 establishing a closed ghetto (Keneally 1983: 47, 76–7). In his role as war-profiteer, Schindler has been employing Jewish workers, on Stern's recommendation, before the SS seize the labour of the ghetto. The 'moral discomfort' of using slaves which then arises 'outweighed the economic advantage', but it gives the ghetto an 'economic permanence', and he promises his workers 'if you work here, then you'll live through the war' (Keneally 1983: 80, 84). Having witnessed SS brutality and murder in the ghetto, he resolves to 'do everything in my power to defeat the system' (Keneally 1983: 123, 127). The 'clinching evidence' is the report of one Bachner, who has 'somehow' returned to the ghetto from the 'Baths and Inhalation Rooms' of Belzec with what many take to be a 'dangerous rumour' about the gassing of Jews (Keneally 1983: 130). Contacted by a Zionist rescue organization, Schindler travels to Budapest to document the 'unbelievable' existence of extermination camps at the moment when Untersturmführer Amon Goeth is posted to Kraków to liquidate the ghetto and take command of the forced labour camp under construction at Płaszów. Twice arrested by the Gestapo, Schindler is by this stage in the narrative deeply implicated in a struggle to keep the population of his factory 'haven' from extermination. In its counterpointing of the Schindler Jews' witness of Nazi barbarity with their testimony to the miraculous actions of Schindler, Keneally's subsequent narration of rescue suggests that while the death camps have become one of 'the commonplaces of history' (Keneally 1983: 131), requiring no further corroboration, Schindler hovers on the brink of the mythical. What makes his virtue a risky venture from the storyteller's point of view is not just that it is so unconventional, but that it creates a temporal and causal dissonance: Schindler 'seemed to draw on a knowledge of future [Nazi] intentions' (Keneally 1983: 18).

In *Schindler's List* (1993), Steven Spielberg constructs Oskar Schindler's relation to this knowledge in a very different way. Keneally's hero has a nature to be sought through the fictional narration of cause and effect. By contrast the film seeks credibility at the level of characterization. Liam Neeson's Schindler belatedly discovers his role as rescuer: the inner nature of the good German is called forth by Stern, in whom three characters from the novel (two Jewish, one Austrian) are combined.[3] Spielberg's hero is denied the authority that attaches to a 'knowledge of future intentions', indeed he is presented at the outset as a collaborator with race policy (hiring Jewish workers from the SS because they are cheaper than Poles) who must be compelled to recognize that his profiteering has provided shelter to Jews long after the 'machinery of destruction' has been perfected. Keneally's problem with the presentation of virtue is resolved by creating what amounts to a conversion narrative which rehearses the West's tardy recognition of the Holocaust. This means that the events of the Holocaust are presented in a different way to the novel, where they are assumed to need no corroboration. The extermination of the Jews is, in the temporality of the film, something happening as for the first time. The importance of this in the film's popular and critical receptions is manifest in the stunned adulation and the controversy which was generated by Spielberg's decision to reconstruct events of the Holocaust through a quasi-documentary presentation of the workings of Nazi genocidal techniques and technology.

The film does attempt to qualify its hero-centred structure by incorporating echoes of the testimony of Jews reported by Keneally's narrator. For instance, it is in relation to the subjectivity ascribed to Jewish characters that the reconstructions of the ghetto and Auschwitz are mediated to the audience. Schindler watches events leading up to the liquidation of the Kraków ghetto from horseback in an overlooking park. But it is the Jews who feature in the glimpses of daily life overlaid by the soundtrack of Goeth's address to the SS ('Today is history…') who are identified via reaction shots as witnesses to murder: Stern, Mrs Dresner, Poldek Pfefferberg. Only then does Schindler track the progress of the girl in the red coat who passes out of sight as a group of adults are lined up and shot. The reaction and point-of-view shots which establish Schindler's sightings of the girl have a different function as part of a narrative schema connoting character psychology (Hansen 1996: 305). Schindler's second sighting of the coat completes a frame around the pivotal episode in the development of his altruistic personality. Told that the Jews in Płaszów say his factory is a haven from random killings, he modulates his evasive 'What am I supposed to do?' into an invitation to think of things from Goeth's 'point of view'. The cut to Stern's secondhand account (via voice-over flashback) of Goeth's 'reprisal' execution of twenty-five men from the barracks of an escapee answers this rationalization with testimony to the nature of the camp regime. Schindler, who has for a second time employed Goeth's trope of the Jew tempter/temptress to accuse a Jewish pleader of entrapping him in an infringement of the Race Laws, now acts wittingly to protect Jewish lives. Stern draws forth the act for which Schindler's own earlier witness is a kind of dormant motivation, and turns him from bystander to rescuer. His second sighting of the red coat – the corpse of the girl is incinerated as Płaszów is closed down, the evidence of its product destroyed – points towards Spielberg's bathetic addition of Schindler's self-recrimination ('I could have got more out') at the film's close. The function of this remodelling of Schindler is underlined by comparison with the red coat episode in the novel (the second sighting is Spielberg's invention). The presence of the girl as a witness confirms for Keneally's Schindler that there will be no witnesses: if the men carrying out the executions can allow a child to see such things, they can have no shame, and if they have no shame, there must be official sanction (Keneally 1983: 123). Her witnessing confirms the future to Schindler, whereas in *Schindler's List* it is Stern's testimony of another's witness which reaches out to produce it (Hansen 1996: 303–4).

The same narrative structure which defers Schindler's knowledge of the significance of the actions he, unlike the Jews, is empowered to risk taking, also defers visual registration of the extent to which the 'machinery of destruction' had been perfected to the goal of destroying all witnesses. In this sense, the audience's exposure to the Holocaust (dramatic reconstruction of genocidal acts is the basis of some of the exorbitant claims for and against the film) is correlated with the viewpoint of Schindler, and the Jews who by virtue of the luck of coming within the orbit of his factory are fated to survive the Holocaust. This is reinforced by the cinema's power to denote reality sensuously. The narrative alludes to the existence of death-factories like Auschwitz at key points in the hero's progression, when he pulls Stern, on whom his profiteering is dependent, off a transport ('Where would I be?'), and when he has the packed rail trucks standing in stifling heat at Płaszów station hosed with water. But the film only establishes the existence of Auschwitz in terms of its dominant representational mode of authenticating historical reconstruction towards the end of the narrative sequence (which is the end of the war, and liberation). This approach to Auschwitz is emplotted as a bureaucratic mistake, and diegetically constructed through a dispersed sequence of shots establishing Mila Pfefferberg's progressive realization of what is happening there. Her report of a rumour of extermination ('They gassed them') is rejected by the women in the barracks at Płaszów: 'It doesn't make any sense' – if they gassed them all, how did the story get out? She alone sees the boy who draws his finger across his throat, which is the first sign of the transport's real destination, and it is in relation to Mila Pfefferberg's point of view that shots of the crematorium chimney and the plumbing of the underground chamber are sutured into the narrative.[4]

Two issues arise in relation to Spielberg's use of the narrative conventions of fiction and cinema's economic and rhetorical capacity to generate the appearance of a self-authenticating reconstruction of the past. One, to which we will return in a consideration of the arguments of Spielberg's fiercest critics, concerns the ethical and ideological implications of Hollywood's relating of history and the assimilation, appropriation or denial of traumatic events. The other is the meanings of a story of rescue and survival in the context of public knowledge of the Holocaust.

Because the exceptional nature of rescue is perceived as being at odds with the registration of the exceptional nature of the Holocaust, the very story that Spielberg filmed a decade after he was first shown Keneally's book has become controversial. Stories of the saved distort because they exclude stories of the drowned (Bartov 1997: 47). For other critics, the historical events retold in the film 'cannot but remain a fairy tale in the face of the overwhelming facticity of "man-made mass death"' (Hansen 1996: 298–9). But although rescuers and survivors are atypical figures in the statistical record of the Nazi genocide, altruistic behaviour and resistance are significant dimensions of historical research, and raise important interpretative and ethical issues in relation to knowledge and understanding of the Holocaust. If the representation of rescuers and survivors is problematic, it is in part because images of individuation and liberation contradict the concept of inescapable mass extermination. While criticism of *Schindler's List* has been chiefly addressed to the consequences of the way Spielberg encodes the rescue narrative, it also registers the problems created by the increasing heterogeneity and complexity of the historical record and of scholarly interpretations of the Holocaust. The issue here can be stated as the difficulty of making or preserving the distinction between the facts of rescue reported in Keneally's book, and the narrative forms which have been attached to them. The decision to base a screenplay about the Holocaust on *Schindler's Ark* is readily explicable in economic terms: the book supplies a hero-centred narrative, and Oskar Schindler's wartime story has a redemptive conclusion. But is the subject of rescue itself to be considered homologous with Hollywood's narrative conventions? Do screenings of *Schindler's List* make audiences likely to locate the meanings of the Holocaust in the ethical drama of rescue and survival *instead of* in the actions of the SS and their collaborators, and the hopelessness of their victims?

Escape is a trope of human agency which, in its ubiquitous cultural reproduction, works to makes the 'Grey Zone' inconceivable:

> Perhaps it is good that the prisoner's condition, not-liberty, is felt to be something improper, abnormal – like an illness, in short – that has to be cured by escape or rebellion. Unfortunately, however, this picture hardly resembles the true one of the concentration camp.
>
> (Levi 1987: 386–7)

Escape, resistance and rebellion invoke ideals of free agency and moral determination which in themselves connote subjectivities and realities alien to the regime of the death camps. Arguments that the Allies did little domestically, diplomatically or militarily to rescue the Jews, which have shifted the perception of these states from a role as saviours (in resisting and destroying Nazism) to bystanders, may be infected by a compulsion to conceive of opportunities where they were unconceived or inconceivable.[5]

But the history of the Jewish experience of the Holocaust, rather than of the actions of the Nazis, cannot be written without documenting and seeking to understand the place of acts of resistance, rebellion and rescue. As Yehuda Bauer notes, '[a]ttempts at rescue from the Holocaust were a side show, but their implications are very significant', in particular for the 'questions of personal and public ethics with which we grapple in the generations after the Holocaust' (Bauer 1994: 2). The extension of historical knowledge brings with it the problem of integrating, at the levels of analysis and imagination, manifold perspectives on events which escape us as we try to bring them under familiar descriptions. If, as Hilberg suggests in *Shoah*, big questions get small answers because the Holocaust will never be explained, investigation must attend to the detail of what, where, who and how, in the manner in which Lanzmann interviews survivors and perpetrators, or in which Martin Gilbert has chronicled genocide (Gilbert 1985). Josh Waletzky, the director of the film *Partisans of Vilna* (1986), takes the optimistic view that public knowledge and understanding is synchronous with this cumulative recovery of the past: 'the public value of the Holocaust in America has always been to stress the tragedy. It's certainly the overriding reality. So it's not surprising that one particular aspect – which was seen as a countervailing one – has been late in coming out. Death and destruction are more important in the overall scheme. Resistance becomes significant after the basic facts are known and assimilated into the culture as a whole' (Insdorf 1989: 166). But Spielberg's critics have sought to confound this buoyant inference of progressive enlightenment. Hilberg has argued that in inflating the rescuer's role the film reproduces a 'need for heroes' which can in this context only lead to revisionist distortions; Lanzmann asserts that '[t]he project of telling Schindler's story confuses history' (Fensch 1995: 221–2).

The difficulties that *Schindler's List* raises in its interpretation of rescue are most evident in its closing phase, from the farewell sequence in which Schindler weeps over the gold Nazi Party pin which could have bought 'one more person'.[6] As a 'profiteer of slave labour' he is now hunted, the Jews are free. The historical and psychological implausibilities of this perspective are compounded by the disguise – the striped uniform of the concentration camp – which Schindler dons for his departure (his robing as a victim anticipates the promotion of the film as a vehicle for a politics of universal victimhood). The film's capacity to signify the reality of liberation is as fraught with conflicting messages as is its passing through Auschwitz. References in the dialogue to there being no other survivors are transcended in rhetorical terms by the shot of the Schindler Jews cresting a hill, line abreast. The connotations of this image are quite different to those of the scene of liberation which closes Wajda's *Korczak* (1990), as a wagon-load of Auschwitz-bound orphaned children appear to escape into the Polish countryside. By staging the *fantasy* of rescue, Wajda confronts us with the gap between a faith in goodness (Korczak is the epitome of the virtuous rescuer) and the exitlessness of the Holocaust. But with its soundtrack allusion to the Six Day War (Naomi Shemer's 1967 hit 'Jerusalem of Gold') and imagery redolent of the imaginary communities of Coca Cola and British Airways commercials, *Schindler's List* portrays a triumphalist exit from history. This conflicts with more sober and disturbing accounts of the survivor's return home: '[i]n that moment in which they felt they were again becoming men (that is, responsible), the sorrows of men returned' (Levi 1989: 52). The Technicolor sequence in Jerusalem constitutes the film's documentary titles, or title, visually identifying survivors with the actors who play them, and underlining the trope of Schindler as father of the 'family' of survivors' descendants who outnumber, as a subtitle assures us, the Jews of Poland today. How many of the film's audience would unpack the way the closing location reads the Holocaust in relation to the establishment of the State of Israel is a matter of debate (Bartov 1997: 45).[7] More explicit is the implication that liberation closes off the past, and that life is resumed. Video-taped testimony by the son of Schindler survivors, with its graphic registration of the persistence of trauma, contradicts this message:

> The 'reunion' between Menachem S. and his parents is a traumatic meeting that violates all traditional notions of closure and afflicts consciousness with an overpowering sense of the *im*possibility of restoring interrupted family unity. His father, more than six feet tall, weighs eighty-eight pounds. His rotted teeth are hanging loosely from his gums. Menachem S. looked at him and didn't recognize him as his father. His emaciated mother did not resemble the woman in the picture she had left with him. 'I just couldn't believe that they were my parents,' he reports....For some period after that, he called them Mr and Mrs S. instead of mother and father, unable to restore continuity to the disrupted story of his life.
>
> (Langer 1991: 111)

In comparisons with Lanzmann's *Shoah*, which does not restore the past but interrogates its traces in the present, *Schindler's List* looks either naively unself-conscious or culpably manipulative in its bridging of fifty years to spell out the lessons of the Holocaust for the late twentieth century (whether these relate to propaganda for multiculturalist pedagogy or for Zionism). In appearing to restore the past, the film trivializes or appropriates it. But, as I shall suggest, criticism of the film is also prey to the problems of restoration, particularly where it forgets the complex developments of Holocaust awareness in those fifty intervening years.

The scale and intensity of intellectual and academic opposition to *Schindler's List* is unprecedented for a commercial movie. Dissent from popular and industry acclaim has not been limited to the articulation of more exacting aesthetic and ethical judgements on Spielberg's representation of the past: it also voices alarm at the film's hegemonic status in defining the meaning of the Holocaust. But this scenario, not least where it is associated with sanctions which imply some proper mode of addressing the Holocaust, only makes it more difficult to address questions about the sociology of knowledge of the Holocaust in contemporary culture. Ideas about the power of Spielberg's movie to silence all other representations, and about an absolute knowledge of the Holocaust are, in this debate, mutually reinforcing extremes which pre-empt reflection on the contradiction that the Nazi genocide must and must not be talked about.

Hansen identifies four themes which consistently appear in the critique of *Schindler's List*: it is a product of the culture industry; it employs the form of fictional narrative; it narrates events from the perspective of perpetrators; it violates the taboo on representation (Hansen 1996: 296–300). The first and last positions are not primarily correlated to the form and content of *Schindler's List*, but call into question all commercial or institutional mediations of the Holocaust, not just those of the media industries but also instructional and memorial representations which are consumed at the interface of education and leisure. The entertainment business adapts and trivializes history in line with its economic and ideological imperatives: 'everything is looked at from only one aspect', that of exchange value (Adorno and Horkheimer 1979: 158). To relate or visualize the Holocaust promises to misrepresent or even desecrate a disaster whose nature, it is often claimed, is such that it cannot be grasped. On this line of argument, the attempted assimilation of the unspeakable to conventional modes of representation amounts to denial or sacrilege. But the *Schindler's List* debate raises the question of how far the thesis of the 'crisis in representation' brought about by the Holocaust – 'the death taint of Nazi jargon has irretrievably corroded language and symbolic expression…the experience of horror and genocide remains in some sense outside the boundaries of language' (Horowitz 1997: 121) – has become an article of faith which predetermines the kind of conclusions that are drawn about who can speak of the Holocaust. The second and third critiques are, by contrast, concerned specifically with *Schindler's List*'s narrative content (its hero is a German) and its devices (for example the choice of film stock and cinematographic apparatus to create illusions about the provenance of its images, citation, the deployment of suspense, and the distribution of point of view). In these respects, Spielberg has been arraigned for making a film which displaces extermination with liberation, and engages its audience ethically only through its simplistic presentation of the conflict between good and bad Germans.

It is hard to dissent from the detail of these interpretations of Spielberg's film, and they are well-warranted in the light of the cultural significance attributed to 'the first studio film to deal directly with the enormity of the Holocaust' (Loshitzky 1997a: 1). At the centre of the debate is the issue of the impact of commercial culture on historical consciousness, in particular the power of cinema and television to shape our knowledge of the past. Because these questions are formulated both in aesthetic and demographic terms, the slippage in critiques of *Schindler's List* between conclusions about form and about public effect is less obvious than it might be. Thomas Doherty's observation that '[t]he medium that in 1945 indelibly confirmed the rumors of war now passes information to a new generation – with film-makers like Spielberg the custodians of an awful legacy' (Fensch 1995: 124), highlights what lies at the bottom of much discussion of the film's deleterious impact, namely guardianship of the past. Hansen (1996: 294) suggests that the controversy over *Schindler's List* (which was released in the year that the United States Holocaust Memorial Museum opened in Washington, D.C.) reflects not only conflicts over remembrance and the Americanization of the Holocaust, but also the attitudes of intellectuals to mass culture. In this respect, disagreement about how Spielberg's movie should be judged reflects differing positions on the project of disseminating knowledge about the Holocaust. The way in which the significance of the film's distortions has been weighed with the significance of its impact has reinforced a tendency towards a categorical scepticism about the possibility of a public knowledge of the Holocaust which is not already compromised by bias and manipulation.

Assumptions about public knowledge are objectified in the frequent comparisons of *Schindler's List* and *Shoah* 'as two mutually exclusive paradigms of cinematically representing or not-representing the Holocaust' (Hansen 1996: 294). *Shoah* locates the traces of the events of the early 1940s which persist into the years of its production (1974–85): the memories of victims, perpetrators and bystanders, the remains of the infrastructure of extermination in the Polish landscape. *Shoah* does not present a view of the past, but of the present: 'if there had been...a film actually shot in the past of three thousand people dying together in a gas chamber...I would never have included this in the film. I would have preferred to destroy it. It is not visible. You cannot look at this' (Lanzmann *et al.* 1991: 99). This is what *Schindler's List* threatens to show us, and then draws back by narrative fiat. It requires us to look (by creating suspense through the build-up to a dramatic reconstruction of the scene of mass murder) and it renders reality whole by figuring disaster as something bypassed. The form of Spielberg's film, which culminates in triumph, correlates with the way it is positioned (in the words of Gertrude Koch) 'at the end of film history', as a culmination of cinematic representations of the Holocaust (Loshitzky 1997b: 104). *Schindler's List* supersedes *Shoah* technologically and economically, both by showing what (in Lanzmann's view) must not be shown, and by showing it to millions who will in all likelihood never see Lanzmann's nine-hour film. This challenge to the idea that images of catastrophe are a kind of sacrilege is a complex one, for the conventions by which Auschwitz is visualized produce a resistance to the intention of forcing the Holocaust into public consciousness.

'Everybody knows six million have been killed, which is an abstraction'. *Shoah* relentlessly searches out concrete detail – 'in Treblinka the train was pushing the wagon...at Auschwitz the wagons were pulled' – to counter the sway of disembodied generalization (Lanzmann *et al.* 1991: 92). Lanzmann hired a locomotive to retrace arrival at Treblinka station (the rail spur to the extermination camp having been dismantled). This intervention led to an unforeseen discovery he regards as crucial to his film's construction, the sign made by the Polish locomotive driver, cutting his throat with his finger: 'I didn't expect that the man would suddenly do this gesture....I did not ask him to do this because I could not even imagine he would do it, and I did not know at this time that the gesture was made.' This sequence becomes 'the proper way' to approach Treblinka. What occurs here is the opening of a gap between the name 'Treblinka' at the station, which has become a synecdoche for the Holocaust, and the sign which, when it was already too late, signified 'passing in another circle, call it whatever you want, of hell' (Lanzmann *et al.* 1991: 83). The film works its harrowing effects by declining to recycle familiar images of Nazism (Loshitzky 1997b: 113).

Where Lanzmann uses place to invoke what is absent, Spielberg assiduously replicates the past. The train carrying the Schindler women enters his simulacrum of the gas chambers and crematoria (constructed outside the camp) through the familiar structure of the Birkenau gatehouse. The integrity of the illusion matters more than the integrity of its construction, for the train we see has departed from *inside* Birkenau itself, an ironic underscoring of the film's passing through Auschwitz. If Spielberg's film 'challenges ["the limits of representation"] by making the unimaginable imaginable, the unrepresentable representable' (Loshitzky 1997a: 2), in doing so it has seemed to a number of critics to cover both its tracks and the contradictions involved in its pursuit of authenticity. Leon Wieseltier, observing that the film 'is designed to look like a restored print of itself' (Fensch 1995: 117), points to the problem of the fiction film's potential to seem more real than the events it recreates.

That reality effect, as Gertrude Koch argues, is the product of a recycling of the already imagined (Loshitzky 1997b: 104). Spielberg cites *Shoah* when Mila Pfefferberg glimpses a child making Lanzmann's chanced-upon gesture. A reprise in slow motion, as seen through the bogies of the train, is a more explicit homage to Lanzmann's film, the soundtrack of which is marked, in de Beauvoir's words, 'by the almost intolerable din of the train rolling towards the camps' (Insdorf 1989: 254). But the narrative's destination makes this a misreading (it is not, in this instance, too late). The sign is adapted, modified for new conditions, by its insertion into a structure that redresses its function in *Shoah* where, we might agree with Felman's overall conclusion, it 'revives the Holocaust with such a power...that it radically displaces and shakes up not only any common notion we might have entertained about it, but our very vision of reality as such, our very sense of what the world, culture, history, and our life within it, are all about' (Felman 1991: 40). In *Schindler's List* the sign has become an abstraction, like the name Treblinka in the history books.

The burden of the critique of *Schindler's List* is that Spielberg, for all his efforts to transcend his earlier treatment of the Second World War in *1941* (1979) and *Always* (1989), and especially in the comic-book Nazis in the Indiana Jones films, has subdued the Holocaust to a Hollywood version of reality. The force and the limitations of this reading are evident when we consider the way the visual repertoire of *Schindler's List* has itself become the subject of adaptation. In the otherwise monochrome television advertisement created for Euro RSCG Wnek Gosper's UK Peugeot campaign, a girl in a red coat is rescued from the path of a American tractor-trailer juggernaut by a car driver, with a soundtrack featuring M People's 1995 top-ten hit 'Search for the Hero'.[8] We could read here (irrespective of denials of intention by the creative team and the agency), a sequence in which the trope of rescue occludes the destruction of lives. But can we infer that *Schindler's List* sponsors a cognitive denial of the Holocaust as complete as that generated by the advertisement in respect of the economically justified road-deaths with which the likes of Ralph Nader have indicted the car industry? A second example makes the point about confusing judgements of the form of the film with the sum of its effects. Typing the eponymous list, Stern remarks that for every cigarette Schindler has smoked he, Stern, has smoked half. This almost subliminal propaganda for the passive-smoking lobby may introduce a momentary friction between the values of a culture obsessed by risks to the prolongation of life, and the death sentence enacted on European Jewry, but the latter is not thereby reduced to equivalence with the medical warnings of the Surgeon General. This is the *reductio ad absurdum* of the argument that Spielberg's film about survival, whatsoever we conclude about its failure to be another *Shoah*, reduces the Holocaust to a 'reality effect' in a fiction about overcoming adversity, and thereby destines its audiences to a facile relation to history. In one sense, the fate of Spielberg's imagery tends to confirm the most pessimistic conclusions about trivialization: the image circulates at the expense of its referent. But it is also a warning about overly reductive or polarized accounts in which *Schindler's List* colonizes all discourse about the Holocaust. As David Thompson observes, the film is 'good enough to let us realize that movies are never good enough and that they threaten to replace life' (Fensch 1995: 97).

It is an irony that criticism of *Schindler's List*, while denigrating its version of the Holocaust, has accepted at face value the claims made about its demographic significance as a vehicle of remembrance:

> For the moment at least, the most audible public discourse on the fate of the European Jewry under the Nazis is being framed by the context of Spielberg's movie. The worrisome question is how long this moment will last. There is a cultural version, as well as an economic one, of 'Gresham's Law': 'bad money drives out good,' and in the way a society takes up and defines the issues that engage its attention, the success of an appealingly facile articulation can set to the side, or even silence altogether, more complex and troubling expressions. This is why to speak about a '*Schindler's List* Effect' is by now perhaps more useful than to concentrate exclusively on the film.
>
> (Bernstein 1994: 431)

We might identify another, parallel *Schindler's List* effect in this movement beyond the film to the economy of Holocaust discourse. However the film's function as a metonym for cultural banality reflects an enduring dichotomy between minority and mass modern culture. A decade earlier, Irving Howe advanced the possibility that amnesia or ignorance might be preferable to commercially-engineered remembrance: 'Those of us who used to fear that the Holocaust might be forgotten now confront the possibility that it could suffer a worse fate...the Holocaust has become popular, the mass media are "into" it' (Blatter and Milton 1982: 10). The screening of NBS-TV's *Holocaust* in 1978 was an equally significant episode in the culture industry's addressing of itself to history: denounced by many as soap opera, *Cahiers du cinema* noted that 'the fiction of *Holocaust* has more effect, *today*...than all the documentary material ever accumulated on the genocide of the Jews' (Insdorf 1989: 6).

The problem of this TV and cinema takeover needs to be related to a fifty-year-long history of the making of our knowledge of the Holocaust, a process which takes in the recovery and preservation of testimony, legal prosecutions, the promotion of political ideologies, historical scholarship, commemoration and pedagogy. The power of the moving image to shape perceptions of history must be considered in the light of the reluctance to write the Holocaust into the mainstream historical narrative of the twentieth century. For the thesis that bad representations drive out good implies not only that the good have been in circulation, but also that the assaying of intrinsic value is straightforwardly and publicly undertaken. But much of the concern over the impact of *Schindler's List* rests on the assumption that the film shapes perceptions of the Holocaust in the absence of other representations: 'the Holocaust is currently at risk of being presented, if only in people's first exposure to the subject, chiefly as the factual "basis" of Spielberg's movie' (Bernstein 1994: 431). In the light of the narrative and visual strategies of *Schindler's List*, 'first exposure' might refer not only to spectators ignorant of the Holocaust, but also to those who have not 'seen' it. In either case, we are invited to think of the film as an adaptation, not of Keneally's novel, but of the Holocaust itself.

The charge of adaptation brings with it assumptions about origins and criteria of fidelity which ultimately reinforce an adversary binarism in thinking about public and professional understanding. Michael Marrus is right to observe that 'the study and the popular presentation of the Holocaust run into difficulties when they have been deliberately undertaken to make us "feel better" – to confirm our political judgements, to enhance understanding of the Jewish predicament, or even to improve "human understanding"' (Hayes 1991: 119). If '[a]llowing *Schindler's List* to stand as a master-narrative of the Holocaust seems ethically irresponsible' (Horowitz 1997: 138), a responsible stance toward the 'difficulties' of which Marrus writes might begin by addressing the relationship between the academy and popular culture, rather than that between popular culture and history-as-it-happened. The power to form belief about the Holocaust invested in *Schindler's List* is in part a projection of professional powerlessness: critiques of mass-cultural trivialization are intimately bound up with the rituals of the critic's affiliation to a community antithetical to a public sphere which is indifferent to its ideals. Bartov's remarks about turning scholarly disapproval into involvement in the production of popular narratives and memorials posit the surrender of an attitude to the ownership of understanding, not standards (Bartov 1997: 58). While he tells us little about how such negotiations might be opened up, the explicitness of the goal of 'greater public awareness' is worth pondering. The critique of *Schindler's List*, which consistently slides into judgements about the intrinsic value of public knowledge, entertains the idea that such popular awareness of the Holocaust is itself the difficulty: when there is 'no danger of people forgetting it', remembrance may be the 'worse fate' (Bristow 1997: 34; Howe, in Blatter and Milton 1982: 10).

Jeffrey Katzenberg (boss at Walt Disney film studios) would be surprised at the way Spielberg's critics have literalized his claim that the film 'will affect how people on this planet think and act' (Fensch 1995: 146). Where they have attested to the scale of its negative influence, they have done so largely rhetorically and anecdotally. In the process, they have reinforced the presumption that only the critical guardians of history can tell the difference between a story about the past and what happened. But this authority assumes an access to past events which contradicts what might now seem the overly-categorical hypothesis that the past lies beyond representation. *Schindler's List* is viewed as a baleful influence because it persuades its audience that the Holocaust can be represented within commercial conventions, and because its story shapes those events into a triumphalist or redemptive pattern. Thus the existence of the film would seem to make it all the more necessary that its audience know about the Holocaust. However, what the critique often implies is that they need a proper master-narrative, for mass audiences are vulnerable to both Hollywood trivialization and the complexity of the historical record. But this is precisely what is impossible given the premises on which the film has been found wanting. If the debate about *Schindler's List* has made little progress with issues about how knowledge and understanding of the Holocaust are disseminated, it is because this question has been foreclosed by assumptions about who has the capacity for selfconsciousness about the contingency of knowledge. The tendency to extrapolate from the well-documented shortcomings of Spielberg's film to the conditions of public awareness has served only to entrench a conviction that the Holocaust is so important that only those who believe that it is unspeakable ought to speak of it. We might note, in this connection, Michael Bernstein's recent reflections on the absolute of catastrophe invoked in talk of the 'radical unspeakableness' of the Holocaust. Trivialization and distortion are not monopolized by mainstream culture. It is timely, too, to question that privileging of catastrophic suffering, which leads to a 'perverse veneration of the "final solution" as a fitting "final judgement" before which all our beliefs and practices must ultimately be weighed and by whose dark light everything else is necessarily found wanting and trivial' (Bernstein 1998: 8).

Notes

1 The novel is the chief source on Schindler in Oliner and Oliner 1988 and Gutman 1990.

2 In the film, Schindler suggests that a letter to the commandant at Auschwitz will secure 'special treatment' for Stern: *Sonderbehandlung* is part of a 'whole new language' which Schindler does not know.

3 The Austrian is Raimund Titsch, whose clandestine photographs of Płaszów, donated to Yad Vashem by Leopold Pfefferberg, are a source of Spielberg's imagery in *Schindler's List*.

4 This sequence is an expansion of what Keneally's free indirect discourse implies is a report of Mila Pfefferberg's testimony about Auschwitz in the last week of the gas chambers' operation: '[she] was troubled by rumours of the type most prisoners of the Reich had by now heard – that some shower nozzles gave out a killing gas. These, she was delighted to find, merely produced icy water' (Keneally 1983: 303–4).

5 For a discussion of these arguments, see Rubinstein 1997.

6 This is Spielberg's invention: 'Everyone was too unnerved to make formal goodbyes' (Keneally 1983: 378).

7 The 1998 Oscar for Best Documentary Feature was awarded to a film about the post-war migration of survivors to Israel, Mark Jonathan Harris's *The Long Way Home*.

8 The advertisement was screened in the UK early in 1996 and again in the autumn of 1997 (coincidentally at the time of the first terrestrial TV broadcast of *Schindler's List*).

10

SPEAKING OUT

The transformations of *Trainspotting*

Derek Paget

Janespotters and trainspotters

In March 1996, a Sunday newspaper article alleged that audiences in British cinemas were self-selecting as either 'Janespotters' or 'Trainspotters'. The film of Irvine Welsh's novel *Trainspotting*, adapted by John Hodge and directed by Danny Boyle, had captivated the Trainspotters, while the Janespotters were championing Emma Thompson's adaptation of Jane Austen's *Sense and Sensibility*, directed by Ang Lee. In almost every respect, said writer Martin Wroe, the two films were different: 'One is about insensible smackheads in Edinburgh, the other about sensible bonnet-heads in middle England. One is about chemical highs, the other about romantic highs.' Difference was even more evident in the films' respective audiences: 'Trainspotters are younger, Janespotters older. One audience comes out speeding, the second weeping.' The article even had an inset panel to help you decide which camp you belonged to, offering two columns of taste-markers (clothes, food, bands, drugs, etc.) under the heading: 'Two films that define the sensibilities of the nation' (Wroe 1996: 13).

Wroe's (stereo)typical *Trainspotting* audience was either out of work or studying, and relatively poor. They were likely to be interested in illegal substances, rock music and football, and as often as not went to the film in groups (not exclusively male, but dominantly so). The atmosphere at screenings was lively and interactive, the film's mordant humour in particular being relished by a young-to-youngish audience. Janespotters, by contrast, were altogether less obviously tribal: they were young-to-middle middle-aged – post-war baby boomers, so to speak – well-heeled and going grey, out for the night revisiting a classic text of their undergraduate youth. They had young families, salaries and careers, and were likely to be interested in heritage sites, classical music and frocks-and-bonnets fashion. Couples predominated, and the atmosphere at screenings was appreciative but sedate.

Sense and Sensibility, produced by major Hollywood studio Columbia, was financed on the back of Thompson's burgeoning reputation as a 'bankable' movie star. *Trainspotting*, meanwhile, had been produced for a niggardly £2 million under the innovative auspices of British TV's Channel Four and its cast

128

were mostly unknowns. But whatever their differences, both films were hugely successful at the box office. The outward appearance of the published screen-plays of both films reinforces some of the differences in their provenance. *Sense and Sensibility: The Screenplay* is fronted by a sepia, soft-focus shot of Emma Thompson and Kate Winslet in costume as Austen's Elinor and Marianne. A banner in heritage gold at the top of the front cover proclaims: 'Winner of the 1996 Academy Award for Best Screenplay'. John Hodge's screenplay for *Trainspotting* carried the snappy *Sight and Sound* comment: 'A book no student bedsit should be without.' The cover illustration shows Ewan McGregor as the novel's Mark Renton. In poster form, it is to be found on the walls of many a student bedsit, and the look it celebrates is still fashionable.

Those who saw both films at the time of release could regard themselves as cultural oddities judging from Wroe's article. The audiences just did not seem to mix, he claimed, with the *Trainspotting* audience 'rarely above 30 years old' while 'over-30s are everywhere' at screenings of *Sense and Sensibility*. The purpose of recalling this tongue-in-cheek journalistic stereotyping is to note the way it drew attention to a distinct 'Two Nations' 1990s cultural climate. The film *Trainspotting* marked a moment of self-definition for a mainly youthful audience out of tune with their elders. In retrospect, things were probably not quite so simple: a recent survey of student reading (and other) habits showed that, while Welsh held the number one spot as 'favourite writer' (forty per cent of arts, thirty-five per cent of science students preferring his work, with *Trainspotting* by far the most popular title), who should be second but the redoubtable cynosure of the Janespotters, Jane Austen herself.[1]

Trainspotter and Janespotter tribes may not have been totally oil-and-water entities, but there was a clear sense of two particular kinds of Britishness being articulated in these two contrasting films. Their divided condition was marked out by age, gender and class, as well as taste. If *Sense and Sensibility* was in part a nostalgic harking-back to the imagined elegance and civilization of a former period (always provided you ignored the very tiny class fraction encountered in Austen's novel), *Trainspotting* acknowledged the underbelly of Heritage Britain, observable to anyone daring to venture beyond the tourist sites of British cities. It focused on a social group marginalized in almost all senses, and its drug-taking 'schemies' from the Edinburgh estates became metonymic of young, ghettoized and dispossessed city-dwellers everywhere.

If flower-children became the symbol of an idyllic 1960s 'alternative society' of the young (with San Francisco their New Jerusalem), Welsh's Trainspotters have fulfilled this function in the largely negative idyll of the 1990s. Edinburgh is still the dystopian Golden City of our time, as the 1998 BBC2 drama series *Looking After Jo Jo* recently illustrated, sharing time, place, star (Robert Carlyle) and subject-matter with *Trainspotting*. The novel and its adaptations gave voice to a generation, and allowed them to speak out in a variety of media. This chapter will examine the implications of the Trainspotter cultural moment, through an analysis of the transformations of Welsh's novel that were effected for stage and screen.

Transformations and textual 'fidelity'

One thing the oil-and-water audiences of these two films almost certainly had in common was knowledge of the source novels. Those who had not read these works beforehand, or who did not do so shortly afterwards, were probably few and far between. Part of the purpose of the *Observer* comparison was to demonstrate an emergent 'classic' status for the novel *Trainspotting*: already it was being read and talked about as much as a major text from the English Literature canon. The film adaptation built on the cultural pulse-taking of Irvine Welsh's novel, and both film and book have become modern classics in their own media. It is only necessary to look at the subsequent careers of the actors involved to illustrate how influential *Trainspotting* has been in film. If Emma Thompson and Kate Winslet were well ahead in the reputation stakes in March 1996, Ewan McGregor, Johnny Lee Miller and Robert Carlyle have more than made up ground since.

Trainspotting was Irvine Welsh's first novel, and essentially it bears out John Hodge's description of it as a 'collection of loosely related short stories about several different characters' (Hodge 1996: ix). Welsh's acknowledgements offer clear evidence of the 'loose' relation of the parts to the whole (he even refers to 'the following stories').[2] Loose or not, publication history indicates how swiftly the novel found its audience. First published by Secker and Warburg in 1993, Minerva published a paperback edition in 1994. Six reprints of this in 1994 were followed by nine in 1995. Reprinting has continued, providing sufficient evidence both of the novel's continuing success and of the boost given to sales through 'cross-marketing' of an equally successful film.

Questioned about the film adaptation, Irvine Welsh has commented:

> I think that as an author the first thing you have to tell yourself is: I wrote the book but somebody else is making the film. The whole point of it – the exciting part of it – is that it's going to be transformed in some way. The more transformation the better from my point of view. People go on about a 'faithful interpretation', but you can't have a faithful interpretation of something; you can maybe have it in spirit, but it's going to change as it moves into a different medium.
>
> (Hodge 1996: 118)

Hodge himself says that Welsh was 'a saintly model of non-intervention' (Hodge 1996: x), a remark confirmed not only by the above quotation, but also by Welsh's own generous view about the stage version. Welsh says of Harry Gibson, the stage adapter, that he: 'dramatised the book with enormous empathy' (Welsh 1996b: 8). Welsh's name appears on the title page of the play although, as he cheerfully remarks, 'I had next to nothing to do with [*Trainspotting*'s] adaptation for the stage' (Welsh 1996b:1).

For the film, as Welsh himself notes, Boyle's masterstroke was to put him in it: 'It stops the author from criticizing the film because you can't say, "Oh, my God, they've ruined my book!" because you've been a part of the whole process and you've joined in' (Hodge 1996: 119). But Welsh is clearly not one to set great store by 'fidelity' in adaptation. One can only wonder whether Jane Austen would have been prepared to 'join in' like he did (a cameo as Lady Middleton, perhaps, or maybe Mrs Jennings?). Janespotters are often opposed to what they see as exploitation of their idol by the modern media, but this may have more to do with the privileging of written texts in our culture.

Discussion of film/TV adaptation of novels is often troubled by the vexed question of fidelity to 'prior texts' deemed to have inherently greater cultural standing. Inevitably, the 'not a bit like the novel' argument is often heard (along with its extension – 'not as good as the novel'). Such arguments are more stridently heard when the work of classic authors is at issue. It almost seems to constitute a kind of perverse pleasure for those jealous of canonical literature's supposed superiority to continue to argue for the primacy of print. When the author in question is, say, John Grisham or Catherine Cookson, defenders of the cultural faith tend to be less plentiful. The notion of an inherent hierarchy of texts mostly privileges canonical novels and constructs their film adaptations as flawed and inferior – inauthentic – works.

Brian McFarlane proposes a notion of 'relative transferability' between texts in different media in order to escape such low-level discussion (McFarlane 1996: 13–5). He returns to those functions in narrative called 'cardinal' and 'catalyser' by Roland Barthes, and 'kernel' and 'satellite' by Seymour Chatman, in order to 'establish some [non-judgmental] guidelines for exploring the different natures of the experiences of the two related texts' (McFarlane 1996: 197).[3] Audience experience is important to a consideration of the pleasures involved in the reshapings of adaptation. The pleasures of reception, positive and negative, have been too rarely considered.

McFarlane argues that adapted narratives must logically be based on cardinal/kernel functions without which a certain basic recognition of similarity would be impossible. These are more or less directly 'transferable' and have little need of major transformation. Such basic recognition constitutes part of the pleasure of the well-read audience. The paradigm shift between conceptual (print) and perceptual (audio-visual) media makes inevitable a difference in the realization of catalyser/satellite functions, however. These must by necessity be transformed through equivalent functions specific to the new medium. The whole purpose of the adaptation exercise (in terms both of production and reception) is to effect this series of transformations. McFarlane is talking, of course, about the difference between 'narrative' and 'enunciation', and the connections obvious and otherwise between them. Cardinal/kernel functions can relatively easily be linked across media, and have fairly unproblematic equivalence; the comparison of catalyser/satellite functions is always likely to be more problematic to compare (because in some ways they will be non-equivalent), but more pleasurable because of this manifest difference.

131

At the point of reception, comparison is best pursued, he argues, through acknowledgement of the inherent 'intertextuality' of all texts (McFarlane 1996: 10). The process of intertextuality can be characterized as follows: the well-read audience recognizes, acknowledges and even enjoys the transference between media of cardinal/kernel narrative functions; they then compare and contrast (and further engage with) differences in catalyser/satellite enunciation. These readerly exercises are simultaneous during viewing, and constitute part of the pleasure of seeing something already 'known' transformed into something 'similar-but-different'. If a text is not 'known' by having been previously read, there may be compensatory pleasures (wondering what the source text is like; anticipating reading it). Potentially the activities of comparing, contrasting and projecting are far more interesting than either low-level 'fidelity' issues or those hierarchies which tend to overvalue one medium against another for primarily elitist reasons.

The 'showing through' of one text into another is a major feature of the theory of intertextuality. Even when someone is apparently unconvinced about the issue of fidelity, they are often still drawn to participation in debate about book and representation. In novel, play and film there are significant differences in both narrative and enunciation which illustrate the extent to which the challenge of *Trainspotting* was accepted both by Harry Gibson (stage) and John Hodge/Danny Boyle (film). In all cases, enunciative possibilities in reception are extended by creative decisions taken.

'Idiolect' and 'character'

Welsh's novel, as Hodge so perceptively says, 'is an incredible book: its characters, language, narratives, and tone of aggressive entertainment were like nothing I had seen before' (Hodge 1996: ix). It is more than interesting that Hodge uses the verb 'see' rather than 'read' here. Welsh's novel is highly visualizable, partly because the reader 'sees' so often through the eyes of first-person narrators (eight of them in all). The characters and their language form the novel's major dynamic: as Hodge goes on to say, it is only later that the novel's narrative becomes continuous with its gradual focus on Mark Renton and his escape/exile from Edinburgh. The eventual concentration on a handful of characters, and the linking of several major themes through the plot device of the Big Drug Deal, drive what hitherto might have seemed rather a formless novel towards closure.

The laconic first sentence alerts the reader to the challenge to follow: 'The sweat wis lashing oafay Sick Boy; he wis trembling' (Welsh 1996a: 3). It is immediately necessary to hear this voice to make sense of it. The typographical rendering of the Scottish voice (varied slightly for each major speaker) compels a 'sounding out' of both dialogue and narrator's voice. This tends to slow down the process of reading initially (for most non-Scottish readers anyway). The strength of idiolect in the novel is ultimately the element most 'transformable' in terms of acted performance on stage and screen. 'Idiolect' (a term from

132

linguistics) conflates the prefix 'idio-', or personal and private, and the suffix '-lect', or language system. The word was coined to provide an individualized equivalent to the collective 'dialect' (or shared local/regional language system). 'Idiolect' has been defined as: 'The linguistic system of an individual, differing in some details from that of all other speakers of the same dialect or language.'[4] It is a kind of vocal fingerprinting.

It is true that dialect plays a big part in *Trainspotting*, and it is necessary for those unfamiliar with Edinburgh patois to pick up clues to the meaning of words like 'radge' and 'poppy' as they go. But the multiple first-person narratives make it more than just a collection of short stories, more than just a 'dialect novel'. The most frequent narrator is Renton, with the omniscient narrator not far behind, but seven other characters of varying centrality narrate (Spud, Sick Boy, Begbie, Kelly, Second Prize, Tommy and Davie Mitchell). Welsh mixes their sections judiciously with third-person narrative, thus providing periods when one can 'stand back' from the characters.

The attention to idiolect in the novel refines the distinctiveness of dialect in terms of rhythm as well as vocabulary. Idiolect becomes character in *Trainspotting*. This is, perhaps, most obvious in the case of Spud, with his trademark 'likesay, ken?' interrogative, and his idiosyncratic, semi-hippy locutions ('catboy', for example). But all the principal first-person narrators (Renton, Begbie, Sick Boy, Spud) have traits of speech which become a kind of recognizable signature tune for their character. When they 'speak out' in other sections, the reader can hear these rhythms from another perspective, as well as taking a view of the character alternative to their own. This is particularly evident in the case of the 'hard man' Begbie, whose psychopathic reversions to violence are treated by himself as perfectly justified (see Welsh 1996a: 110) and by others as terrifyingly random (Welsh 1996a: 79, for example). The overall effect is as vivid as the individuality that Chaucer confers on his Canterbury pilgrims, or Mark Twain gives to Huckleberry Finn. The 'voicings' allow much of the narrative to be relayed through enunciations which are always more than just first-person narratives, and which add up to something greater than the sum of the individual parts.[5]

In the theatre, the real-time possibilities of a transformed enunciation of this narrative were realised in 1994, when *Trainspotting* was directed by Ian Brown for the Traverse Theatre, Edinburgh. The cast included Ewen Bremner, who went on to play Spud in the film. Harry Gibson developed the version which played the Edinburgh Festival and toured in 1995, then ran in the West End in 1996 (Ambassadors and Whitehall Theatres). The published text is written for four actors, who share roles but are named as 'Mark', 'Tommy', 'Franco' and 'Alison'. The staple theatrical techniques employed are those perfected in the post-war alternative theatre: direct address to the audience, rapid transformations of time, place and character through 'open' declaration of theatrical process (as against the elision and concealment used in bourgeois, boulevard theatre).[6]

All these techniques are basically non-naturalistic, and depend upon an audience's willingness to be active in the construction of meaning. The novel's individualized, 'stream-of-consciousness', multiple points-of-view were transformed in the theatre into the collective role-exchange of actors busily transforming themselves and their settings before the eyes of their audience: in effect, inviting the audience into the creative process. In the film, the multiple technique in narrative was split away from character (Renton becoming the main storyteller), and carried instead through a formal experimentation unusual in mainstream fiction films. If direct address is a tricky technique for actors to bring off (but easier – and more common – in small-scale theatre) the film version's use of voice-over and direct address of the camera is equally non-naturalistic, rare and, in some ways, even more daring.

Transforming 'The First Day of the Edinburgh Festival'

As a representative scene for analysis, 'transformed' in highly innovative ways in both adaptations, I will take the one in which Renton goes to Mikey Forrester to get the 'final score' he needs in order to come off heroin. Forrester gives him two opium suppositories: 'Custom-fuckin-designed fir your needs' (Welsh 1996a: 22). Suddenly loose-bowelled as his previous hit fades, Renton rushes into a betting-shop and uses their vile lavatory. In his haste, he forgets the all-important suppositories, and is reduced pathetically and comically to fishing around for them in the very toilet bowl into which he has just 'empt[ied] ma guts' (Welsh 1996a: 25). The scene is so vivid in the novel, so full of hideous yet hilarious detail, so typical of the grasp *Trainspotting* has on the pity and horror (and gallows humour) of junkie-dom, that it would be difficult indeed to leave out. Arguably vital to the cardinal/kernel functions of narrative with its distinctive account of drug-taking, the scene presents formidable problems for catalyser/satellite enunciation. For the enunciative modes of stage and screen, with their predominantly visual imperatives, it represents a challenge indeed.

In the novel, the scene is effectively the second chapter (Welsh 1996a: 14–27). The first, 'The Skag Boys, Jean-Claude Van Damme and Mother Superior', introduces Renton, Sick Boy and friends, their drug habits and fascination with films (Welsh 1996a: 3–13). Welsh then uses the surreal drug-experience interlude 'Junk Dilemmas No. 63' to interrupt narrative continuity (Welsh 1996a: 14). These surreal sections punctuate the whole novel, are numbered consecutively, but start (suitably perversely) with 'No. 63'. Renton's success in coming off the skag later on is then signalled by a section titled, suitably logically, 'Straight Dilemmas No. 1' (Welsh 1996a: 299–301).

In 'The First Day of the Edinburgh Festival', the famous arts festival ironically counterpoints Renton's narrative, vividly contrasting Two Nations' different experiences of the day (Renton only remembers the festival as a comic afterthought). Significantly, it is one of the sections about which Welsh acknowledges: 'Versions...have appeared in other publications.' It bears all the hallmarks of its short-story origins, being a complete incident in itself. The closed mini-narrative contains characters the reader never again encounters: Forrester himself, the presumed ex-prisoner Donnelly (who Renton mentally christens 'Johnny Saughton' after the Edinburgh jail), and 'Fat Sow' ('a gross bitch with a broken leg'), as well as the denizens of the betting shop (one of whom Renton in his characteristic way names 'Charles Bronson' because he looks like a disapproving vigilante). The link to the rest of the novel is the narrating voice of Mark Renton – at this point in *Trainspotting* the only voice the reader has encountered.

The stage version re-orders the novel's narrative sequence and locates this scene as the seventh in 'Part One', the first act (Welsh 1996b: 30–3). It is rendered entirely in direct address to the audience by the actor named in the text as 'Mark', and in stage time would probably run about ten minutes. Direct address is a stage technique which demands the building of a relationship between actor and audience if it is to work. The demands on performance have more in common with the working methods of the variety performer than with those of the classical actor. It is true that Elizabethan soliloquy employs direct address, but the demands of this stage convention are rarely as direct as those the stage version of *Trainspotting* makes.

Like the comedian, or the MC in a night club, 'Mark' has to assume an anecdotal relationship with the audience, friendly but in control. So far from laying bare mental processes and advancing a plot (the work of the soliloquy), he assumes the intimacy of friendship, which involves prior acceptance and understanding – empathy in a word. The macro-narrative is held up while the audience is invited to relish the mini-narrative's detail. Successful performance creates a bond between actor/character and audience. The 'voicing' of the novel speaks out in the theatre as an actual individual (actor 'in character') faces his audience in real-time, making eye contact, providing the facial expression and vocal inflection which the reader can only imagine. 'Mark' even acts out the dialogue with Mikey (named only as 'the skag merchant'), supplying his voice as well. The whole stage adaptation relied on this anecdotal technique, and it tended sometimes to make things difficult to follow.

However, this scene works because, as in the novel, it turns primarily on two dramatic moments: Renton's hilariously accurate re-animation of a cliché, and the desperate toilet-bowl search. There is thus an aural and a visual dimension to the scene which has to be transformed. The aural joke occurs after Renton has inserted the suppositories. He says to Forrester: 'For aw the good they've done ah might as well huv stuck thum up ma erse' (1996a: 23). In the novel, this gives Renton a brief advantage in the status-game he is playing with the dealer he likes least of those with whom his habit obliges him to negotiate. The absence of 'Johnny Saughton' and 'Fat Sow' in the theatre has the effect of constituting the audience as the observers (and appreciators) of his brief moment of triumph. The search of the foul toilet bowl is rendered theatrically in eleven lines of direct address (Welsh 1996b: 32–3), slightly truncating the fifteen lines of description in the novel (Welsh 1996a: 26). The novel's description of the capture, squashing of and calligraphy with a dead fly is omitted. Some of the more baroque description is also simplified – for example: 'Ah rummage fastidiously and get one ay ma bombs back straight away' (Welsh 1996a: 26), becomes 'Ah slosh around down there and get one ay ma bombs back straight away' (Welsh 1996b: 32). Something is lost in the omission of the phrase 'rummage fastidiously', but something is gained theatrically by the directness of the alternative.

To conclude the stage monologue, Mark says to the audience: 'It was a swelterin hot day. Ah remembered somebody hud said that it wis the first day ay the Edinburgh Festival. Certainly got the weather fir it. Back in ma room – ah coundnae face those three broon buckets' (Welsh 1996b: 33). The buckets featured in the earlier inventory of necessary items for Renton's attempt to clean up (see Welsh 1996a: 15; Welsh 1996b: 30–1). It is significant that the stage version should revolve around these items, given the inevitable scatological focus of the monologue after the narrative detail of the novel has been pared away, and given the real-time need to end the scene with a punchline.

The effect of the stage version is to concentrate the 'voicing' evident in the novel to the level of comic monologue to be expected, for example, in the great tradition of Scottish music-hall. This tradition of revealing character through turns of phrase, runs from George Robey to Chick Murray and on to Billy Connolly. It was notable for the subtle inflections performers could give to knowledge (and self-knowledge). This lively and popular art-form opened itself up historically to working-class life, and provided a contrast with, and critique of, dominant Anglo-Scottish high culture. The politics of *Trainspotting* lie in this formal technique, in a broadly similar way to the theatre company 7:84's more obvious employment of it to thrust home their polemic in the 1970s.[7]

The film treatment takes a different route to arrive at some of the same destinations. There is no mention of the Festival at all (the line 'It's the first day of the Edinburgh Festival' becomes a stage direction for a later scene – see Hodge 1996: 52). Beginning with the inventory, the scene moves swiftly to incorporate the meeting with Mikey Forrester. This face-to-face dialogue is telescoped, and the punchline made more economical, by having Renton insert the suppositories in front of Mikey rather than 'retir[ing] tae the toilet and insert[ing] them, wi great diligence, up ma arse' (Welsh 1996a: 23). Forrester in the film (a Hitchcockian guest appearance – admirably deadpan – by Welsh himself) has a flat almost totally bare of furniture. No one else is present, so once again the audience is sole witness to the dealer/junkie status-game. Renton's somewhat pyrrhic 'victory' is confirmed by Ewan McGregor's expression and aggressive thrust of the head as he delivers his key line.

The treatment of the toilet-search is what makes Hodge/Boyle's work distinctively different in enunciative terms, however. Their decision to express the scene's pity, horror and humour surrealistically lifts the film sequence onto an entirely different plane. Prior to the voiding of the suppositories, the film is reassuringly social realist. Renton then enters, according to the stage direction: 'the most horrible toilet in Britain' (Hodge 1996: 12; compare Welsh 1996a: 24–5). For the next page of the screenplay, there is no dialogue at all, but the stage directions gradually indicate the stylistic direction. The search of the toilet bowl 'seems to take ages'; Renton cannot find the suppositories, even after sticking his arm in 'further and further':

> His head is over the bowl now. Gradually he reaches still further until his head is lowered into the bowl, followed by his neck, torso, other arm, and finally his legs, all disappearing.
>
> (Hodge 1996: 13)

The screenplay then posits a shift to: 'INT. UNDER WATER. DAY', with Renton diving in search of the suppositories 'which glow like luminous pearls'.

As filmed the scene lasts just over five minutes (Hodge 1996: 9–14). It follows the credits/main titles, and is thus the first scene proper of the film. Audience reaction in the cinema can usually be described as a combination of fascinated horror, disbelief and amusement. The ensuing laughter and gasps of disgust signal an audience's appreciation of the film's acceleration out of social realism into surrealist fantasy. Boyle's embellishments of the screenplay provide further comic, non-realistic detail. As Renton goes through the door labelled 'Toilet', a graphic pastes words to the sign to make it read: 'The Worst [Toilet] in Scotland'. Renton's pearl-diving is accompanied by ironically gentle ambient music. Finding the suppositories, he utters a triumphant cry: 'Yeeesss, ya fuckin' dancer!', which is distorted by the underwater environment, then swims to the surface and to reality (of a sort – he's still 'in' the toilet bowl).

This richly ironic evocation of a junkie's nightmarish dive for his indispensable treasure is often received with a laughter which is partly relief (that this, at least, is not real) and partly pleasure (at the inventiveness which can 'transform' the scene in this elegant way). Renton's gasping 'surface' from his dive, his extraction of himself from the toilet and its contents (in which he finds himself both literally and metaphorically covered) returns the audience, by degrees, to the social realism the scene has so triumphantly vacated. The film dispenses with the details of the re-insertion of the suppositories, the walk back through the betting shop, and the wait for the Number 32 bus. It dispenses too with the stage version's reversion to the 'three broon buckets'. In the final frame, Renton soggily re-enters his flat. The iconic, hard-won, suppositories are revealed glowing in his hand to give point to his words: 'Now I'm ready' (Hodge 1996: 14).

Boyle omits two things from Hodge's script: a shot of the interior of Swanney's flat, and a montage sequence intended to be ironic. The former is clearly designed to explain, as the novel does, why Renton has to go to Forrester in the first place (Swanney and company 'all lie inert while the telephone rings' – Hodge 1996: 9; compare Welsh 1996a: 16–7). This is precisely

Figure 10.1 Trainspotting (1996). Renton (Ewan McGregor) surfaces in the notorious toilet scene

the kind of point which, however useful and interesting in a conceptual narrative mode, is redundant in a perceptual narrative which needs to move forward. Just as the audience for the stage version only need to know Mikey as 'the skag merchant' (and do not hear at all about any other dealer), so Renton's appearance in the flat needs only to be linked in the film through the action of one telephone call (with the visual joke that, having barricaded himself in his flat, he has to break down his own barricade in order to access the hall telephone).

Hodge's suggested montage undoubtedly evokes on the page the scale of Renton's release from constipation: 'A lorry on a building site dumps a load of bricks, B52s shed their load on Vietnam, the "Blue Peter" elephant, etc.' (Hodge 1996: 13). However, Ewan McGregor's animal noises, the accompanying sound effects and a camera angle that turns him into a head on a lavatory pan are a wittier and more economical way of conveying this. Boyle's editing and filming of the scene has the added advantage of keeping audience, as well as Renton, in 'The Worst Toilet in Scotland' and making the pearl-diving fantasy more dynamic (because unique).

An additional dimension is brought to the sequence by non-diegetic music. As Renton goes through his 'cold turkey' shopping list, the screenplay adds 'soothing music' to Welsh's original list – cueing music from Bizet's 'Carmen'. It is heard throughout the scene with Mikey Forrester. After diegetic sound for the betting shop, 'Carmen' returns as elegant and ironic counterpoint at the moment Renton capitulates to his junkie need and sinks himself into the repellent toilet pan. The final, triumphant, chord sounds as his feet disappear from view. The pearl-diving music, Brain Eno's 'Deep Blue Day', then underscores the contrast between underwater peace and tranquillity and surface vileness.[8]

'Simply a snapshot'? The cultural moment of *Trainspotting*

The playwright David Greig argues that 'it isn't any [political] use, however entertaining it may be, and however interesting it may be, simply to take a snap-shot of a group of people...in the way that a film like *Trainspotting* did.'[9] The degree to which any novel, play and film can be politically 'oppositional' or 'counter-cultural' will always be arguable, but the triumph of the *Trainspotting* artworks surely lies in the way they facilitated the release of a group (let's call them the Trainspotters) into wider cultural prominence and more visible expression. Welsh himself made the following observation about the scene just analysed:

> I would have been disappointed if it had been a kind of worthy piece of social realism. I think there's more to it than that. It's about the culture and the lifestyle in a non-judgemental way. It's about how people live their lives and how people interact. To see it as just another kind of reaction to social oppression, to social circumstances, is to rip some of the soul out of it and to make the characters into victims. I don't think they really are. I think that they're people whose ideals and ambitions perhaps outstrip what society has to offer them, but I think they've got great strength in spite of that.
>
> (Hodge 1996: 118–9)

He notes that a Ken Loach-style treatment might have dulled the edge of his novel's attack on the stereotypical image of the junkie.

In eschewing social realism and overt politics, Hodge and Boyle (and before them Brown and Gibson) did not avoid the pity of Welsh's *Trainspotting*. It remains a work in all three media which can freeze the smile on the face of the reader/audience. The toilet scene is at once a comic *tour de force* and baleful observation of the compelling nature of junkie needs. One is never in doubt that drugs do you serious harm, as well as offering a pleasure better than orgasm (Welsh 1996a: 11). But neither novel nor adaptations fall into the trap of simplifying at the levels of aesthetic representation and ethical judgement.

This is what has enabled the novel and film in particular to tap into a youth movement which has seen much recent positive, oppositional action in a society grown lazy about its rights in the Thatcherite 1980s (consider, for example, the well-organized and wittily-constructed environmental protests of the 1990s). Irvine Welsh was describing his book as 'dated' when interviewed in the penul-timate week of filming, giving the actual historical moment of *Trainspotting* as 'between 1982 and 1988' (Hodge 1996: 119–20). This is not unimportant, but the salient point about the cultural moment of *Trainspotting* is that the experiences of which it spoke fitted it for its 1990s role. This was about communicating to (and for) the condition of the contemporary young. The potential of this mainly youthful constituency had been misread, overlooked and downgraded, while an older generation in Britain allowed itself to be heritaged half to death. The *Trainspotting* moment signalled the rejection, at least temporarily, of one kind of Britishness – the kind that routinely looked away from, and denied, anything with which it was not comfortable.

Notes

1 See Wishart (1997: 18): Nick Hornby completed a fashionable triumvirate of authors.
2 The edition I am using is the 1996 Minerva one (unheaded acknowledgements face the 'Contents' page). Compare the arch 'Acknowledgements' in Thompson's *Sense and Sensibility: The Screenplay*: 'I should like to acknowledge the profoundest debt (for my having developed a sense of humour) to Jane Austen, Monty Python and The Magic Roundabout' (Thompson 1996: facing title page).
3 McFarlane takes Roland Barthes' theoretical concepts from the 1966 essay 'Introduction to the Structural Analysis of Narratives' (see Barthes 1977), and Seymour Chatman's from his 1978 book *Story and Discourse: Narrative Structure in Fiction and Film*.
4 *Shorter Oxford English Dictionary* (1993: vol. 1, 1305).
5 The comparison with Twain extends also to Welsh's penchant for using the same characters in other works – several of the *Trainspotting* characters (Renton, Spud, Begbie) turn up in his short-story collection *The Acid House* (1995) and in his second novel *Marabou Stork Nightmares* (1996).
6 For accounts of this movement, see Craig 1980 and Itzin 1980.
7 John McGrath's 7:84 company made use of such techniques in plays that included the 1973 *The Cheviot, the Stag and the Black, Black Oil*. See also McGrath 1981.
8 Music is used to great effect in the film, and the first soundtrack CD included several songs performed by musicians cited in Welsh's text – Iggy Pop and Lou Reed, for example. The CD was a commercial success in its own right, launching Reed's twenty-three-year-old song 'Perfect Day' into new fame. In 1997 the 'Trainspotting 2' CD was released to coincide with the first television transmission (Channel Four, 26 November 1997). With only five tracks actually taken from the soundtrack this was altogether a more dubious marketing exercise.
9 Greig was speaking about political theatre at 'About Now', the eighth Birmingham Theatre Conference, Birmingham University, April 1997. This quotation is reprinted in *Studies in Theatre Production* 15, June 1997: 102.

Part III

FROM SCREEN TO TEXT
AND MULTIPLE
ADAPTATIONS

11

INTRODUCTION

Deborah Cartmell

As in the previous section, this part of the book moves from (what some may regard as) the sublime to the ridiculous, beginning with Virginia Woolf – who discretely 'borrows' cinematic codes in her writings – and concluding with Walt Disney – whose productions unashamedly bury their literary sources, giving priority to the visual image and the commodification of the Disney 'product'.

The following chapters contain a wide range of issues, each focusing on certain aspects and forms of adaptation:

Chapter 12   Virginia Woolf's 'cinematic' writing and Sally Potter's *Orlando* (1993).

Chapter 13   Jane Campion's 'literary cinema' – *The Piano* (1993), *The Portrait of a Lady* (1996).

Chapter 14   Adaptations from television to film (the case of Star Trek).

Chapter 15   Adaptations of comics – from 'low' to 'high' culture (the case of Batman).

Chapter 16   Animated adaptations.

Chapter 17   Walt Disney and the place of 'low' cultural productions within the study of adaptations, and live-action versus animated adaptations (the case of *101 Dalmatians*).

The influence of film on literature must, surely, be included in the study of adaptation. In the first chapter in this section, Sharon Ouditt concentrates on Virginia Woolf's essay 'The Cinema' in the light of Sally Potter's adaptation of *Orlando*. Rather than an attack on the cinema, as is usually thought, Ouditt sees the essay as containing a sneaking admission of cinema's potential and worth. Woolf's growing dislike of the novel is read in the context of the emergent film industry and, undeniably, the cinema gives birth to a new form of fiction; in *Orlando* Woolf absorbs cinematic devices, adapting zooms, change-in-focus, close-ups, flashbacks, dissolves and tracking shots. Although coinciding with contemporary modernist writing, Woolf's *Orlando* is almost written as a screenplay: a gift for Sally Potter.

Which comes first: the word or the picture? This question is continued in Chapter 13, Ken Gelder's 'Jane Campion and the limits of literary cinema'. While Virginia Woolf's *Orlando* can be described as 'cinematic literature', Gelder argues that Jane Campion's *The Piano* and *The Portrait of a Lady* can be defined as 'literary cinema'. In the latter film, Gelder demonstrates how Campion thematizes what constitutes literary cinema, in its entanglement of aesthetic and popular taste, negotiating a space for itself between the restricted circulation of a literary text and the much wider 'mainstream'. While *Portrait* is an adaptation, *The Piano* isn't: in the absence of a literary source, Kate Pullinger and Jane Campion provided a 'novelization' of the film. Yet, strangely, the novel restricts the imaginative scope the film offers. It is the very 'openness' of the film, Gelder demonstrates, that was the selling point of the movie, almost always praised by its critics. According to Gelder, 'literary cinema' (epitomized by Jane Campion's two films) privileges the symbolic over the verbal, and in doing so intimates that a film can be more than a novel: in other words, showing is better than telling.

Yet this suggestion would be considered, in some circles, near blasphemy, and undoubtedly it is the case that literary studies lag far behind other disciplines in refusing to entertain the notion that a film can better its literary original. On the one hand, novelizations of such films as Jane Campion's *Piano* can be seen as a means of enhancing the film's status by pretending the existence of a literary source. Yet the disappointment generated by these books of the films suggests that they had the opposite effect. More significantly, however, these novelizations (which are unanimously agreed to be inferior to their filmic sources) shake a fundamental belief that in the beginning was the word.

Literary studies, perhaps, is also slow to recognize the disappearing boundary between 'high' and 'low' culture. Taking a cue from Roy Lichtenstein, who successfully transformed disposable kids' culture into high art, the next chapters 'boldly go' where the study of literary adaptation has, so to speak, never been before: to the adaptation of mass-cultural products, moving from popular television series to comic book to cartoon. Once we allow screen-to-text adaptations (in addition to the more 'traditional' text-to-screen adaptation), then the door is open for a host of other forms.

Ina Rae Hark pushes the boundaries of 'adaptation' further in Chapter 14, examining translations from television to film, with particular attention to the case of *Star Trek*. Hark considers Hollywood's reluctance to remake television series into feature films until the popularity of the six films of *Star Trek* (1979–93), which successfully cashed in on a nostalgia for the 1960s television series. Adapting television into film reverses the traditional hierarchy in which film is seen as appealing to an elite, and television to a mass-cultural audience.

The case of *Star Trek* proves that it is possible to succeed without slavishly clinging to the 'original': when William Shatner and his crew were no longer available to play their original roles, others could and did successfully take over, with different identities and objectives. Thus a text could be adapted by fundamentally changing the original. In Chapter 15, Will Brooker demonstrates how far the film adaptations of Batman are from the original comic text. While personally lamenting the disappearance of the original, Brooker concludes that the original is of minimal importance to the Batman adaptations' successes and merits: each adaptation is free to impose its own stamp on the character. Implicitly, instead of one author, Batman now has many.

In the survey of animated adaptations in Chapter 16, Paul Wells demonstrates how the original text is present merely for the purposes of anchorage: an animator is unashamedly unconcerned with the fact that something happens, but is rather interested in the *way* in which it happens, interested in it not 'as it is' but 'as it would be'. The words of the literary sources of the animated adaptations are ultimately secondary to the determining language of cinema: animation can and does visually interpret the words of Kafka, even Shakespeare, through unique and penetrating readings. Wells argues that the minutiae of detail involved in the animation process is not to be underrated, but rather should be regarded as a visual equivalent to the complex codes and conventions of the written word. The pictorial takes precedence over the verbal – the visual is shown to 'speak louder' than the literary text on which it is ostensibly based. In Chapter 17, Imelda Whelehan demonstrates a similar change to expected hierarchies of 'authenticity'. She accounts for why, in Disney's two productions of *101 Dalmatians*, the author Dodie Smith is of little or no importance in terms of the films' receptions. It is argued that the animated version of the film is streets ahead of the live-action adaptation, reversing the traditional hierarchy of book, live-action film, then cartoon.

Thus in many ways this book comes full circle, insisting on the importance, possibly the primacy, of the determining language of the visual image (through what is often regarded as the lowest of the low: the cartoon). This brings us back to the analysis of Shakespeare on screen, where the identification of cartoon images can provide highly sophisticated shorthand interpretation/replacement for Shakespeare's words. As we have argued, it is ironically 'the look' of the production, rather than the retention of words, that is of importance in the fidelity debate. Adaptation is, perhaps, the result of an increasingly post-literate (not illiterate) world in which the visual image dominates. Reactions to this idea range from the hysterical fear that the book is finished to the expectation that film and television will prove to be the natural successors to the literary text.

Finally, this book does not pretend to offer a comprehensive account of literary adaptations – indeed the very nature of the subject prevents this. However, *Adaptations* does reveal just how 'open' the study of adaptation must become.

12

ORLANDO

Coming across the divide

Sharon Ouditt

'I am coming across the divide to you', sings an angel, towards the end of Sally Potter's film of *Orlando*. The angel is poised above Orlando and her daughter, resplendent and androgynous, pealing out the ecstasy of being 'neither a woman nor a man', its (only *slightly* mournful) exuberance inviting the audience to celebrate the eradication of chronology, distance and gendered characteristics. The mind opens out to consider not only Orlando's previous incarnations within the film, but also the previous incarnation of the film itself, in the form of Virginia Woolf's novel. But the angel croons on: 'I am born and I am dying.' Are we catching echoes of the death knell of the printed book? Do the formalities of literature have to be expunged so that cinema can live? Or can we see a much more fruitful relationship between these two texts, and one in which we can grant Woolf a degree of prescience with which she is rarely credited: that of glimpsing the potential of the cinema, and of developing its formal possibilities in the context of her own work?

Virginia Woolf was one of the earlier critics to comment on adaptations from text to screen, but in a way that showed little faith in the transition. In 1926, in an essay entitled 'The Cinema', she dismisses the ruthless parasitism of the cinema on 'the famous novels of the world': 'What could be easier and simpler? The cinema fell upon its prey with immense rapacity and to this moment largely subsists upon the body of its unfortunate victim' (Woolf 1994: 350). It has been suggested that this image is implicitly gendered, that the 'victim' is a feminized literature, defenceless against the untrammelled desires of a masculine film industry (Shaughnessy 1996: 43). While I wouldn't want to dismiss a reading of that kind – the image may well suggest a gendered positioning – I would want to question its broader implications: that Woolf is the hired advocate for the aristocrat of the arts, namely literature, indicting the cinema as greedy and barbarous, defending the grace of the word against the crassness of the moving image.

My reading of Woolf's essay is that she is providing not a case for prosecution, but an impressionistic account of the development and potential of the cinema. The extract cited above is but a brief step in her argument, which goes on to explore what the cinema might do 'if left to its own devices' (Woolf 1994:

350). It is true that for Woolf literature lives and breathes and provides the primary forum for her aesthetic activity, whereas the cinema had a much broader, democratic appeal. It is also true that, in a number of publications, she defends literature, thought and intellectual independence as the province of the female as much as of the male – and for that she has had to put up a fight against the institutions of male power which have deprecated women's contributions.[1] Woolf, in other words, has an ambivalent relationship towards tradition: she loves literature but is aware that its history has been based on the exclusion and derision of women. As a means of negotiating this ambiguity, it becomes part of her active intellectual life to seek out new forms, both for her own use and for wider consumption. And she recognizes in the cinema just that – immense potential for formal innovation: 'Is there, we ask, some secret language which we feel and see, but never speak, and, if so, could this be made visible to the eye?' (Woolf 1994: 351). Cinema's problem, as far as she is concerned, is that its technology is rapidly outgrowing its aesthetic accomplishments. Thus the 'unnatural disaster' that has befallen the relationship between cinema and literature, the thing that has prevented eye and brain from working 'in couples' (Woolf 1994: 350), has more to do with 'classic' literary texts being too rumpled and familiar for the youthful, vigorous cinema, than with the ferocities of the battle between the sexes or a kind of class warfare.

The problem, then, lies in inequality of experience. The cinema, in attempting to take lessons from literature, makes some basic mistakes and the viewer's mind – already conversant with the emotional complexities of, say, *Anna Karenina* – is affronted by their impoverished representation in the form of indicial signs: 'A kiss is love. A smashed chair is jealousy. A grin is happiness. Death is a hearse' (Woolf 1994: 350). Just as the literary tools of one generation are seen to be useless for the next, so, for Woolf, this kind of relationship has no future. Film, she suggests, should break away and explore its own forms: 'the cinema has within its grasp innumerable symbols for emotions that have so far failed to find expression' (Woolf 1994: 350). Shadow, for example, might function in various forms as an analogue for extreme emotional states. Woolf is also intrigued by the 'speed and slowness' of thought, its 'picture-making power', its 'dart-like directness and vaporous circumlocution' (Woolf 1994: 351). She is beginning an exploration, in other words, of the relationship between the emotive and formal capacities of the moving image and, very probably, considering them for use in her own work. 'The most fantastic contrasts could be flashed before us with a speed which the writer can only toil after in vain', she says (Woolf 1994: 352). Isn't this something she has tried to achieve in *Mrs Dalloway*? 'The past could be unrolled, distances annihilated' (Woolf 1994: 352). And isn't this precisely the method applied in *Orlando*?

What I'm trying to suggest here is that, far from being an innocent victim of the rapacious triumphs of the modern cinematic age, literature, in Woolf's eyes, could learn from the more abstract potentialities of the use of the moving image, and from its different ways of handling narrative. Film appears effortlessly to dispense with the omniscient narrator: one of Woolf's comments on the documentary side of cinematic production is that 'we see life as it is when we have no part in it' (Woolf 1994: 349). We might relate this to Isherwood's narrative viewpoint as 'a camera', or to the London scenes in Woolf's *Mrs Dalloway* in which the observations of Mrs Coates, Mrs Bletchley and Rezia Warren Smith are linked only by the commercial aeroplane, zooming in and out of view, spelling letters that are variously interpreted. This rendering of the rhythms of city life, of the anonymity of ordinary individuals (Mrs Coates and Mrs Bletchley are 'extras' in the cast of the novel) is surely related to her observation that 'it seems sometimes as if movements and colours, shapes and sounds had come together and waited for someone to seize them and convert their energy into art' (Woolf 1994: 352).

It is clear from a number of her essays and diary entries that Woolf was impatient with the idea of 'the novel', and that she invested much of her creative energy and critical acumen in expanding its shape and redefining its terms. She hazarded the idea that *To the Lighthouse* might be called an 'elegy'; she declared in a 1927 essay entitled 'What is a Novel?' that 'there is no such thing as a novel' (Woolf 1994: 415); in February 1928, she confided to her diary: 'I doubt that I shall ever write another novel after O[rlando]. I shall invent a new name for them' (Woolf 1982: 176). Writing in 'Poetry, Fiction and the Future' (1927), she mentions writers in England, France and America who are 'trying to work themselves free from a bondage which has become irksome to them' (Woolf 1994: 439). The bondage is the inheritance of the social realist novel; the freedom may take the shape of allowing other forms – poetic, abstract, psychological – to propel the 'novel' further into the twentieth century.

It is perhaps significant that the hero/ine of *Orlando* is, ultimately, a poet, who has taken about three hundred and fifty years to produce her prize-winning, best-selling 'stammering answer' to the relationship between poetry and nature, entitled 'The Oak Tree' (Woolf [1928] 1945: 187). The image of an oak tree suggests something of the stable, organic, enduring nature of Englishness ('the spine of the earth'): it is a primary symbol in both the novel and the film of *Orlando* – a point of rest, recuperation and meditation; its appearance in the plot of the novel usually suggests a turning point, as if the sap were rising to wrench out new life. In the film it frames the entire narrative, overlooking first the blank page on which Orlando makes his earliest scratchings, and last Orlando and her daughter, catching images on video. Woolf uses an image of a tree towards the end of 'The Cinema'. Speaking of the obstacles that lie in the path of the artistic innovator, she reminds us 'how the smallest twig even upon the oldest tree offends our sense of propriety. And here', she goes on, 'it is not a question of a new twig, but of a new trunk and new roots from the earth upwards' (Woolf 1994: 352). There is a strong similarity between her next image and the final sequence of Potter's film. Woolf is sure that 'the time is coming, and that art of the cinema is about to be brought to birth' (Woolf 1994: 352). The last section of the film is entitled 'Birth' and, as

Orlando sits at the roots of the oak tree, filmed by her daughter's video camera, an androgynous angel sings to her that s/he 'is coming...across the divide to you.' These images of competing traditions, of the birth of the new offending the 'proprieties' of the old, of the bridging of a division between gender, perhaps, or aesthetic/cultural conventions, suggest some of the issues that arise from a consideration of 'adaptations' in general, but which also apply specifically to these texts. *Is* Potter's angel saying that literature must die to make way for the new – i.e. cinema or, more radically, video (Shaughnessy 1996: 46)? Or is the 'divide' between Woolf and Potter much like that between masculine and feminine, old and new – capable, that is, of recognizing each other in themselves? Is Potter killing the 'angel in the house', a revered but inhibiting figure, or looking back through one of her mothers?

I shall return to that question at a later stage but, for the moment, let me take the argument back a few paces in order to explore further Woolf's interest in stylistic innovation. I have already suggested that she may have been influenced by some of the characteristics of cinema. Her passing comments about that medium suggest that she thought it intensely visual: 'We have sat receptive and watched, with our eyes rather than with our minds, as we do at the cinema' (Woolf 1994: 403). This sense of spectacle (a feature of both the novel and the film), of being captivated by visual images, is something that Woolf displays with self-conscious lavishness. She mesmerizes us with rapid, jewelled sketches of the past, mocks up some exotic Eastern residences, and creates an absurdly elaborate tableau to announce the change of her main character's sex. Woolf is, after all, engaged on a project of mockery. She is writing a spoof biography of a 'made up' Vita Sackville-West, which takes her and her beloved country house, Knole, through about three-and-a-half centuries of trying to balance life, love and poetry with her inheritance (the house, its land) and the various spirits of its ages. Woolf's sardonic assumption is that women writers have no history prior to the eighteenth century so, obviously, Orlando had to be a man until that point and then undergo a quick change of sex. As far as Woolf was concerned the book was to be all 'satire and wildness', with a hint of sapphism; her own lyric vein was to be mocked, it was to be 'an escapade', 'great fun to write', 'a writers [*sic*] holiday' that would 'revolutionise biography' (Woolf 1982: 131, 177; Woolf 1981: 429). In order to achieve this mocking tone, she dispenses with the conventional unities of time, place and gendered identity. She draws attention to individual eccentricities and contradictions 'which it is the aim of every good biographer to ignore' (Woolf [1928] 1945: 10), and parodies 'contemporary evidence' in the form of letters and diaries. The apparent climax of the biography, the award of the literary prize, is hoicked out of a stream of consciousness rather than crowning the narrative at the end, for, says the narrator, 'when we write of a woman everything is out of place' (Woolf [1928] 1945: 179).

The use of intensely visual images, which we might think of as being related to camera shots, helps to achieve this sense of being out of place, of mocking the pedestrian certainties of the dutiful biographer. Take one of the early scenes in which the vista from Orlando's oak tree is described:

> It was very high, so high indeed that nineteen English counties could be seen beneath; and on clear days thirty or perhaps forty, if the weather was very fine. Sometimes one could see the English Channel, wave reiterating upon wave. Rivers could be seen and pleasure boats gliding on them; and galleons setting out to sea; and armadas with puffs of smoke from which came the dull thud of cannon firing; and forts on the coasts; and castles among the meadows; and here a watch tower; and there a fortress; and again some vast mansion like that of Orlando's father, massed like a town in the valley circled by walls. To the east there were the spires of London and the smoke of the city; and perhaps on the very sky line, when the wind was in the right quarter, the craggy top and serrated edges of Snowdon herself showed mountainous among the clouds.
>
> (Woolf [1928] 1945: 12)

This can be read as a panning shot which takes in the southern view and zooms in on pleasure boats and puffs of smoke, before taking in details of the English countryside on its way round to sight London. A sharp cut to the west then brings the Welsh mountains into view. The changes in focus and the range ('thirty or forty counties') point up the ludicrousness of this being physically possible: it is a parody of the convention of England being laid at the feet of the noble lord as he surveys his territory.

This might be complemented by a 'close-up' of the hand of the great Queen Elizabeth, which is also a point-of-view shot from the perspective of a boy who has spent too long in solitude when he should have been honouring a royal guest:

> Such was his shyness that he saw no more of her than her ringed hand in water; but it was enough. It was a memorable hand; a thin hand with long fingers always curling as if round orb or sceptre; a nervous, crabbed, sickly hand; a commanding hand too; a hand that had only to raise itself for a head to fall; a hand, he guessed, attached to an old body that smelt like a cupboard in which furs are kept in camphor; which body was yet caparisoned in all sorts of brocades and gems; and held itself very upright though perhaps in pain from sciatica...
>
> (Woolf [1928] 1945: 14)

And so it goes on, parodying the 'close reading' that close-ups on indicial signs might give rise to, the very proliferation of image suggesting the absence of any 'concrete' detail that is 'likely to be of use to a historian', confessing at the end of the paragraph that it was 'nothing; or only a hand' (Woolf [1928] 1945: 14).

This scene is replayed in Potter's film, as is the visually and metaphorically stunning image of the frozen bumboat woman, suspended within the transparent ice 'in her plaids and farthingales with her lap full of apples, for all the world as if she were about to serve a customer' (Woolf [1928] 1945: 22). Here we have life transformed into art, or at least spectacle, for the merriment of a bluff old king. Peasant life comes cheap and its transformation into an object, while pointing up the commodification of human life for the entertainment of those with privileged access to it, sits slightly uncomfortably with the idea that Woolf is performing a similar act of transformation upon Sackville-West (cf. Hanson 1994: 95–6).

There are further examples of 'montage' which suggest that Woolf might have adapted cinematic techniques to form her own narrative process. There is, for example, the 'cross-cutting' from Orlando's introspective vision to the vision of his house (Woolf [1928] 1945: 62); the 'flashbacks' from the orderly London scenes of the eighteenth century to the huddle and violence of Elizabethan times (Woolf [1928] 1945: 129), and from the viewpoint of a twentieth-century woman to that of an Elizabethan male ([1928] 1945: 174). A 'dissolve' is used as the ink-blotted face of a princess mutates into the face of a poet, indicating Orlando's change of emphasis from love to poetry, and described as the way in which 'one lantern slide is half seen through the next' ([1928] 1945: 47). And, as Orlando makes her way out of the city in her car, there is something which seems to imitate the 'tracking shot' taken from the perspective of the moving vehicle:

> Long vistas steadily shrunk together. Here was a market. Here a funeral. Here a procession with banners upon which was written 'Ra—Un', but what else? Meat was very red. Butchers stood at the door. Women almost had their heels sliced off. Amor Vin— that was over a porch....Nothing could be seen whole or read from start to finish.
>
> (Woolf [1928] 1945: 176)

'Nothing could be seen whole'. This at once seems to repudiate the synoptic vision of the 'Edwardians' and to speak to the spirit of the modern age, both in terms of motorized transport and conceptual perspective. It is followed, a couple of pages later, by its interior, psychological equivalent as Orlando projects flickering, partial images of her selves:

> 'What then: Who, then?' she said. 'Thirty-six; in a motor-car; a woman. Yes, but a million other things as well. A snob, am I? The garter in the hall? The leopards? My ancestors? Proud of them? Yes! Greedy, luxurious, vicious? Am I? (here a new self came in). Don't care a damn if I am. Truthful? I think so.'
>
> (Woolf [1928] 1945: 178)

And so it goes on, as if replaying in jerky, rapid motion (equivalent to the movement of the car, but running through time instead of across space) some of the major scenes of her life. The admission that 'nothing can be seen whole' along with the biographer's confession that only six or seven out of the many thousand possible selves have been called upon, suggests that we might relish this text more for its spectacle, its pageantry, than for its image of aesthetic coherence.

But while the novel is something of an extended joke, there are some serious points to be made, and those points concern gender and the idea of literary inheritance. Soon after Orlando first becomes a woman, she becomes conscious of her body – the fact that the display of her ankles might cause a sailor to fall from the masthead, and of the infinite hours to be spent in 'staying and lacing', 'washing and powdering' and 'changing from silk to lace and from lace to paduasoy' (Woolf [1928] 1945: 91). She notes that the 'wits' of London society are delighted to accept her hospitality, but likely to scorn her in her absence: 'Women are but children of a larger growth…' (Woolf [1928] 1945: 23). She is informed that, as a woman, she cannot inherit property, and her status amounts to much the same thing as being dead. More ambiguously, pending the outcome of the law suits against her, she is to remain 'legally unknown'. This gives space for a significant amount of playfulness in gender terms, and for the development of a scenario which echoes that of the idea of 'androgyny' in *A Room of One's Own*. 'Different though the sexes are', says the narrator, 'they intermix. In every human being a vacillation from one sex to the other takes place, and often it is only the clothes that keep the male or female likeness' (Woolf [1928] 1945: 109). So Orlando changes sex as s/he changes clothes, finding 'no difficulty in sustaining the different parts' (Woolf [1928] 1945: 127). Despite the improbability of Orlando being able to live up to the implications of the *double entendre*, this seems to be making a strong case for the idea of gender as a performance, using the arbitrary props and roles provided by any historical period. It also has interesting implications for the representation of sexuality. It is not clear whether Orlando 'is' a man or a woman when she absconds to the Low Countries 'with a certain lady' (an echo of Vita Sackville-West's escapade with Violet Trefusis). It is, however, the case that, although Orlando's affair with Sasha is narrated in heterosexual terms, it is recalled as a relationship between women. The novel was published in 1928, when Radclyffe Hall's formally conservative but sexually groundbreaking *The Well of Loneliness* was tried for obscenity. The formal experimentation in *Orlando* thus provides a camouflage (which Hall's novel lacks) for the 'Sapphic' element.

The nineteenth century, however, leaves less room for ambiguity. In an extended metaphor of what we might now think of as 'writing the body', Orlando finds the most insipid sentimental verse dripping from her pen, while her body quivers and twangs until pacified by the presence of a wedding ring. It is only once she is legally declared female and safely married that she can write at all, and even then an invisible censor interrogates her with regard to the propriety of her sexual imagery. She thus produces what we assume to be a rather old-fashioned meditation on the relationship between truth, nature and humanity, which Sir Nicholas Greene (a replay of the Jacobean satirist Nick Greene, who earlier sabotaged Orlando's literary reputation) seizes and has published immediately. The formal innovation of Woolf's own literary style, then, is not matched by that of her heroine. Orlando's art lies in her negotiations with the spirit of the age. She has a son, thus ensuring that her inheritance stays within her grasp, and she has a husband, whose existence shields her from a certain amount of moral scrutiny. The free-form nature of the marriage, the gendered ambiguity of herself and her husband, the house flickering with history like a movie-screen may not in 1928 (the year in which women were granted the vote on an equal basis with men) represent a banner for social progress, but they do represent a celebration of idiosyncratic bravura which inspired Woolf's delight in her friend, Vita Sackville-West.

What, almost half a century later, does Sally Potter make of this? Cinema has now shrugged off its younger sibling image; Potter is known for her avant-garde productions and for her interest in gender politics (she used an all-female crew for *The Gold-Diggers*, 1983); we have been through the second wave of feminism and, in the early 1990s, were struggling with the effects of AIDS and a re-elected Conservative government that apparently wanted to stake its future on the imagined values of the Victorian past. What is the potential for a 1990s screen adaptation of a novel whose representation of freedom depends on privilege?

This brings me back to the question I asked earlier: is Potter looking to do away with the angel in the house, or is she more interested in establishing a dialogue with her female predecessors? I think there is some truth in both of these possibilities, so, with due deference to the postmodern conventions with which this film engages,[2] I shall go for 'both/and' rather than 'either/or' and try to chisel out some suggestions, beginning with the second of the propositions.

It seems to me that Woolf and Potter are engaged in similar kinds of projects. They are of different generations and they use different semiotic systems, but they are both interested in prising open the sex–gender duality that has been reinforced by tradition, inheritance and convention, and amounts to a resilient, but certainly flawed gendered ideology. Woolf interweaves her fantasy with the life of an aristocratic writer, Vita Sackville-West, for whom freedom is dependent upon privilege; she employs a panoply of mockery, allusion, selfconsciousness and parody as her subject collides with the conventions of the last three-and-a-half centuries, in order to undermine the idea that male and female are separate and fixed opposites. Potter is less constrained by that particular biography. One could argue that for her the novel is 'material', rather than a 'literary love letter'; a commodity to be recycled into yet another commodity (like the frozen bumboat woman) in a further development in the relationship between the arts and capitalism. But I think that there is a stronger political edge to the adaptation than that. Potter also uses a fair armoury of parody and intertextuality. The film could be read as another episode in the seemingly endless series of country-house costume dramas, that might cover anything from the televization of *Brideshead Revisited* (1982) to the glamorous Merchant–Ivory productions. The architectural appearance of the garden ornamentation and the water mechanics recall Peter Greenaway's *The Draughtsman's Contract* (1982). The costumes are stunning and all but upstage the actors. The past unfolds, a visual feast, a celebration, apparently, of English manners and the opulence of our heritage. But the disjunction between the understated acting style and the overstated garments, the ingenuous 'on what grounds?' (as Orlando questions Harry's assertion that she belongs to him) and bemused half-smiles, prevent us from settling in to devour it all with the eye and not the brain. Just as Woolf mocks the reader, so readers of the film have their gaze returned by Orlando's to-camera interjections. The symmetry of the film and its inverted logic (from 'Death' to 'Birth'), its 'dutiful' use of establishing shots, its intertitles – a wry reference to the days of silent movies and possibly to Woolf's comment on 'words of one syllable' (Woolf 1994: 350) – all suggest that conventions are not only ways of making us see, but ways of making us see that we are looking.

It is interesting to note those one or two scenes when Potter does transpose almost directly from the text. The 'close-up' of Queen Elizabeth's hand becomes just that in the film. The image of the bumboat woman is there, and the meeting between Orlando and Shelmerdine on the moors is fairly close to the literary version. But the film lasts a brief ninety-three minutes, which not only suggests numerous omissions from Woolf's dense and garrulous text, but also that there must be some condensation and invention. Thus the enormous constrictions imposed by eighteenth-century morals on the female spirit are suggested by Orlando's clothes: she is laced, stayed, pulled, pushed (in a manner recalling the opening scenes of *Dangerous Liaisons*, 1988) and then has to shuffle and manoeuvre with some awkwardness and little speed among the equally heavily-dressed items of furniture in her house. Similarly the debilitating obsession with the manners of the Victorian drawing room are indicated by Orlando's facing her house (and the camera) against a background of tea-cup topiary, her own arm crooked, providing a visual index of the domestic ideology that had invaded her mind as well as her body.

Where the novel makes use of flashbacks, the film will frequently dwell on an image or a face, inviting the viewer to explore its associations. Thus, in the scene in which Orlando bathes Shelmerdine's feet, the camera lingers on the kettle: a metonym for the clutter of Victorian domesticity, for the subjection of women, but also an analogue for the bowl of rose-water which Orlando held out to the Queen, in which she washed her hands. This is a different kind of servitude. Later, in the 'sex' scene, the camera runs over the 'lines' of Orlando's 'form' while she does the same to Shelmerdine. Her long look at his face and his smile, and the physical similarity (especially around the eyes) between Billy Zane and Charlotte Valandrey, encourage the viewer to imagine Orlando thinking back through that founding love affair, exploring the likeness between Sasha and Shelmerdine.

This is one effect of imaginative casting. There are others which draw more radical attention to the idea that Woolf raises in her novel of gender as performance. First, an actress was chosen to 'play' Orlando throughout. We know, despite the mitigating plea that the fashions of the time did something to disguise the fact, that Tilda Swinton is a woman. Thus the scenes between Orlando and Sasha don't even have to be recalled in terms of a same-sex relationship: the implication is there, obscured only by costume. We are similarly tantalized into trying to unravel the relationships between gender and power in the interplay between the 'ageing Queen' (played by Quentin Crisp) and the young Orlando. A man acts the part of a woman – Queen Elizabeth I – who was known to play the part of a prince. Without spelling out the layers and cross-currents in terms of political power, the acting fraternity, sexual preference, the relationship between age and youth in terms of sexual appeal and the ownership of property, I'm sure it can be seen that the idea of essential gendered identity becomes so shot-through with costume, performance and sexual ambiguity as to be almost meaningless; the serenading presence of the gay rights activist, Jimmy Somerville, reinforces this.

Just as Jimmy Somerville inaugurates the process by which Orlando inherits the house, so he presides over the ending of the film, by which point she has lost her property. For Potter's Orlando has a daughter, not a son, which means that the lineage is broken and the house passes into the hands of the heritage industry. We have seen some aspects of the way in which Potter takes up some of Woolf's points, and either transposes them directly, translates them into a different kind of semiotic unit, or adds to them by dint of cinematic practices that rely on knowledge of the careers of the actors involved. But, as I suggested earlier, she does more than looking back through this particular predecessor, and if she doesn't quite kill the angel in the house, she questions some of her assumptions. Potter's Orlando is brought more or less up to the present. She is not a poet, but is a writer of some kind. She no longer owns her house; this is seen to be a liberation rather than a loss. The past is seen to be a trap, something that enforces inappropriate gendered identities, and the house that represents that past should be left behind and permitted to take its role in capitalist production as a commodity: English heritage. The present permits, even endorses as an adjunct of style, the appearance of androgyny. Potter's Orlando needs neither marriage nor son. She can leave behind her class-consciousness and exult in the 'ecstacy' of sexual ambivalence, being, in the words of the song sung by Jimmy Somerville's angel, 'neither a woman nor a man'. The angel has been liberated from the house and is restored to its androgynous identity. The voice-over and the final song, in other words, take issue with Woolf's class-consciousness, and develop her idea of androgyny beyond the safety net of needing a husband and a son. The future (and here Orlando's child looks at her mother through a camera) is in the hands of her daughter.

Does this signal the triumph of film and the demise of the queen of highbrow literature? Clearly the ending is polysemic in a way that resists absolutes, and this in itself seems a good reason to assume that no such truimphalism is indicated. The angel's announcement that it is coming across the divide implies that there is space to be traversed not only between women and men, but between women artists of different generations and between different art forms. The film itself alludes to so many forms – literature, obviously, but also painting, choreography and music – that to suggest that one of those should be expunged would seem, well, suicidal. Furthermore, there is a pacifist argument implicit in the film that, although present in others of Woolf's works, is less obvious in this novel. Woolf's Orlando is happy slicing at heads, engaging in duels, and generally taking part in bellicose masculine activity. Potter's Orlando, however, refuses to kill: it is Archduke Harry's instruction that a dying man is not a man but the enemy, that precipitates Orlando's sex change. She suggests to Shelmerdine that freedoms won by killing might not be worth having, and that one might choose not to be a 'real man' should that situation arise. In the light of this added emphasis, it would seem odd, perhaps, that the only victim should be literature, or indeed that literature (especially given the lucrative link between the two in the modern film industry) should have to die in order for film to thrive.

Both art forms deal with ideas and the means of representing ideas. It seems likely that some of Woolf's formal innovations may have been inspired by the cinema, and that she used some innovative techniques to make comments on gender (among other things) that are still worth paying attention to. Although she wasn't, in any literal sense, a screenwriter, Woolf's consciousness of the interplay between word and image, her openness to the capacities of form to convey meaning, her visual imagination and interest in multiple perspectives, make this modernist text quite a gift for Potter. Potter seems to accept it, to embellish it, but also to take issue with some of the ideas (class, marriage, patri-lineage) that no longer seem appropriate in the 1990s, and invites viewers to take part in the dialogue which she has established.

Notes

1 The most obvious examples of this argument are to be found in *A Room of One's Own* ([1929] 1977) and *Three Guineas* ([1938] 1977).

2 For detailed commentary on the relationship between the film and postmodernism, see Humm (1997: Chapter 6).

13

JANE CAMPION AND THE LIMITS OF LITERARY CINEMA

Ken Gelder

Jane Campion's film *The Piano* (1993) poses some interesting problems in terms of the relationship between literature and cinema. We can begin by noting that the film itself attracted the kind of sustained analytical criticism which worked to designate it as 'literary', even though it was not actually an adaptation. This meant that when the novel-of-the-film appeared a year later – co-written by Jane Campion and Kate Pullinger – it could only be identified as somehow *less* literary than the film: as if the film was more of a novel than the novel itself. The novel-of-the-film in fact answered some of the film's over-hanging enigmas and resolved some of its ambiguities. In other words, it clarified (even simplified) the film, and no doubt for these as well as other reasons it received almost no critical attention as a literary text. Certainly it is unusual to come across a case where a film is seen as more complex, nuanced and worthy of sustained 'literary' critique than the novel to which it is attached. In Campion's next project, a 1996 adaptation of Henry James's novel *The Portrait of a Lady* (1881), quite the opposite would seem to be true: that such a great novel would inevitably remain more complex and nuanced than the film. On the other hand, Campion's reputation by this time was secure enough for her scriptwriter, Laura Jones, to restructure this conventional view of novel-to-film adaptation by imagining Henry James to be 'turning [in his grave] with pleasure' at the film version (see Jones 1996: x). For Jones, novel-to-film adaptation involves an initial loss and a subsequent gain: 'you empty out in order to fill up' (Jones 1996: vi). Indeed, her screenplay even 'widens James's circle a little, stretches it a fraction' (Jones 1996: viii), returning us to the sense provided by *The Piano* that – those initial losses in an adaptation notwith-standing – a film can actually become something *more* than a novel. At the very least, then, a certain kind of productive entanglement occurs between the 'literary' and the 'cinematic'; let us also note that this entanglement works to limit possibilities, too, as the following discussions hope to show.

Literary genealogies and postcolonialism

Campion herself had given *The Piano* a precise kind of literary genealogy,

157

speaking of her special debt to Emily Brontë's *Wuthering Heights* (1847). In an interview with Miro Bilbrough in the Australian journal *Cinema Papers*, she pays tribute to Brontë, as well as the American poet Emily Dickinson. For Campion, *Wuthering Heights* is 'a powerful poem about the romance of the soul' (Bilbrough 1993: 6) which provided an inspirational precursor for the not dissimilar narrative of *The Piano*: a thoroughly constraining arranged marriage (in the 1850s in this case) to a cold bourgeois property developer, and a tempestuous love affair with a man more in tune with nature and sexuality which, by contrast, is thoroughly liberating. More interestingly, the stark landscape of the moors in *Wuthering Heights* seemed to Campion to translate perfectly to the location of *The Piano*, the west coast of New Zealand's North Island, as if Brontë's novel and her film had somehow become synchronic:

> For me, and for many New Zealanders, the relationship with very wild beaches, especially the black sands and the west coast beaches around Auckland and New Plymouth, and the very private, secretive and extraordinary world of the bush, is a kind of colonial equivalent to Emily Brontë's moors.
>
> (Bilbrough 1993: 6)

Campion's remark in *Sight and Sound* that 'I feel a kinship between the kind of romance that Emily Brontë portrays in *Wuthering Heights* and this film' (Bruzzi 1993: 6), plays up this compatibility. In this sense, *The Piano* is quite a different project to Jean Rhys's *Wide Sargasso Sea* (1966), which had itself turned to Charlotte Brontë's *Jane Eyre* (1847) in order to emphasize not the synchronicity between texts and locations but, rather, their incommensurable differences. For Rhys, the Caribbean – being so *unlike* Brontë's England – worked to estrange *Jane Eyre* from itself, providing a postcolonial point of departure from that earlier novel. Campion, however, fuses her own project and *Wuthering Heights* together, to the extent – especially through the unrelenting rain-sodden images of the forests, and the beach in the opening sequence which is so turbulent as to make landfall a sheer impossibility – of making New Zealand strange instead. As a consequence, the postcolonial project of *The Piano* is much more internally compromised.

The grafting of a *Wuthering Heights*-based sensibility onto mid-nineteenth century New Zealand in fact ran the risk of obscuring issues specific to the latter's postcolonial development. The role of Maori, for example, who mostly shadow the film or appear fleetingly in ambiguous poses – like the 'effeminate' Maori reclining on a branch of a tree in one scene – has proved a source of contention among critics. Stella Bruzzi's homage to the film in *Sight and Sound* manages to ignore the role of Maori altogether, reading the film entirely through its *Wuthering Heights* framework – and both broadening and consolidating the film's European literary genealogy by comparing its heroine, Ada, with Flaubert's Madame Bovary (Bruzzi 1993: 8). For Bruzzi, the binary of austere patriarchal culture (repressive) and a feminine, sexual nature (liberatory) provides the key to *The Piano*; its modernity lies in Ada's ability to '*transcend* the limitations of such disempowered nineteenth-century heroines as Emily Brontë's Catherine' through 'self-knowledge' (Bruzzi 1993: 7; my italics). Bruzzi's article attracted a response in *Sight and Sound*'s letters pages from Richard Cummings, who sees Ada's romantic attachment to Baines in *The Piano* as a 'cop out' since, although the latter has Maori facial decorations, he nevertheless 'remains an Englishman' and manages to save Ada by getting her out of New Zealand and back to civilization (Cummings 1994: 72). 'In a post-colonial world', Cummings says, 'this is not only condescending, but so Eurocentric as to be totally anachronistic' (Cummings 1994: 72). Bruzzi's counter-response perhaps only exacerbated the problem, seeing Cummings' account as 'reductive' and defending Campion's portrayal of Maori in the film *à la* Margaret Mead by claiming them as 'a positive force who remain unfettered by colonial notions of sin and guilt and do not censor sexuality or desire', adding that they 'in some way represent the unconscious of suppressed – and oppressed – characters such as Ada's husband Stewart' (Bruzzi 1994: 64).

This romantic view of indigenous people as the 'unfettered' unconscious of a repressed civilized world simply extends the binary which underwrites Bruzzi's article, of course – but it is also pertinent to the 'literary' appreciation of the film itself, which (in spite, or perhaps because, of the marginal presence of Maori) talked up the role of the 'unconscious' in *The Piano* and linked it to the feminine, the 'lyrical' and the poetic. In 1995 the film journal *Screen* published three articles which polarized *The Piano* by seeing its use of the repression (civilization, patriarchy) versus liberation (nature, sexuality, femininity, Maori) binary either positively as the key to the film's literariness, or negatively as something inhibiting and overly romantic, especially from a postcolonial perspective. One of the articles is by Stella Bruzzi, and extends the tribute she had paid to *The Piano* in *Sight and Sound*, seeing the film as an expression of Ada's capacity to 'unbalance' patriarchal restrictions (Bruzzi 1995: 266). A second article, by Sue Gillett, is a kind of lyrical panegyric to *The Piano* which tries to mimic the feminized (or feminist) 'unconscious' of the film through its very letter. But the third article, by Lynda Dyson, sees this turn to the 'unconscious' – and the association of the unconscious with Maori in the film – in negative terms only, as 'primitivist'. For Dyson, the grounding of the film in the kind of 'romantic vision' associated with Brontë's *Wuthering Heights* is precisely responsible for both the 'primitivist' representations of Maori and the obscuring of this feature in the film's critical reception. *The Piano*'s 'critical acclaim', she suggests,

> not only ignored the film's colonial setting but, by focusing on links between *The Piano* and the English literary canon, Campion and her work were appropriated as distinctly 'European'. While this appropriation can be understood within the context of the relationship between

the metropolitan centre and the periphery – historically the 'privileging norms' of the European cultural canon have defined 'cultural value' in the colonial context – it also seemed to consolidate the 'whiteness' of the text.

(Dyson 1995: 275)

For Dyson, then, the literariness of *The Piano* – owing so much to 'the European cultural canon' – inhibits its postcolonial potential. It prevents the film from functioning critically in relation to that canon, in the way that (for example) Rhys's *Wide Sargasso Sea* does in relation to *Jane Eyre*. By Campion's own account, as we've seen, the film transplants *Wuthering Heights* onto colonial New Zealand, as if the novel and the place are somehow made for each other.

Where is New Zealand in *The Piano*?

There never was a great nineteenth-century New Zealand novel: in this sense, the film of *The Piano* fills a literary gap. Yet the 'New Zealand' it evokes – derived from the atmospherics of Brontë's English novel, 'unconscious', feminine, lyrical, turbulent – may raise, rather than solve, problems of authenticity and appropriateness. In fact, the New Zealand identity of the film itself was contested, partly because Campion at the time of production had been living in Sydney, Australia, and partly because the film was financially backed by the French company CIBY 2000. The New Zealand film journal *Onfilm* noted these facts but claimed 'Kiwi sensation' Campion as a New Zealander all the same, albeit of a certain bohemian type (Pryor 1993: 25). Former Australian Prime Minister Paul Keating had claimed Campion's film for *his* country, however, praising *The Piano* as 'another triumph for the Australian film industry' (cited in Burchall 1993: 17). Some commentators had placed *The Piano* primarily in the context of earlier Australian – rather than New Zealand – films, taking it as broadly 'antipodean'. Although she emphasizes *The Piano*'s Anglo-European literary precursors, Stella Bruzzi nevertheless positions it cinematically alongside Gillian Armstrong's 'Australasian' film *My Brilliant Career* (1979) and Peter Weir's *Picnic at Hanging Rock* (1975), both 'high quality' Australian period costume dramas. But she also internationalizes *The Piano* by discussing it in relation to Caryl Churchill's *Cloud Nine* (1979) and, in fact, she invokes a range of contemporary British and American films and novels throughout her discussion by way of further comparison, including A.S. Byatt's *Possession* (1989). Other critics extend this international framework of influence – in particular, citing other examples of 'literary cinema', as well as novels themselves. For the *New Statesman & Society*'s film critic Jonathan Romney, *The Piano* 'bears obvious comparison' with John Fowles's *The French Lieutenant's Woman* (1981) through its depiction of 'Victorian mores from the standpoint of twentieth-century irony' (Romney 1993: 33). Jan Epstein compares Ada's muteness in *The Piano* with Oskar in *The Tin Drum* (1979), 'who at the age of three stopped growing by an act of will' (Epstein 1993: 20). Bruzzi also mentions Sally Potter's *Orlando* (1992) and Christine Edzard's *Little Dorritt* (1987).

Australian novelist Helen Garner had regarded the plot of *The Piano* as 'so original and seductive that I can hardly resist' (Garner 1993: 32), disavowing influences from elsewhere altogether. Other commentators have seen not just influence, however, but derivation. For Richard Cummings, *The Piano* 'has its roots in the original Rudolph Valentino version of *The Sheik*, in which another white woman awakens her eroticism with a pseudo-Third World character' (Cummings 1994: 72). The New Zealand location of Campion's film disappears entirely under the broad sweep of this comparison: from 'antipodean' to 'Third World'. The colonial romantic drama, of course, is a well-established cinematic genre and it would be quite possible to talk down *The Piano*'s uniqueness – and specificity – by situating it in this context. Think, for example, of Ken Annakin's film *Nor the Moon By Night* (1958), which has a woman go out to a similarly rain-soaked, muddy Kenya to marry a man who is cool towards her, only to be attracted to the man's brother – who, like Baines, is coded as close to nature and speaks the Zulu language fluently. But perhaps New Zealand returns to *The Piano* through another, more localized example of the colonial romance. Jane Mander's *The Story of a New Zealand River* (1920) has probably been the least acknowledged of all the sources for Campion's otherwise 'original' film. This colonial romance – a minor novel in early twentieth-century New Zealand literary history which, incidentally, has no Maori characters in it at all – concerns Alice and her daughter, who travel up river to the North Auckland frontier to meet Alice's husband-to-be, Roland, an enterprising but cold-hearted forester. Alice, however, finds herself attracted to David Bruce, an altogether more compassionate man. There certainly are clear comparisons to be drawn between this novel and *The Piano* in the exacting framework of colonial romantic drama. Alice even brings a piano with her – but this is the focus only of the earlier part of Mander's novel, and is never given the kind of symbolic resonance it has in Campion's film. Campion's treatment of Ada's piano in fact works to lift the film out of the generic constraints of the colonial romantic drama, making it seem 'original' once more – and allowing a suitably 'literary' mode of criticism to flourish in relation to it.

Reading *The Piano* (the film)

The combination of a symbolically enriched piano and a mute, impassioned heroine enabled commentators to talk up the 'literary' features of Campion's film. *The Piano*'s metaphors were seen as always open and ambiguous, and necessarily so. For Vikki Riley, Campion's film manufactures 'an entire system of signs and symbols, a Manichean universe which must be interpreted as a synergy of separate, albeit ambiguous motifs and gestures...Campion delights in matching and mismatching the symmetrical and asymmetrical implications of its design principles' (Riley 1995: 62). This may be why Riley sees Campion's feminism as 'out of sync with...feminist debate in the English speaking world' and yet at the same time 'so refreshingly accurate' (Riley 1995: 63): somehow asymmetrical and symmetrical at the same time. For cultural critics Ruth Barcan and Madeleine Fogarty, *The Piano* actively prevents viewers from arriving at 'any "one" interpretation...rendering a final interpretation unperformable' (Barcan and Fogarty 1995: 28). These two critics trace some of the differences of opinion found in commentaries on the film, and attempt to 'deconstruct' them – asserting, finally and liberally, that *The Piano* 'validates a position of ambivalence' (Barcan and Fogarty 1995: 27).

Openness (to different interpretations) and ambivalence (where even polarized interpretations are each true in their own right) give Campion's film its special 'literary' qualities: like a novel, *The Piano*'s meanings seem unable to be reduced or closed off. Philip Bell makes exactly this point: 'the film', he says, 'resists...reductionist analysis through the integration of its various modes of story-telling and its rich *mise-en-scène*' (Bell 1995: 59). Bell is particularly keen not to reduce the piano itself to a symbol of 'the female unconscious' (Bell 1995: 59). Nevertheless, he is also compelled to invoke the explanatory force of French psychoanalytical theory, thus running the risk of being reductive in spite of himself: 'Without reducing this complex figure [the piano] to one psychoanalytically specific term, it might be seen as signifying what Kristeva calls the "semiotic" realm...of pre-oedipal subjectivity' (Bell 1995: 59). Kristeva's 'semiotic' becomes the master key to the meaning of the piano in the film, and, as Bell sees it, Ada's task as she bargains over the keys is to retain as much of this feminized 'pre-oedipal subjectivity' as she can under the pressures of a 'patriarchal' symbolic order. For Bell, Ada and her muteness come to stand for the predicament of all women, particularly the female film-goer:

> the 1990s women watching *The Piano* are once again constituted as a *movie* audience, a reminder that the meanings conveyed by the moving images on the big silver screen are more like those set in motion by the ontological flows of music than by the digital or discrete signs of realistic literary (verbal) forms. Such an experience is not easy for the audience to talk about. They therefore 'love' the movie without analysis or critique.
>
> (Bell 1995: 58)

Here Bell uses the predicament of 'literary cinema' to polarize – rather than entangle – the two terms in this partnership. He sets up a binary which in fact recovers the 'cinematic' at the expense of the 'literary', triggering off a string of unimpeachable oppositions: film and novel; visual and verbal; lyrical and realistic; feminine and (by implication) masculine; mute and analytical; the unconscious and the symbolic order. These binaries segregate the 'literary' and the 'cinematic' in ways not dissimilar to some earlier film theorists, such as Rudolf Arnheim in *Film as Art* (1957) and Siegfried Kracauer in *Theory of Film*

(1960). Bell's representation of women in this passage (as film-goers, but unable to conceptualize, replacing analysis with 'love') is obviously patronizing. But at the same time he suggests, through the example of *The Piano*, that film is nevertheless something *more* than the novel, something that can transcend the kind of analysis that depends on or is constrained by words alone (a position represented in the film itself by Ada's husband Stewart). Helen Garner agrees, seeing Campion's film as unleashing an 'unconscious' which, by its very nature, would seem to resist the closure of analytical literary criticism: 'to talk narrative would allow me a luxury that is denied to reviewers but which all Campion's work urges us towards – holding back as long as possible from analysis, letting the film's imagery work on us privately; as Jung would say, "letting the unconscious take precedence"' (Garner 1993: 32). In this sense, then, *The Piano* is something more than 'literary cinema' itself: it transcends even this particular genre.

The turn away from analysis is seen positively here, as if the film exceeds verbal critique to take its viewers into the realm of ecstasy. But a subsequent 'backlash' against Campion's film showed that analysis could be withdrawn for quite different reasons: because the film's symbols and metaphors weighed so heavy upon it as to render *The Piano* virtually unreadable (see, for example, Grimes and Barber 1994: 3; Martin 1994: 14). Film critic John Slavin gave perhaps the most considered account of the film in these terms. For Slavin, Campion's foregrounding of the 'subconscious' of her heroines means that she forgoes 'the requirements of coherent narrative in favour of a paradigm of isolated and exaggerated signifiers' (Slavin 1993: 28). Slavin's main objection is that the piano is simply unable to carry the kind of symbolic weight it seems burdened with. The implication that it represents Ada's 'voice' and 'independence', for example, does not properly explain why she so quickly acquiesces to Baines' 'improper suggestions', giving herself and her piano over to him (Slavin 1993: 30). Slavin, however, recognizes that he is showing a preference for what Bell had disparagingly called 'realistic literary…forms':

> It may be argued that in contrasting narrative and symbolic constructions in the film I'm judging it as though it is a literary text, that what I'm presenting is once again a case for the long playing debate of naturalistic depiction against the symbolic/geometric of which modernism has been such an energetic exemplar.
>
> It is certainly true that there is a prevailing philosophy in our film schools of 'Show, don't tell!', that is, of the striking visual moment as superior to the written or spoken word…
>
> I have no argument with a cinema of signs. In such a cinema the symbolic brings order to the imaginary and in the process aestheticises it. Signs, however…emerge out of the organic/dramatic nature of the narrative text and that text is the negotiating agent between them and their socio-political context.
>
> (Slavin 1993: 30)

We have already seen critics valorizing the 'Show, don't tell!' approach in *The Piano* – which makes it seem more literary than literature in its privileging of the symbolic over the verbal. Slavin, however, requires a restrained, monogamous relationship between the two, where symbols bring 'order' to the 'imaginary' (in which case, the 'unconscious' is now much *less* 'unfettered') and are themselves entirely compatible with the verbal/narrative. In Campion's film, however, the 'striking image dominates the *mise en scène*, the dramatic development' (Slavin 1993: 30); it is excessive rather than restrained and compatible, promiscuous rather than monogamous. 'Her symbols', Slavin concludes, 'are hysterical high points of a subtext turned inside out' (Slavin 1993: 30).

Reading *The Piano* (the novel)

Slavin's commentary sees *The Piano* negatively, as too symbolic, too metaphorical. It is a film that destabilizes, rather than transcends, the otherwise monogamous partnership between terms in the genre of 'literary cinema'. Other critics, however, such as Bell, Riley and Garner, see this same feature as a positive thing, a mark of *The Piano*'s distinctly 'cinematic' or hyper-literary character. No matter which critical view prevails, the subsequent novel-of-the-film could only be seen in the wake of all this as *lacking*. The novel of *The Piano* certainly seems to provide the kind of monogamous, settled relationship between word and image that Slavin yearns for. It has a primarily explanatory project, filling out the missing histories of various characters (Ada in particular) and accounting for how they came to be as they are. Its task is, in fact, to make the film more coherent. In this sense, the novel can be seen as restricting the film's imaginative scope. Interestingly, Campion's co-author Kate Pullinger laid part of the blame for this on Campion herself, who had written two initial chapters: 'She [Pullinger] was…restrained by Campion's first chapters, which covered Ada's motherlessness, her father's decaying estate, her life until the age of sixteen and her music teacher – and restrained again by her willingness to fax pages to Campion for amending, then picking up with the details as Campion saw them…' (Field 1994: 8). This sense that the novel is 'restrained' in relation to the film is consistent with those earlier readings which had seen the film as excessive, as open and ambiguous. 'Everything in the film is much more open to interpretation,' Pullinger says. 'For instance, a lot of people who have seen the film think that Ada was married before, because the evidence in the film which says she wasn't is so easy to miss' (Field 1994: 8). Her interviewer, Michelle Field, agrees, and as a consequence is also unable to see the novel's project in positive terms (Field 1994: 8).

These perspectives help to fix the novel-of the-film in a secondary, slighter role as something less than the film. The novel's project is first and foremost to explain rather than to allow the imagination a free, 'unfettered' rein: not 'Show, don't tell!' but 'Tell, don't show!' It thus completes a film which had valorized incompleteness, and in doing so it runs the risk of saying *too much*. In this sense, of course, the novel is not restrained at all; it, too, has its own mode of excess, performing the sort of explanations that some of the commentators cited above had wilfully foregone in relation to the film.

The novel-of-the-film certainly makes the symbolic role of the piano clearer – and in the process reveals a theme which it shares with the film, and which speaks directly to the characteristics of Campion's kind of 'literary cinema'. In her earlier life as a child (which the novel details) the piano comes to stand for Ada's mother, and her attachment to it is pre-Oedipal: 'as she played Ada conjured a soft, warm figure composed of music and polished wood and called it "Cecilia"' (Campion and Pullinger 1994: 35). Her music teacher, Delwar, seems to underwrite this attachment with his own playing, which transports Ada 'into another world where everything had the texture of silk and all was warmth and small rooms made cozy by hearthfires at night' (Campion and Pullinger 1994: 171). Their relationship is more erotic than disciplinary – so much so, that their sex flows naturally from a duet they play together. More importantly, the piano helps them fit 'naturally' together, sharing the same 'rhythm' (Campion and Pullinger 1994: 171), as if the pre-Oedipal attachment to the piano is not disturbed by Delwar, with Ada retaining the autonomy it had given to her. Playing the piano, then, is linked to pleasure, even ecstasy, and this in turn is linked to an image of the autonomous self and an 'unfettered' unconscious. The unconscious is privileged, in other words, while the disciplinary role – which requires restraint, learning, culture, work and *someone defined as other to you* – is given a greatly reduced significance.

In New Zealand, however, this relationship is traumatically unsettled. Ada's daughter, Flora, already sees the piano in a disciplinary way, refusing to practice (Campion and Pullinger 1994: 148); her betrayal of Ada may very well follow on from this refusal. When he purchases the piano, Baines asks Ada to teach him how to play, placing *her* in a disciplinary position and so compromising her autonomy. The piano recovers its unconscious, pre-Oedipal character, however, when their relationship becomes sexual: 'George Baines was not her husband; now he was no longer her pupil either' (Campion and Pullinger 1994: 146). Yet the unconscious/discipline binary does not fully separate itself out here. Rather, it becomes entangled. During the sex with Baines, Ada feels 'lost to the world' (Campion and Pullinger 1994: 151), still pleasured and playful and in the realm of the unconscious. Yet negotiating with Baines for the piano keys (she only ever partially recovers her piano) and learning more about sex from him at the same time, Ada is also aware that her body is 'no longer her own' (Campion and Pullinger 1994: 150). The novel both knows this and occasionally forgets it: sometimes the piano-as-Baines *is* associated only with pleasure, play and the 'unfettered' unconscious. By contrast, Stewart, Ada's husband, is associated with the denial or suppression of pleasure: with organization, work and production, with discipline and its virtues. (Like Ada, the Maori in the novel and the film are seen as 'naturally' unproductive.) When he punishes Ada and Flora by locking them inside his house, the novel tells us: 'Stewart had decided to teach Ada a lesson' (Campion and Pullinger 1994: 161). Lessons/work are seen here as restricting, restraining; pleasure is seen in contrast to this, as excessive and unrestrained and therefore always potentially compromised. Ada is a character, then, who tries to recover as much pleasure as she can. But the novel, like the film, stops short of presenting her as utterly unrealistic by putting her in a relationship which requires her to negotiate for her pleasure, to see pleasure-as-excess (improvisation, autonomy) always in a dialectical relationship with work-as-restraint (learning lessons under the guidance of others: negotiating and bargaining, rather than being autonomous and 'unfettered').

So the novel presents us with a sense of the unconscious/pleasure not as 'unfettered' at all, but as always potentially compromised, always coming up against its own limits. The piano might well signify this anyway: the heaviness of the instrument keeps it on the beach for a time, and people literally have to work together to get it up the cliff and into the house. This is one of the few 'material' moments in the film, when the work of others is shown as the means to a pleasurable end for the piano's owner, when the 'unfettered' imagination is seen to depend upon organized labour. The piano thus has both a symbolic force and a material presence: it produces pleasure for Ada, but it is also – albeit reluctantly in this context – there to be worked upon, negotiated over, transacted, compromised, the subject of deals and directions with and by other people, autonomous and yet commercial.

Its role, in fact, speaks directly to the location of the film itself in what Pierre Bourdieu has called 'the field of cultural production' – which may well explain why the film takes the piano for its title (Bourdieu 1993). *The Piano* was the first of Campion's feature films to achieve substantial commercial support, thanks to the work of her producer, Jan Chapman – a 'tough negotiator' who managed to secure an 'extraordinary deal from CIBY 2000' (Connolly 1993: 7). But *The Piano* is also an 'arthouse' piece of literary cinema which would otherwise wish to distance itself from the compromises built into commercial deal-making. Campion has accounted for her own film-making history in this way: 'My first idea of cinema wasn't commercial cinema, it was personal-expression cinema. I still like to think that the two aren't mutually exclusive – and I hope that *The Piano* proves that' (Connolly 1993: 7). These comments polarize the commercial and the arthouse/personal at the same time as trying to reconcile them: as if they, too, can live monogamously with one another. In the interview in *Onfilm*, Campion represents CIBY 2000 as a commercial venture which has, in spite of itself, come to recognize and privilege the value of arthouse cinema:

> I think the curious thing about CIBY 2000 is that it's really a vision of one man, Frances Bouygues....His years on earth were numbered and he wanted to leave a sort of tribute...he chose to do that through alternative cinema, art cinema. What I love about it is he actually loves

art. You've got so much money, what are you going to do with it? I think in the end the thing that meant something was to have his heart moved, his soul, his spirit.

(Pryor 1993: 25)

This sentimental account of the other party in Jan Chapman's 'extraordinary deal' puts a corporate backer in a role which is even more idealized than Ada's in Campion's film: as someone who actually *does* recover the kind of 'unfettered' pleasure or ecstasy associated with playing (or in his case, paying for) the piano. Indeed, in the context of women making deals with men, CIBY 2000's French representative is comparable not so much with Baines in *The Piano* as with Delwar (who is only in the novel-of-the-film); he certainly does not resemble Stewart, apparently having no repressive or constraining function at all as far as film production is concerned. Campion and her financial backers, in other words, fit together in terms of their position in the cultural field as smoothly as Ada and Delwar as they play their duet together. But we should remember that this duet was a pre-Oedipal moment in the novel-of-the-film which later events undermine. Campion's happy synthesis of commercial transactions and the 'spiritual' world of art is not unlike her earlier blending of the atmospherics of *Wuthering Heights* and New Zealand: two incommensurable places are yoked together. But it relies on a disavowal of commercial pressures. In another interview, Campion proclaims: 'I'm not really trying to sell myself....I don't need to sell myself, I've got work' (Schembri 1993: 13). The interviewer wonders if those pressures help to make her film more 'conventional' than it might have been:

> Under fire, she slips into arrogance. So suggesting that Campion opted for a more conventional shooting style in *The Piano* compared with her previous films, for instance, draws a duly liberal, if slightly uncomfortable, response. 'I don't agree with you at all about that. I don't think this is conventional at all.'
>
> (Schembri 1993: 13)

This disavowal of one of the consequences of commercial negotiation in film production – selling one's self, 'selling out' – helps Campion retain an image of *The Piano* as an autonomous and 'unfettered' form of 'personal expression'. Such an image no doubt assists in the identification of the film as 'literary cinema', even though it was never actually adapted from a novel, and it also allows *The Piano* to be received through a mode of literary criticism which valorizes these qualities. This is in spite of the fact that the ethics of 'selling out' or compromising one's self is the central theme of Campion's film, a point which the Australian critic Kerryn Goldsworthy registers with something close to horror:

But what seems to me to be the inescapable moral of this movie is that a gifted woman must pay with her gift for true love. And the idea of the spectacularly gifted Jane Campion's beautiful and inspired film conveying this message makes my hair stand on end.

(Goldsworthy 1993: 47)

We have seen a set of critical responses to *The Piano* that, in their privileging of the unconscious, of metaphor, of the imagination, displace the role of commercial transactions in the film – or, as in the last example, mention it only in order apparently to wish it wasn't there. For so many commentators, *The Piano* comes to stand for 'literary cinema' in its purest form: so pure, in fact, that the cinema is the only place for it. Any other place, including the place of commentary and criticism, seriously 'reduces' *The Piano*'s force. So the production of the novel-of-the-film becomes a kind of abject event – in which case, it may not be surprising to hear Kate Pullinger rebelliously admit 'that while I was writing it, I had this other version in my head which I called *The Anti-Piano*' (Field 1994: 8). Here the novel and the novel-of-the-film are coded as opposites: one is appropriate to the field of literature, while the other is inappropriate. This is because, in this case at least, the movement from film to novel is seen as regressive, as a debasement – not entirely unlike the movement from film to video. Indeed, for Philip Bell *The Piano* is precisely a film made to 'be seen at the theatre, not on the video', as if its cinematic location simply cannot be transgressed. This, he says, is because the film 'needs a space of black, or silence, as a zone to ward off the world which clatters and hums outside...' (Bell 1995: 60). In this account, *The Piano* must remain cinematic so that its autonomy is never compromised; it must remain sealed off in some kind of pre-Oedipal dark space, utterly separate from those other forms (the novel-of-the-film, the video of the film, the outside world 'which clatters and hums', analytical commentary) which seem to refuse to allow it to be what it is.

The making of a literary adaptation

In Jane Campion's 1996 adaptation of Henry James's *The Portrait of a Lady*, autonomy – as something both desirable and impossible – turns out to be a central theme. Isabel is a heroine who wishes for independence and yet finds her independence increasingly compromised as she goes along. This theme may carry over into the adaptation itself, which begins by announcing its own independence from James's novel through an apparently unrelated prologue which presents a number of young Australian women talking about 'the kiss'. For Lee Marshall, the prologue immediately secures the film's autonomy from its literary source: 'this is a film which renders the debate about faithfulness to the source text irrelevant....This is clear from the title sequence, which features a group of Aussie girls discussing love' (Marshall 1997: 9). Lizzie Franke, in her article on the film in *Sight and Sound*, initially sees Campion's prologue in the same way: 'The opening few minutes of Jane Campion's *The Portrait of a Lady* are sublimely designed to disorientate any viewer corseted into certain expectations of the literary-adaptation piece' (Franke 1996: 6). Identifying with the Australian girls, however, Franke goes on to recall her own teenage years and, as a consequence, recovers the literary tradition the film seemed at first to have disavowed: 'For those were the years when we started cramming our heads with ideas and aspirations, reading Austen, George Eliot, the Brontës, James and others' (Franke 1996: 6). An otherwise 'disorienting' scene that was initially viewed as independent of James's novel thus comes to evoke a field of great literary precursors (including James himself), in relation to which Campion's literary adaptation is then more properly and respectfully located. With *The Piano*, the issue was one of cinematic uniqueness, as if this work of 'literary cinema' is – in spite of its own literary genealogies – nothing other than cinematic. But even the scene that is most 'irrelevant' to James's novel in Campion's *The Portrait of a Lady* reminds Franke that this work of 'literary cinema' remains literary first and foremost.

How independent – how autonomous – can a work of 'literary cinema' hope to be? Of course, if the literary source remains unread, then from a film-goer's point of view the cinematic adaptation is all there is. Campion herself has noted that only '[o]ne in 10,000 people reads the novel, and of those who read it, many don't bother finishing it' (Campion 1997: 72). From this directorial perspective, the novel is 'finished' by the film itself, as if the adaptation somehow completes or even replaces James's own work – giving us quite the opposite relationship to the one we had seen with the film and novel of *The Piano*. Philip Horne, on the other hand, tries to recover the authority of Campion's literary source by seeing her adaptation as much *less* independent from Henry James, the Australian prologue notwithstanding. In particular, he notes that the dialogue in the film is often lifted wholesale from James's original novel (Horne 1997: 20). For Horne, Henry James sets up the terms of judgement for an adaptation of his own novel: Campion's film could not be any less autonomous from its source than this! Brian McFarlane also restricts the scope of the adaptation, regarding the prologue in Campion's film as 'downright silly', complaining about 'some artfully or pointlessly angled shots' and arguing overall that the 'film is at its least impressive when it seems most earnestly straining to be "cinematic"' (McFarlane 1997: 37). This last remark re-opens the binary implicit in the otherwise monogamous partnership of 'literary cinema', disparaging the latter term and in the process curtailing an adaptation's ability to secure at least some kind of independence from its source. In *Novel to Film* (1996), McFarlane discusses the film adaptations of five classic novels, including Peter Bogdanovich's 1974 adaptation of Henry James's novella *Daisy Miller* (1878). His emphasis is on an adaptation's faithfulness to the narrational mode of the literary source, the criteria for which in this case are again laid out by Henry James himself: 'By this, I mean the Jamesian device, variously described by the author and his critics as the use of a "centre of consciousness"'

(McFarlane 1996: 139). At the same time, McFarlane recognizes that in cinema a character's inner turmoil 'is also…shown rather than told'. We return here to the question of a proper relationship between literature and cinema – proper enough to keep the 'literary cinema' partnership faithful and monogamous. For McFarlane, the slide toward a 'cinematic' independence from the source novel is the thing that most unsettles the properness of this partnership: 'The problem', he concludes, 'lies in deciding what exactly is being shown' (McFarlane 1996: 139). This is, indeed, the problem: an undecidability inhabiting the relationship between literature and cinema which enables the latter to be faithful and independent, monogamous and promiscuous, restricted or compromised by the source novel, and yet 'separate' or autonomous from it, all at the same time.

As I have noted, the theme of autonomy – as desirable and yet impossible – is central to Campion's adaptation of *The Portrait of a Lady*. The heroine, Isabel, wants to be able to 'do what she likes', to travel broadly and take 'chances', and she is encouraged along these lines by the small fortune provided by her generous benefactor, Ralph Touchett. We might observe in passing just how Touchett's relationship to Isabel recalls Frances Bouygues' relationship to Campion – as a benign corporate backer 'who wanted to leave a sort of tribute' which works inevitably to produce Campion, as Ralph does with Isabel, as a transnational. A new introduction by Regina Barreca to the 1997 Penguin film tie-in edition of James's novel talks up Isabel's autonomy in order to characterize her as a new heroine for the 1990s: 'At the end of the novel', Barreca says, over-enthusiastically, 'Isabel Archer is free' (James 1997: xv). Scholarly articles on Henry James and his heroine, perhaps not surprisingly, offer a more restrained view: Debra MacComb sees Isabel Archer as someone who negotiates her space within the framework of a partnership (MacComb 1996), while Jessica Berman takes the Jamesian woman as someone who, like America itself at the time, needed to 'temper its tendency to individuality' in relation to others (Berman 1996: 73). Campion's film certainly remains faithful to this particular theme, showing Isabel to be continually compromised by her various relationships with men, Gilbert Osmond in particular. Yet faithfulness itself is rendered unstable in the film, with Isabel imagining the possibility of being promiscuous (as in the dream-sequence where she is fondled by all her admirers) even as she acknowledges the restrictions that marriage to Osmond imposes upon her.

A certain kind of female masochism works itself out through this tension, as Mark Nicholls has noted in an article entitled 'She Who Gets Slapped' – where he also seems to suggest that Campion relishes the fact that Isabel's yearnings for independence remain unsatisfied (Nicholls 1997: 43–7). But another approach to this theme may be taken by turning back to available distinctions in the field of cultural production. Campion's film is also all about 'taste': it sets up a binary between tastes which are open, and tastes which are closed or restricted. The aesthete Gilbert Osmond cultivates the latter, as Ralph tells Isabel: 'I should have said that the man for you would have had a more active,

larger, freer sort of nature....I can't get over the sense that Osmond is somehow
– well, small...I think he's narrow....He's the incarnation of taste' (Jones 1996:
63). Isabel, however, thinks that Osmond's tastes are 'large' and 'exquisite'
(Jones 1996: 64). The film shows her to be quite deluded about Osmond's
highly refined tastes, while at the same time it suggests that Isabel is drawn to
them precisely because they *are* so 'narrow' (which is where her 'masochism'
really lies). The film thus sets up a predicament for its heroine that shows her
openness and independence to be compromised by tastes that, although
'exquisite' and attractive to her, nevertheless work to restrict her freedom and
compel her faithfulness. In other words, the film speaks about its *own* predicament as a literary adaptation. This is recognized in the partnership built into the
generic term 'literary cinema', which articulates the sense that one is drawn to a
form of cultural production that is itself restricted in terms of circulation ('One
in 10,000 people...') but which requires one to cultivate a certain faithfulness
or respect towards it – and yet, because cinema exerts its own influences and
can have a much broader circulation than the literary source anyway, a certain
kind of openness or unfaithfulness (or even a kind of promiscuity) is achieved at
the same time. Literary cinema may thus very well be in Isabel's words both
'exquisite' and 'large', as if there is no contradiction between these two features.
It is a cross-over form of cultural production in this respect, negotiating a space
for itself between the restricted circulation of the literary source and something
altogether much broader or 'mainstream'. We can return to Pierre Bourdieu
here, noting – as Bridget Fowler does in her book *Pierre Bourdieu and Cultural
Theory* (1997) – his unimpeachable opposition between aesthetic taste on the
one hand, and popular taste (the 'popular aesthetic') on the other (Fowler
1997: 160). Elsewhere, Simon During has talked about what he calls the
'global popular', mostly referring to the movie blockbuster form which is
'distributed and apparently enjoyed everywhere' (During 1997: 808). We have
seen that *The Piano* was also a transnational film, and so is *The Portrait of a
Lady*, yet their global popularity is tempered by their generic identification as
'literary cinema' and their association with 'narrow' or 'exquisite' – or literary –
tastes. Perhaps we can mutate During's term accordingly, by seeing literary
cinema as an example of what might in this case be called the 'restricted
(global) popular'.

14

THE WRATH OF THE ORIGINAL CAST

Translating embodied television characters to other media

Ina Rae Hark

When works of literature are adapted for the screen, the chief tasks facing the film-makers involve embodying the characters in actors whose material attributes do not offer a violent contradiction to the images generated in the typical reader's mind and repackaging the literary work's diegesis to fit the limitations of the filmic medium. When a television series is produced in a big-screen version, the challenges are substantially different. The appeal of a television series lies less in its narratives than in its continuing characters and general situation. The appeal of the characters is to a greater or lesser extent constituted also by the actors who embody those characters. Therefore, an ideal filmic adaptation of a television series would retain the characters and actors but insert them into a diegesis enhanced by the various advantages that film possesses over television as a medium: larger, sharper visual field; bigger budget for settings, costumes, effects, guest actors; more time for plot development than the usual thirty- or sixty-minute episode (although, of course, far less than the multi-episode entire series run). Such an ideal is graspable for films produced simultaneously with the broadcast run of the series. When, however, the desire arose to adapt television series to the big screen many years after the shows had ceased production, the requirement to retain the originals' embodied characterizations was difficult (or impossible) to satisfy. This chapter will explore some of the strategies adopted by the industry to deal with this problem.

A brief history of television to film adaptation

Very early on, Hollywood saw the benefits of putting television series into cinemas while the programmes were still running: examples include *Molly*, a 1950 feature-film version of the popular Gertrude Berg series, *The Goldbergs* (1949–54) and the *Dragnet* movie made in 1954 in the middle of the series' 1951–9 run. In the 1960s and 1970s such transfers became increasingly common, with quickie features like *McHale's Navy* (1964), *McHale's Navy Joins the Air Force* (1965), *House of Dark Shadows* (1970), *Night of Dark Shadows* (1971), and a number of 'amplified' episodes of *The Man from U.N.C.L.E.* rushed into cinemas at intervals during the series' entire 1964–8 run. The small number of feature-film releases during this time of 'product shortage' meant that exhibitors were more than happy to screen these media hybrids. By the 'blockbuster era' of the 1980s, however, productions like these would have looked far too television-like to compete with the visual spectacles that were dominating screens. Thus 'movies' featuring the original-cast performers were more likely to be based on recently cancelled series and to remain on television (the series of two-hour *Columbo* or *Alien Nation* TV-films, for example), while nostalgia for series of past decades produced a number of 'reunion' TV films. (The one major exception, the *Star Trek* films, will be the focus of the second part of this essay.)

This same nostalgia, fuelled by constant reruns of old shows on cable television – especially by *Nick at Nite*, whose programming strategy was built on the loving re-presentation of the televisual past – led in the 1990s to their recast, big-budget re-creation. While the previous films based on television series had involved a transfer from one medium to another, these many 1990s adaptations, which were spurred by the success in 1991 of Barry Sonnenfeld's *The Addams Family*, involved *remaking* the television series as films.[1] Sonnenfeld cast familiar film character-actors Anjelica Huston, Raul Julia and Christopher Lloyd in the roles played on television by Carolyn Jones, John Astin and Jackie Coogan. Subsequent remakes cast major film stars like Mel Gibson, Harrison Ford and Tom Cruise in the roles of characters whose original embodiers could not realistically play the parts because they were now either dead or too old. Sometimes links to the original were preserved by featuring the television-series performers in small roles. *The Brady Bunch Movie* (1995) had cameos by Florence Henderson, Ann B. Davis, Barry Williams and Christopher Knight. James Garner, TV's Bret Maverick, played a substantial supporting role in the *Maverick* feature film and was revealed at the conclusion, in a nice twist, to be the oft-invoked but never seen 'Pappy' whom both TV and movie Brets were always quoting. This practice of using original performers had, however, already been established with some remakes of features, as in the appearance of Kevin McCarthy in the 1978 *Invasion of the Body Snatchers* or the cameos by Gregory Peck and Robert Mitchum in the 1991 remake of the 1962 *Cape Fear*.

The box-office success of at least some of these adaptations of old television series as feature films with new casts (*The Addams Family, The Fugitive*, 1993; *Maverick*, 1994; *The Brady Bunch Movie, Mission: Impossible*, 1996) proves that nostalgia for characters and situations can in fact suffice when nostalgia for the stars of the series cannot be satisfied. Indeed, the prior television incarnation guaranteed initial audience interest, much as did the name of a Tom Clancy or John Grisham, providing a 'pre-sold' commodity to studios. In re-incarnating such series, the film-makers did not feel – any more than those adapting a novel do – overly constrained by the original from making fairly substantial changes.

The Fugitive completely changed the circumstances of Helen Kimble's murder and the apprehension of the one-armed man from how they had been portrayed in the series, created a new murderer for whom the one-armed man was simply acting as hired killer, moved the action from Stafford, Indiana, to Chicago, transformed Dr Richard Kimble from a paediatrician to a surgeon, changed police Lt Philip Gerard to U.S. Marshal Sam Gerard, and so on. *Mission: Impossible* presented TV's super-patriot team leader Jim Phelps as a burnt-out traitor. These alterations in no way prevented each film from earning substantial box-office rewards.

As Nick Gillespie observes, careful reconceptualization and recasting of the roles of regular characters may be a key to the quality of such adaptations:

> Since [*The Fugitive*] compresses events, Harrison Ford's Kimble is by turns, flustered, disoriented, and rage-filled. Since the experience of being chased is new to the filmic Kimble, there is a greater sense of urgency and terror. In the TV show's two-part finale, by contrast, David Janssen's Kimble, understandably worn out by four years of false leads, false hopes, and false endings, is almost devoid of any affect.
>
> (Gillespie 1994: 55)

Reactions to *The Addams Family* in two non-professional Internet critiques posted to **rec.arts.movies.reviews** also reveal that recasting could succeed with those who treasured the performances of the original cast, and that for many others the original cast is not even a memory. Frank Maloney, evidently an aficionado of the television series, gushes:

> The performers represent a dream cast, the kind of inevitable choices that result from a lot of selling and looking around. Anjelica Huston is the only woman in the U.S. who could have played Morticia as well as Carolyn Jones did nearly 30 years ago, at least she surely gives us that impression....Whether Raul Julia comes up to manic John Astin's mark as Gomez Addams, Julia gives it a great shot....And of course, Julia looks and sounds a lot more like a Gomez than Astin did.[2]

On the other hand, reviewer Brian L. Johnson felt it necessary to announce: '*The Addams Family* is based on an old black-and-white television show by the same name. The actors/actresses have been changed. I have never seen the television show so I don't know if it's like the film' (Johnson 1992). As these contrasting takes on the cast changes indicate, when 1960s television shows are remade as 1990s films, the combination of baby boomers who remember the original and younger viewers who do not can ensure a fairly wide demographic for the film's audience, provided that the adaptation has been skilfully done: 'The demand for nostalgia, it seems is extremely elastic and depends less on the product's track record than its present performance' (Gillespie 1994: 54).

Thus it is certainly possible for television series to be adapted successfully for the screen, not simply transferred to it. Given that adaptations of literary works for the screen, and remakes of previously filmed material, have been common practice since the beginnings of cinema, it is quite astonishing that television was nearly fifty years old before the same types of regular film remakes of programmes from this medium occurred. Given that single episodes of dramatic television from the 'Golden Age', like *Marty* and *Requiem for a Heavyweight*, had become films, and that hundreds of movies had travelled the other way to become prime-time television series with a few, like *M*A*S*H* and *The Odd Couple*, having long runs, clearly the two media were no more incompatible than film and literature. Thus the prolonged hesitancy to remake television series as feature films is quite puzzling at first glance. I would like next to theorize about some possible explanations for it.

First, despite countervailing examples like the 'novelizations' of films, adaptation has generally been conceived as a one-way street leading from older, more elite media to newer, mass-cultural media. It therefore seemed a natural trajectory for Grace Metalious' bestseller *Peyton Place* (1956) that it should be adapted into a feature film in 1957 and then a long-running television series in 1964, or for *Anna and the King of Siam* that it should go from Margaret Landon's 1944 literary text to Hollywood movie (1946) to Broadway musical *The King and I* (1951) to musical film (1956) and then to a much shorter-lived television series *Anna and the King* (1972). Reversing this trajectory, however, struck many as highly unnatural. Richard Corliss claimed that: 'The lemming rush to televidiocy reveals a movie industry close to creative exhaustion' (Gillespie 1994: 53). In a similar vein, Joe Brown (reviewing *The Addams Family*) complains that 'Hollywood must have run out of comic book characters to blow up on the big screen, because now it's sending screenwriters into the vaults to exhume baby-boom era TV shows' (Brown 1991). As Gillespie asserts, these reactions are entirely predictable:

> The film industry's recent use of TV shows, then, is a reversal of the traditional hierarchy of big and small screens, a turnabout which no doubt bothers film mavens. For the cinema to turn to TV for ideas is an aesthetic double-cross, akin to finding out that the camera angles in *Citizen Kane* were stolen from comic books.
>
> (Gillespie 1994: 54)

The 'mavens' tolerated these reversals only in the case of high-quality, dramatic television anthology series episodes, which were virtually a theatre of the airways.

For continuing series, however, several complications appeared to militate against the adaptation to film, in addition to the relative newness and low cultural status of the medium. One is the difference in narrative form between a series and a self-contained film. As John Ellis observes: 'Cinema's single texts tend to inaugurate a novel problematic, a new story subject, for each film. The

TV series repeats a problematic' (Ellis 1992: 154). Therefore, while a film might inaugurate a 'prototype' situation that a television version could profitably repeat, it seems unlikely to Ellis that the oft-repeated problematic of a series would not have exhausted the narrative interest required for the stand-alone cinematic text.

Connected to this repeatability of the series text is the different relationship television actors bear to their regular series characters in comparison to that borne by film actors to the characters they embody in any one particular film. For one thing, the television actor has embodied the character far longer than the average two-hour span of a cinema performance.[3] In addition, many television theorists postulate a fundamental difference in the actor/character dynamics of the two media. Ellis, for instance, believes:

> the television performer appears regularly for a series which itself is constituted on the basis of repetition of a particular character and/or situation. The television performer appears in subsidiary forms of circulation (newspapers, magazines) mostly during the time that the series of performances is being broadcast. The result is a drastic reduction in the distance between the circulated image and the performance. The two become very much entangled, so that the performer's image is equated with that of the fictional role (rather than vice versa).
>
> (Ellis 1992: 106)

And Marshall McLuhan, citing anecdotal evidence, asserted in his influential 1960s work *Understanding Media*:

> The old movie-fan tourists had wanted to see their favorites as they were in real life, not as they were in their film roles. The fans of the cool TV medium want to see their star in role, whereas the movie fans want the real thing.
>
> (McLuhan 1964: 318)

Beginning with the move of some performers from radio (and later stand-up comedy) to television (Jack Benny, Burns and Allen, Garry Shandling, Jerry Seinfeld, Roseanne) in shows that featured them as fictionalized versions of themselves, and progressing to a great number of series (mainly sitcoms) so identified with their stars that the programmes are named after them, and the characters they play share their given names (*I Love Lucy*, *The Andy Griffith Show*, *The Mary Tyler Moore Show*, *Newhart*, *Ellen*, *Everybody Loves Raymond* and countless others), the apparent fusion of character with actor is widespread in television. By contrast, even the most iconic movie stars had to settle merely for above-the-title billing: we never saw *The Marilyn Monroe Movie* (although there was the eponymous *Muppet Movie*, whose puppet players, significantly, originated on television). All these factors undoubtedly made Hollywood producers loath to recast television series for big-screen presentation. That soap operas constantly recast characters, that long-running prime-time series could frequently replace major characters with others, that *Bewitched*'s Darrin could be played by Dick York for several seasons and Dick Sargent for several others, all without significant attrition in viewer engagement, did not sufficiently challenge the prevailing wisdom. Only the healthy box-office receipts for *The Addams Family* and many of its 1990s successors could accomplish this.

The exception that proves the rule?

One 1960s television show that was transformed into a series of big-budget feature films departed from the historical pattern described above. This is, of course, the very special case of *Star Trek*. In six films made from 1979 to 1993, it became the only television series to be adapted to the big screen more than a decade after going off the air[4] that retained its original cast in the principal roles they had created. These actors had become practically welded to their characters by the show's cult status and numerous *Star Trek* conventions, at which the actors appeared year after year, so recasting the roles never really seemed to be an option. This decision in turn created problems of its own, especially because of the action-adventure format of the films and the increasing age of the original cast. These films illustrate productively the strategies necessary to carry off such a project, but also question its necessity. The success of the *Star Trek* films has been cited as one of the things that finally gave Hollywood the confidence to look to 1960s television for source materials, but the films also taught Hollywood a lesson about the need truly to remake such programmes for the cinema, not simply transfer them.[5]

Despite their retention of the original performers, the producers of the films of course never intended a mere big-screen enlargement of the television version. The 1960s day-glo colours, clumsy model shots and the plywood construction of the series' sets no longer looked convincing even on television, so *Star Trek: The Motion Picture* (1979) – which was abruptly reconceived as a full-scale feature film after pre-production work had been done for it as the pilot for a second *Star Trek* TV series (Reeves-Stevens and Reeves-Stevens 1997) – featured a completely refitted *Enterprise*, new-style costumes and extensive special effects. The film announced its intention to differentiate itself from the television series in its opening sequence, prior to the first scenes involving the television cast, by introducing Klingons that were radically altered in appearance thanks to a sufficient budget to take advantage of advanced make-up technology. Balancing the differences in *mise en scène* were certain narrative continuities with the past, including a central plot-line very similar to that of the TV episode 'The Changeling' and the implication that new character Will Decker is the son of Matt Decker, a Starfleet officer destroyed by his obsession with defeating an alien 'Doomsday Machine' in the series episode of the same name.

Star Trek: The Motion Picture also introduced plot elements that would continue to recur throughout the *Star Trek* films, elements that foreground the uneasiness the new films experience with having to retain the old television cast. When the film opens, Kirk has been promoted to the rank of admiral and has been working planet-side as Chief of Starfleet Operations for two-and-a-half years. The completely redesigned *Enterprise* is scheduled to depart under the command of Captain Decker. When the mysterious V'ger threatens Earth, however, Kirk convinces his superiors to allow him to reassume command, leaving Decker temporarily demoted to commander and Kirk unsure which way the turbolifts are. In most of the subsequent films, as well, Kirk's command of the Enterprise is delegitimized in some way. In *Star Trek II* he is supposed to be an observer on a training mission for Captain Spock's cadets when Khan's move against the Genesis project sends them off on a real rescue mission. *Star Trek III* requires that the crew engineer a theft of the soon-to-be-scrapped *Enterprise* in order to retrieve the reborn Spock from the off-limits Genesis planet. During this adventure, Kirk is forced to blow up the *Enterprise*. The final part of this film, and all of *Star Trek IV*, find the TV cast as Federation outlaws piloting an appropriated Klingon Bird of Prey. Since they do save the world, however, their only 'punishment' is Kirk's demotion to the rank of captain so that he can, finally, legitimately be put in command of the new *Enterprise-A*. Yet two films later, in the original cast's swansong *Star Trek VI*, the crew are on the verge of retirement and the *Enterprise-A* is to be decommissioned. Contemplating the bad hairpieces, lined visages and expanded waistlines on display in this film, even the most devoted Trekker has to be thinking: 'And not a moment too soon!'[6]

The films' scripts constantly stress the cast's ageing, from *Generations*' captain's remark about reading of the exploits of the 'living legends' in grade school, to the observation of a young ensign in *Star Trek III* to Uhura that their routine and unadventurous assignment to 'the worst duty station in town' might be all right for a 'twenty-year space veteran...whose career is winding down' but is far too dull for him. But these admissions of the toll taken by time on the original cast repeatedly surface only to be rendered irrelevant. In the clear Oedipal conflicts evoked, the fathers and mothers always triumph. The disrespectful ensign finds himself on the wrong end of Uhura's phaser as she inquires: 'You wanted adventure, how's this?' In the same film the technologically advanced *Excelsior*, a product of 'young minds, fresh ideas' that is meant to replace the ageing *Enterprise* (whose 'day is over') as the Starfleet flagship, is brought to a dead halt when Scotty removes a pocketful of small components from its vaunted transwarp drive.

The younger, usurping generation again and again proves inadequate or unavailable to perform the galaxy-saving assignments that inevitably fall to the *Enterprise*. Decker and the Deltan navigator Ilia, whose characters were to have served as a new generation of *Star Trek* heroes in the abortive *Star Trek Phase II* television series, merge with V'ger to become a higher, incorporeal life form.

Scotty's teenage nephew[7] Peter Preston dies in *Star Trek II*. The coupling of Spock's protégé Saavik and Kirk's son David promised by *Star Trek II* is destroyed in *Star Trek III* when David is killed by Klingons. Saavik appears briefly in *Star Trek IV* and then vanishes from the films. A new Spock protégé, Belarus, introduced in *Star Trek VI*, turns out to be a traitor taking part in a conspiracy to prevent an alliance between the Federation and the Klingons. The films simultaneously remind us that '[g]alloping around the cosmos is a game for the young' and that 'I don't think these kids can steer'. Both the above statements are made by Kirk in *Star Trek II: The Wrath of Khan*. This film most explicitly articulates the *Star Trek* films' strategy for continuing to use the original cast, while acknowledging the increasing unlikelihood that characters so embodied would still be carrying out the kind of space missions portrayed on the series in decades past.

Wrath of Khan is the film most closely linked to the original series. It is a sequel of sorts to the 1967 television episode 'Space Seed', in which the *Enterprise* encounters a group of genetically-engineered twentieth-century humans adrift in suspended animation. Their leader, Khan Noonien Singh (Ricardo Montalban), was a tyrant 'superman' who had been eventually defeated during the Eugenics Wars of the 1990s. Although Khan attempts to take over the ship and kill Kirk, showing little gratitude to his rescuers, the captain has a grudging admiration for him and allows him and his followers to settle on an inhospitable planet, Ceti Alpha V, rather than face imprisonment in a Starfleet facility. *Wrath of Khan* revisits this planet fifteen years later, when the Starfleet vessel *Reliant*, looking for a lifeless planet upon which to test the Genesis device, discovers that the explosion of neighbouring Ceti Alpha VI six months after Khan's group had landed has knocked the planet from its orbit and rendered survival nearly impossible for the voluntarily marooned supermen. Only Khan's superior strength and will, and his hatred for Kirk for not bothering to check up on them in the intervening years, has kept a remnant of the colony alive. Montalban, aged sixty-one, returned to play the role he had created at the age of forty-six.

The film begins, however, not with Khan but with an *Enterprise* bridge staffed by the original personnel, Spock, McCoy, Uhura and Sulu, but with the young Vulcan woman Saavik in the captain's chair. Responding to a distress call from the freighter *Kobyashi Maru*, the ship finds itself in a deteriorating situation that eventually leaves all the bridge crew dead save Saavik. At this point, the events are revealed as part of a simulation used to evaluate how Starfleet cadets deal with no-win situations. It also suggests the necessity for the original cast to make way for a newer generation, a theme reinforced by subsequent scenes of a melancholy Kirk, on his birthday, resigned to his desk job and insisting that his spacefaring days have properly concluded. The series of events set in motion by Khan, the ghost of his more vital youth, ironically renew Kirk's confidence and propel him and the rest of the original cast into four more sequels. The chief metaphor *Wrath of Khan* employs to effect this transformation is the

Genesis device, which generates 'life from lifelessness' (Roth 1987). Apparently defeated by his old enemy, Kirk tells Genesis scientist and former lover Carol Marcus: 'I'm old, worn out'. Taking him to see the transformation of a barren cave that her project has achieved, Dr Marcus replies: 'Let me show you something that will make you feel young as when the world was new'. And after his final triumph over Khan, Kirk reiterates this point when asked how he feels: 'Young, I feel young'.

However, despite all its efforts to rejuvenate its original characters and their ageing embodiers, *Wrath of Khan* was simultaneously abandoning fidelity to the series when expedient. Producer Harve Bennett noted that when he objected to director Nicholas Meyer's suggestion that Kirk should have cheated in order to win the no-win *Kobyashi Maru* test: 'Nick looked at me and said the cruellest words he ever said: "Television Mentality"' (Asherman 1982: 90). Consistency with the events depicted in 'Space Seed' was also intermittent at best. If Khan is now properly white-haired, his followers, played by performers in their twenties and thirties fifteen years before, are now played by different performers still in their twenties and thirties. He does not lead, as he should, a band of middle-aged warriors. And in the apparent gaffe notorious throughout *Star Trek* fandom, Chekov and Khan instantly recognize each other, despite the fact that Walter Koenig, who plays Chekov, joined the cast of the show during the season that followed the airing of 'Space Seed'.

Clearly the desire to feature Koenig overrode any slavish fidelity to the original (John Winston's Kyle, who did meet Khan, is also among the *Reliant* crew, so fidelity could have been maintained fairly easily). Moreover, the *Star Trek* 'universe' provided another way to manage this problem. Starting with the James Blish novelizations of the original series episodes, all the *Star Trek* narratives have had literary incarnations. In addition there is a growing series of authorized *Star Trek* novels, published by Pocket Books under the editorship of John Ordover. And these official publications are far outnumbered by the 'fanfic' that has been productively studied by Constance Penley and Henry Jenkins, among others. All these texts provide a nuance and depth of characterization not possible in the televised and filmed versions. They complement the material representation and vocal expression by embodied characters that, in turn, literature (however liberating it is in refusing to fix character beyond the capacity of the reader's imagination) always lacks. To the vast cultural phenomenon that is *Star Trek* fandom, both the literary extension of what is filmed and the embodiment of original characters in original actors in filmic incarnations have long appeared mutually enriching.

Thus Vonda K. McIntyre's novelization of *Wrath of Khan* (1982) can provide character elaboration for Saavik (a half-Romulan with a deprived past) and Peter Preston (working in the shadow of his Chief Engineer uncle), that ended up on the film's cutting-room floor. It also offers a perfectly logical explanation for the Chekov–Khan recognition: that as 'an ensign assigned to the night watch', he had met Lt Marla McGivers, who became Khan's wife, and that 'when she left the *Enterprise* to go with Khan, Ensign Pavel Chekov had locked himself in his cabin and cried' (McIntyre 1982: 55–6). Henry Jenkins remarks that *Star Trek* fans are able to accept such rationalizations and to believe that Chekov 'was known by Khan before the Russian ensign would have been recognizable to viewers' (Jenkins 1992: 104). In other words, fans can accept that the character Chekov pre-exists his embodiment by actor Koenig.

But would they accept his embodiment by someone other than Koenig? None of the *Star Trek* films featuring the cast of the original series ever went so far as to recast a role played by a series regular or major guest star. The solution to the advancing years of all the performers who had appeared during the series' 1966–9 run came within the television medium, when the success of *Star Trek: The Next Generation* from 1987–94 demonstrated that it was the *Star Trek* ethos, as well as the characters who inhabited it and the actors who played them, that carried a continuing appeal. This generation eventually inherited the film franchise, and in the first Star Trek movie to feature no members of the original series' cast (*First Contact*, 1996), the producers finally dared to recast a major role from the original series in addition to effecting a radical transformation of that character.

The recast character was Zefram Cochrane, the inventor of the warp drive that makes the interplanetary voyages of the *Enterprise* possible, who appeared in the 1967 *Star Trek* episode 'Metamorphosis'. Played by thirty-eight-year-old television leading-man Glenn Corbett, Cochrane was conventionally handsome, with a boyish, gung-ho, all-American charm and striking blue eyes. The television episode posited that Cochrane, a human from Alpha Centauri, had gone off to die in space 150 years earlier at the age of eighty-seven, but had been rescued and rejuvenated by 'The Companion', an energy being who (unbeknownst to the scientist) was in love with him.

In *First Contact*, an encounter with the Borg cybervillains sends *The Next Generation* crew back in time to the day before Cochrane made his first warp-speed flight in 2061, an event that rescued Earth from a period of post-atomic turmoil and led to the hopeful future all the *Trek* stories celebrate. The Borg are determined to prevent this event and so 'assimilate' Earth and eliminate the formation of the Federation. Yet the Cochrane of *First Contact* is a far cry from the man portrayed in either 'Metamorphosis' or the official *Star Trek* novel *Federation*,[8] which was published in 1994, not too long before *First Contact* went into production. While the official *Star Trek* timeline gives Cochrane's age as thirty-one at the time of his historic flight, the scientist here is played by fifty-five-year-old character-actor James Cromwell, an eccentric physical presence at a lanky 6'5' with elongated face and features. Moreover, the somewhat puritanical romantic hero Cochrane has become a self-serving alcoholic, who hangs out in bars putting the make on women and playing 1960s rock music at ear-shattering volume, and whose goal in inventing the warp drive is to earn sufficient money to retire to a tropical island replete with naked females. He is mortified to learn that history has literally put him on a pedestal. The end credits to the film even misspell his name as 'Cochran'. One would like to speculate that this is a tacit admission by the next generation of film-makers of just how far from the original this Zefram has come, but it is doubtless merely an error on the part of the titling department, since the novelization does spell the name correctly.

Needless to say, such a marked alteration in both the character and the appearance of the actor who re-embodies Cochrane did not escape the notice of fans. A representative picture of reactions to the recast and reconfigured character emerges in various exchanges from the newsgroup **rec.arts.startrek.current**:

> >and BOBW, Zefram Cochrane didn't look anything like his TOS incarnation,
> >>Well, seeing as how bringing Glenn Corbet [*sic*] back from the dead would
> >>be a real neat trick...besides Corbet was an atrocious actor. It's called
> >>"recasting". It happens all the time. Remember: a foolish consistency is the
> >>hobgoblin of little minds.
> <chuckles> I've really hit a raw nerve with you here haven't I? Did I say that they should have dug up a corpse to play Zefram? Don't think so. What they COULD have done is pick someone with a superficial likeness to the original, who didn't act *that* bad IMO.

Despite the disagreement between these two posters, we see that both acknowledge that characters from the original series (*TOS*) cannot appear in the 1990s unless they are recast. It is only the results of the recasting that are at issue.

A similar discussion on the newsgroup between Tristan Averett and Dennis Iannicca occurred concerning the changes in the character rather than the actor:

T.A. Perhaps if they had been better at explaining the shocking difference between the Zefram Cochrane of Federation history and the "real" thing, the comparison with [the novel] Federation would be irrelevant. BTW, in the novelization of FC, the author does just that.

D.I. What is the Zefram Cochrane of Federation history? Other than a very old TOS episode I don't remember seeing much about Cochrane at all. I liked the Cochrane in FC. He seemed much more human and down to Earth and care-free....He DID invent warp technology which resulted in first contact with the Vulcans, the eventual birth of the Federation, travel to other solar systems, contact with MANY new races, etc. I could understand how this one (humongous) deed can easily outweigh the fact that he was an aging alcoholic hippy

As Averett indicates, the film's novelization once again intervened to mediate between an original characterization and a discrepant film incarnation. In this book (by J.M. Dillard), we learn that Cochrane suffered from manic-depression previously controlled by implants that had run out during the war years. On the final page of *First Contact* the novel, Dillard suggests that he might subsequently return to the personality of Cochrane as portrayed in 'Metamorphosis', when Dr Crusher gives the scientist an injection that will permanently cure his mental illness. On the matter of the very different physical embodiment of the character, Dillard splits the difference. Zef is 'a worn, fifty-year-old man' (Dillard 1996: 37), not the thirty-one-year-old who created the warp drive according to the *Star Trek Encyclopedia* (Okuda, Okuda and Mirek 1994: 368). Yet his bloodshot eyes are blue (Dillard 1996: 95) like Corbett's, not brown like Cromwell's.

Original cast futures

It is probably no accident that this recasting of a character from the original series occurs only in 1996, after such a practice had proven successful in the many television-to-film adaptations of the decade. *First Contact*'s reception reveals that even *Star Trek* can pull off reinventing and recasting some of its original characters. There may have been grumbling about *First Contact*'s handling of Zefram Cochrane, but that did not stop the film from earning a domestic box-office gross of $92 million in its first four months of release, nor prevent its being ranked fifteenth out of the top 250 films of all time in the Internet Movie Database's ongoing survey. For now, the *Star Trek* films have not moved to recasting the roles of recurring characters, and the creation of three new sets of television series regulars could defer that strategy for some years to come. Still, if the next century finally brings a time when original products of the *Star Trek* franchise have been absent from TV and film screens for a decade or two, a future Barry Sonnenfeld could probably recast Kirk, Spock, McCoy, Scotty *et al.* and get away with it. The 1990s have demonstrated that no matter how fused they may seem, television characters and their original embodiers can always be separated if the surgery is skilful enough.

Undoubtedly there is a much closer relationship between television characters and the performers who embody them, than between actors and the film roles they create. When television-to-film transfers can be done within essentially the same time-period as the TV series' initial run, the strategy of retaining the original cast is sound. For a cult television series like *Star Trek* the strategy was probably necessary, despite the time-lapse in the television-to-film transfer. No doubt similar thinking motivated the decision to produce a feature-film version of the cult 1990s science-fiction series *The X-Files*, starring its television cast and released in 1998, following its fifth television season. Yet the 1990s have proven that the successful remaking of television series as feature films also results in large part from tapping veins of nostalgia. The passage of time necessary to evoke this nostalgia simultaneously renders employment of original cast members in their original roles highly problematic. The first six *Star Trek* films, all produced prior to the beginning of this trend, in many ways constitute a meditation on this paradox. As the 1990s come to an end, the wholesale acceptance of recasting by audiences (even cult audiences) has simply dissolved the paradox.

Notes

1 *The Untouchables* (1987), directed by Brian DePalma, was quite successful both critically and at the box office, as was the same year's comedy version of *Dragnet*, featuring Dan Akroyd in Jack Webb's role, but neither immediately inspired a wholesale rush to adapt television series to the big screen.

2 Maloney undoubtedly means by this last statement that Julia makes a better Gomez because he is a Latino. It is interesting, however, that he can imagine an ideal Gomez separable from his incarnation by John Astin or any other specific embodier.

3 Exceptions to this rule involve characters in film series, like Nick and Nora Charles in *The Thin Man*, Indiana Jones, or James Bond.

4 *The Coneheads* (1993), adapted from a recurring skit on *Saturday Night Live* in the late 1970s, and starring the characters' originators Dan Aykroyd, Jane Curtin and Laraine Newman is a partial exception. The head-to-toe alien make-up helped camouflage the actors' ageing.

5 I am using Brian McFarlane's distinctions between transfer and adaptation (made in *Novel to Film*), with some revisions. In bringing a novel to the screen with fidelity to the original as a goal, film-makers go through a process of '*transferring* the novel's narrative basis and of *adapting* those aspects of its enunciation which are held to be important to retain, but which resist transfer, so as to achieve, through quite different means of signification and reception, affective responses that evoke the viewer's memory of the original text without doing violence to it' (McFarlane 1996: 21). Clearly much more of a television show is capable of direct transfer to film than of a novel, but most big screen versions eschew transferring a considerable amount of the *mise en scène* and performances that the original television series contained.

6 In the prologue to *Star Trek: Generations*, in which the big-screen baton is passed to the cast of *Star Trek: The Next Generation*, Kirk is invited to be a passenger on a public-relations voyage of the newly christened *Enterprise-B*. When once again it becomes necessary for the not fully manned or equipped vessel to take on a real mission, the young captain, Harriman, who used to read of Kirk's exploits when he was in grade school, is forced to rely on Kirk's expertise to save the day.

7 This relationship is not made clear in the film as released, but was a part of the final shooting script (Asherman 1982: 56).

8 In this novel (by Judith and Garfield Reeves-Stevens), Cochrane is portrayed as a conventional romantic hero, who was born on Earth but settles on Alpha Centauri after having invented the warp drive. He makes first contact with the Vulcans, an event also portrayed in *First Contact*, but in *Federation* Cochrane travels to Vulcan rather than, as in the film, meeting Vulcans who have travelled to Earth. The only sign of the character-shift that was to occur in the film surfaces as the aged Cochrane wonders 'when he had stopped being a person. Instead, somewhere in the past decades, he had somehow become an icon, a symbol for this brave new era of humanity' (Reeves-Stevens 1994: 191).

15

BATMAN

One life, many faces

Will Brooker

Having to date been adapted to cinema no fewer than nine times – in two 1940s serials, a 1960s feature, the current franchise of four films and two recent full-length animations – Batman has easily transcended the sphere of his pulp contemporaries like the Shadow, the Spectre, the Phantom and Dick Tracy, and entered the realm of the icon, sharing with Robin Hood, Dracula and Sherlock Holmes a cultural existence which has to a large extent been freed from its roots in an original text, circulating as common knowledge, common property. It is thanks to those films and the television series of the 1960s, not the comics, that everyone knows something of the Batman 'mythos' – his secret identity, the names of his home, his city, his sidekick and his enemies – whereas only a diehard fan could identify Jim Corrigan as the true identity of the Spectre.

There is, then, a certain irony in the fact that many of the key elements of that 'mythos' – emerging in the Batman's first year as a story in *Detective Comics* from May 1939 to 1940, before he gained a title of his own – were themselves appropriated from the cinema. Creator Bob Kane's revelation came, he claims, from a Leonardo da Vinci sketch of a man wearing a bat-like flying machine, but among his other sources were the 1931 film *The Bat Whispers*, Bela Lugosi's *Dracula* and Douglas Fairbanks' performance in *The Mark of Zorro*.[1] Of the supporting cast, the scarred ex-actor Clayface – real name Boris Karlo – was based on Lon Chaney's role as *The Phantom of the Opera* (1926), and Catwoman on Jean Harlow in the film *Hell's Angels* (1930). More generally, the urban milieu of the early stories (which were set in New York rather than Gotham and relied more on generic racketeers and hoods than recurring villains) paid homage to the gangster cycle of the early 1930s – what Jules Feiffer identified as 'that Warner Brothers fog-infested look' (Feiffer 1965: 154) – even featuring a James Cagney look-alike in a story from 1941.

Yet it is the Joker who points to perhaps the most significant motif in the first Batman stories: the Batman's nemesis was drawn from a photo still of Conrad Veidt in *The Man Who Laughs* (1928), and while this is the only explicit nod the early comic gives to the cinema of German expressionism, its gothic spirit broods under every episode in that first year, as the Batman's grim clashes with werewolves, vampires and the death-traps of the Duc D'Orterre co-exist uneasily with the snappy patter of the city hoods and the contemporary detail.

What interests me here is the fact that despite the original concept's obvious debt to the cinema of its time, and cinema's nine attempts to portray the Batman on screen, none of the films can strictly be called an 'adaptation' of the comic book – of whatever period – in anything but the loosest sense. In contrast to the current trend for claiming a return to the 'authentic' ur-text in literary adaptation – *Bram Stoker's Dracula* (1992), *Mary Shelley's Frankenstein* (1994), even Branagh's *Hamlet* (1996) which, despite its play with costume and setting, boasts a fidelity to the original Folio – the recent film versions of Batman, like those before them, must strictly be regarded as free interpretations built around a basic framework, rather than adaptation as we currently under-stand the term. All of them, I will argue here, owe at least as much with regard to visual style, characterization and theme to their surrounding cultural context as to the actual Batman comics of their period; all of them, finally – with the sole exceptions of the relatively little-known animated films – have been and continue to be held in contempt by many 'purist' comic fans, and also by comic writers and artists from Bob Kane onwards.

I should point out that I am not imposing a system of values on the screen texts in terms of their fidelity or otherwise to Bob Kane and Bill Finger's creation of 1939. As I've suggested, the concepts and characters of *Detective Comics* #27 were far from 'original' themselves: just as many of the superheroes who filled comics in the 1940s were shadows of the Batman, so the Batman was an canny amalgam of earlier pulp characters, his origins traceable to the Bat of *Black Bat Detective Mysteries* and the Bat Man in *The Spider* magazine, as well as the multiplicity of cinema icons listed above and the precedents in *The Phantom* and *Dick Tracy*. In turn, the comics and graphic novels from which ABC's TV series and Joel Schumacher's films are 'adapted' are themselves already interpre-tations of the template established by Kane, and so can hardly be held up as ur-texts. I do have my own cards to lay on the table, though, and it may be better if I show them now rather than pretend an academic objectivity which I can never truly achieve.

I first wrote on Batman in 1978, in five colours of felt-tip pen, and I've no doubt that the character was a dominant figure in my seven-year-old life before I sat down to write my story about him and the Penguin. I have an emotional investment in Batman which, like many fans' experience, went through phases of contact with various forms: repeats of the Adam West series in the 1970s, supplemented by the DC comics of the period; a lapse during early adolescence, followed by a rediscovery in Frank Miller's graphic novel *The Dark Knight Returns* (1986); regular cycles of anticipation and disappointment around the four blockbuster films *Batman* (1989), *Batman Returns* (1992), *Batman Forever* (1995) and *Batman and Robin* (1997), and a generalized loyalty to the comic lasting through my mid-twenties, when my academic involvement with the character has led me back to the texts of the Batman's first three decades and to that ambiguous 'original' of 1939.

So I have my prejudices, a whole raft of them – a vague sense of the character's 'betrayal' by Hollywood, a preference for comics tending to the Frank Miller style – but they are complicated prejudices, including a nostalgia for the 1960s TV series whose theme tune I used to dance to in raptures, and a superior, knowing enjoyment of the kitsch and unwitting homoeroticism in the 1950s strips. It is in this sense, I suppose, that I would justify those distancing inverted commas around 'purists' above. My pleasures in Batman are manifold, combining various, often mutually incompatible interpretations from over twenty years' exposure to the character. Inevitably I also have my own platonic ideal of what the Batman would 'really be like': a myth bound up with my notions of fatherhood, the city and moral duty, and dressed with Clint Eastwood's face. The distinction I am making is between imposing this on every Batman text as a dominant reading – excluding any interpretations which fail to fit that mould as 'corrupt' or 'aberrant' – and retaining the eye of a Stanley Fish in the belief that all meanings have an equal validity, with the rider that anyone is entitled to argue for the meaning they prefer. The former line is what I am calling 'purist'. Such an approach has sought to hold up the comic text from whatever period as 'original' and 'true' – ignoring the fact, of course, that this text like all the others holds infinitely diverse readings – in an attempt to show the TV series or Hollywood film as a 'corrupted' version; as I will suggest, this argument has often taken homophobic overtones. My project in this chapter is not 'purist', but I have my prejudices and they will show. As a researcher I find it intriguing that these screen adaptations are so far from the comic text of their period; as a fan, there is sometimes a lingering regret.

It is true that by 1943, when Columbia released its serial *Batman*, the tone and appearance of the comic had altered dramatically from Kane's morbid creation of 1939. The character's 'original' incarnation, now so often cited by comic artists who claim a return to the dark roots of the Batman, actually lasted less than twelve months: that is, up to the cover of *Detective Comics* #38 which announced 'the sensational character find of 1940...Robin the Boy Wonder'. With a brightly-costumed kid at his side who, at the end of that first episode, enthused 'I didn't want to miss any of the fun! Say, I can hardly wait till we go on our next case. I bet it'll be a corker!', Batman could never be quite the same again.

Pearl Harbor gave this grinning hero and his plucky sidekick a new focus, and by January 1943 there were Batman stories called 'Swastika Over the White House', with covers showing the dynamic duo riding the back of an American eagle, selling war bonds or hurling tennis balls at caricatures of the Axis villains. Batman had made the transition from Caligari to Hitler, as Kracauer (1960) would have it, in the space of four years. Yet the fifteen episodes of the Columbia serial, with their Japanese villain Dr Daka attempting to brainwash American citizens into Axis zombies, owed far less to any specific Batman story than to the wider contemporary discourse of anti-Japanese propaganda. The *Batman* serial was to the American viewer of the early 1940s just one addition to a relentless monologue of images and slogans treating the Japanese with a pathological disgust which even the Nazis were spared: other posters caricatured Hitler and Mussolini as individuals, but 'the Jap' was despised as a generic creature.[2] American poster-art quickly established the visual shorthand of round glasses, protruding teeth, squinted eyes, moustache and bright yellow complexion, which was often degraded yet further into images of monkeys, rats or lice; popular songs boasted 'We're Gonna Find a Fellow who is Yellow and Beat Him Red, White and Blue' or 'We're Gonna Have to Slap the Dirty Little Jap, and Uncle Sam's the Guy who Can Do It', while the term 'little yellow men' was used without embarrassment by military analysts, officers, advertisers and newsreel announcers (Dower 1986: 162).

The first Batman serial is clearly informed by this 'way of seeing'. While Daka is no beast or subhuman – in this the serial follows the government directive intended to discourage American complacency by advocating portrayals of Japanese as 'fanatical and ruthless rather than rat-like, yellow and slant-eyed' (Roeder 1993: 87) – he is played as short and cunning, with slicked dark hair, narrowed eyes and a toothy grin under a thin moustache: a more realist variation on the grotesque stereotypes of the poster-art, while retaining the identifying characteristics of the enemy. 'Aha, a Jap!' Batman is able to exclaim when he meets the villain for the first time.

To date, though, I have found no precedent for Daka in any Batman comic of the period. Other titles of 1942–4, such as *Captain America*, *USA Comics* and *Wonder Comics*, echo the crude images of the posters with covers showing yellow-skinned soldiers – complete with the iconography of glasses, moustache and buck teeth – defeated by white superheroes; yet if Batman fought any such villains along with the monocled Nazis who figure so prominently, these episodes have been suppressed into the archive and never reprinted. While Batman stories of the period do regularly feature 'Mongol' goons and swarthy, top-knotted thugs, they also include sympathetic portrayals of Gotham's Chinese citizens, who aid and even pray for the hero. This relatively even-handed treatment (at a time when China was seen by many as a potential threat and conflated into the 'Yellow Peril') could be read as suggestive of a certain liberalism on Kane and Finger's part, and used to support the theory that Japanese stereotypes in the Daka mould never found their way into the comic.

Certainly Kane disliked the serial, though his reasons seem not to have been political. Dismissing it in his autobiography as a 'typical propaganda vehicle', he lambasts the miscasting of 'an overweight chap named Lewis Wilson, who should have been forced to go on a diet before playing Batman' (Kane 1989: 127). His concern is mainly for another kind of vehicle, though, with his discovery that 'the car that was supposed to be the Batmobile was an ordinary gray convertible' (op. cit.), and his interest in the unremarkable sequel *Batman and Robin* of 1948 is limited to its replacement of that convertible with a black

Cadillac. It was not until the 1943 serial was rescreened at all-night marathons in the late 1960s that its racism was recognized and booed by an audience of young people and students. That those viewers also whooped with delight whenever Batman put an arm around Robin's shoulders is testament to a very different context of reception, and to the fact that Batman had by that time been reinvented once again.

The ABC television series *Batman*, which premiered on 12 January 1966 and ran two nights a week until March 1968, has the distinction of being the general public's main reference point for Batman – even after the 'dark' Burton films of 1989 and 1992, most news stories on the character were still using the 'Pow! Zap!' motif in headlines – and at the same time an object of derision among the majority of comic readers and creators, the latter often defining their own work explicitly against the 1960s series and instead, as mentioned above, attempting to align it with Kane's 'original vision'. Alan Moore, for instance, praises fellow writer Frank Miller's achievement in:

> handling a character who, in the view of the wider public that exists beyond the relatively tiny confines of the comic audience, sums up more than any other the silliness of the comic book hero. Whatever changes may have been wrought in the comics themselves, the image of Batman most permanently fixed in the mind of the general populace is that of Adam West delivering outrageously straight-faced camp dialogue while walking up a wall thanks to stupendous special effects and a camera turned on its side.
>
> (Miller 1986: 3)

As Andy Medhurst notes, much of the recent aversion to the TV series and the definition of later works against it is implicitly hostile to the camp overtones of the 1960s show, as evident in Miller's own contempt for 'Adam West and Burt Ward exchanging camped-out quips with slumming guest-stars' and Jonathan Ross's laconic comparisons between the show and 'Elvis Presley's Vegas years or the later Jerry Lewis movies' (Medhurst 1991: 161–2).

The series is still held up by these writers (and many readers) as the Batman 'bad object', at best a misguided interpretation and at worst a betrayal of the character. Yet like the 1940s serial, this take on Batman does have more than superficial roots within the comic texts of the period. In the years following the self-censoring Comics Code, adopted by the industry in 1954 after a witch-hunt spearheaded by Dr Fredric Wertham and his book *Seduction of the Innocent*, Batman had entered a phase of harmless fantasy, magic and science fiction, including a spate of stories in which he changed shape and had numerous encounters with aliens. There was very little of the gothic, the dark or the brooding in 'The Bizarre Batman Genie', 'The Batman Creature!' or indeed any of the adventures with the mischievous elf Bat-Mite or Ace the Bat-Hound, all from the 1960s. Paradoxically, despite the authorial intention to

189

Figure 15.1 The 1960s series of *Batman*, with Adam West as Batman and Burt Ward
       playing his trusty companion Robin

limit the gay subtexts scathingly identified by Wertham in the Batman and
Robin relationship by introducing Batwoman and her niece Bat-Girl, there is a
remarkable sense of camp about many of these stories, some involving a weeping
Robin and hysterical Batman and concluding with the two heroes walking out
arm-in-arm.[3] Again, any direct relationship between the comic and its adaptation must be qualified by looking to a wider cultural context: in this case, not
propaganda but pop.

Andy Warhol had already given up working on enlarged comic images and
abandoned his 'Superman' and 'Dick Tracy' canvases by the time Mel Ramos
exhibited a painting of a chunky, cheap-looking ring, bearing a grinning Batman
in 1962. In the following year Richard Pettibone used images of DC's superhero The Flash in his boxed assemblage, while Jess Collins was transforming
Dick Tracy strips into his surreal 'Tricky Cad' collages from 1953 to 1959. But
it was Roy Lichtenstein who, stealing Warhol's thunder with his blown-up
panels complete with Ben Day dots, brought comics into the realm of pop art
and generated enough hip credibility around what had previously been throw-
away kids' stuff to make the Batman series a success with the sophisticates of
New York's clubs and universities, as well as with under-tens.

Lichtenstein's enlargements and simplifications of comic art are the most
obvious explanation for Batman's enthusiastic acceptance into the pop sphere –
it is interesting to note in passing that the Batman comics of the time closely
resemble Lichtenstein's romance canvases, bearing no likeness to the 'war' series.

There are other links to be drawn, though, between the show and the pop aesthetic. The gaudy, almost day-glo, look of the set and costumes recall Warhol's shift toward 'fauve' colouring – the 'Four Campbell's Soup Cans' (1965) in clashing pinks and greens, for instance, or the predominantly turquoise 'Marilyn' (1964) – and the parade of one-syllable 'Swoosh!'s and 'Biff!'s filling the TV screen during fight sequences can be paralleled with Pop Art's characteristic privileging of the word as image, as in Robert Indiana's 'USA/EAT' and 'USA/HUG' and Edward Ruscha's canvas dominated by 'SPAM', in addition, of course, to Lichtenstein's famous 'Whaam!'. Even the bold, exaggerated sets and props can be seen as an extension of the Pop Art 'installation' with its fake environments built from backdrops and working fittings such as telephones and radios: Tom Wesselman's three-dimensional 'Great American Nude' series and his life-size 'Bathtub 3', Oldenberg's soft-sculptures, Warhol's room decorated with cow wallpaper and silver balloons. Like Lichtenstein's experiments with ceramic models painted to look like comic-book illustrations, *Batman* was an attempt to transform the flat into the three-dimensional, the comic page into the real, while fundamentally retaining its stylized qualities and the simplicity which had made it endearing in the first place.

Whatever else, the *Batman* of 1989 (directed by Tim Burton) was not about simplicity. Mark Salisbury runs through the usual formula in his *Burton on Burton*, effectively summarizing the terms within which the film (and to a large extent its 1992 sequel *Batman Returns*) was critically received and reviewed:

> Burton fashioned a dark, brooding, deeply psychological story for the Caped Crusader which…pitted him against the Joker but was set in a dark, hellish vision of Gotham City that eschewed the campness of the Batman TV series of the sixties and instead went back to Kane's original comic strips of the forties.
>
> (Salisbury 1995: 70)

Never mind that Kane's 'original' strips of the 1940s were mostly gung-ho romps against Hitler's minions. This new *Batman* was clearly defined as other than the TV series and as akin in some way to the better-known graphic novels of the mid-1980s, including Miller's *Dark Knight* and Moore's *The Killing Joke*; that is, it was psychologically-based, visually and thematically 'dark', and aimed at adults as well as children. In fact, Burton admits in Salisbury's book that he 'was never a giant comic book fan', and only a few moments in the film – a replay of the origin sequence and a scene where a thug is suspended off the side of a building – could be read as referring explicitly to Miller's work, just as Joel Schumacher's *Batman Forever* (1995) borrows from Miller only the young Bruce Wayne's first encounter with his totem in the Bat-Cave. Again it would take a stretching of the term to define Burton's film as an 'adaptation' of the mid-1980s comics.

The relation between the *Batman* of 1989 and the graphic novel boom of that decade is twofold, and in the first place a purely financial one. As Eileen Meehan suggests in her article 'Holy Commodity Fetish, Batman!', *The Dark Knight Returns* was of less importance in the eyes of Warner executives than the use of Prince on the soundtrack and of far less importance than the casting of Jack Nicholson, but it was one more guarantee of a crossover audience: the relative success of Miller's graphic novel in mainstream booksellers pointed to a market beyond that of the mere comic collector (Meehan 1991).

What both Burton's films and Schumacher's after them also owed to the graphic novel boom was the rise of a discourse of authorship with regard to Batman's image and character. Until 1964 virtually all Batman stories had been signed 'Bob Kane', regardless of the fact that Kane (an artist of limited talent) had come nowhere near them; it was Carmine Infantino, responsible for the 'New Look' Batman with yellow chest emblem, who first insisted the signature was left off his own work, and shortly afterwards the names of individual writers, artists, even pencillers and letterers, began to appear on the title pages of comics, enabling fans to identify the style of a favourite creator and in turn encouraging those creators to develop their own 'take' on the character. During the 1970s it became common for aficionados to express a preference for an art-style such as the 'Alex Toth' Batman, the 'Neal Adams' Batman, the 'Dick Giordano' Batman; but it was not until the mid- to late-1980s that the work of individual writers was foregrounded in the same way, and it was possible to distinguish the 'Miller' Batman (sardonic, ruthless, efficiently violent) from the 'Moore' (single-minded but characterized by a sense of duty and decency) and those creations from the Batman of others such as Grant Morrison, Denny O'Neil and J.M. DeMatteis.

The tortured Batman of Morrison's *Arkham Asylum* (1989), who exorcizes flashbacks of his parents' death by forcing a shard of glass into his palm with the three cries 'Uh! Jesus! Mommy?', is not the Dirty Harry figure who in *The Dark Knight Returns* tells a teenager: 'So fill me in, punk – the Mutants have a wholesale deal with the Army? You've got a lot of teeth left, and I haven't even touched your tongue...'. Neither of these, in turn, correspond exactly to the dour leader of DeMatteis' in-jokey *Justice League*, giving the order: 'Okay, Mr Sulu – warp seven', or to *The Killing Joke*'s well-meaning liberal whose ultimatum to the Joker is: 'We could work together. I could rehabilitate you. You needn't be alone.'

It was the emergence of this wider auteurist discourse which enabled Burton and Schumacher to place their own distinct stamp on the character; for *Batman* and *Batman Returns* are Tim Burton films before they are adaptations of any comic, while *Batman Forever* and *Batman and Robin* define themselves firstly as 'not Tim Burton films' – Schumacher arguably exhibiting less of a distinctive auteurist style across his *oeuvre* – and are received as such to the extent that Batman fangroups on the Internet are currently polarized by opposing and incompatible allegiances to one director's vision over the other.

Adapting a mood, rather than a specific comic, Burton chose to concentrate on what interested him about the character – his freakishness, his need for privacy and the way he 'dresses up in the most extremely vulgar costumes' (Salisbury 1995: 75). As such, then, his *Batman* not only echoed *Pee-Wee's Big Adventure* (1985) and *Beetlejuice* (1988) with their clown-like eponymous protagonists prefiguring both the Joker and (through Michael Keaton's casting as Beetlejuice) Batman himself, but it also pointed towards *Edward Scissorhands* (1990), another fable of an isolated misfit in black leather, and *Ed Wood* (1994), who also liked to dress up in vulgar costumes. The most careless auteurist would notice other tell-tale signatures: Catwoman's image of sewn-up, wounded femininity was re-enacted as Sally in *The Nightmare Before Christmas*, which like *Batman Returns* and *Edward Scissorhands* is a snowbound picture, and the spookily pretty Danny Elfman score running through all Burton's films would identify *Batman*'s director by the soundtrack alone.

In following his own vision, Burton was fairly cavalier with the Batman 'mythos' established in the comics of the previous twenty years. Burton's Wayne is a diminutive, slightly fidgety outsider who sleeps with the love-interest Vicki Vale during the film; his Joker is stocky and middle-aged rather than lean and spindly, and given a 'real name' after fifty years of anonymity. He is revealed as the killer of Bruce's parents some thirty years ago, then himself killed off in the finale, these events again contradicting the detail of the comics. This rewriting of the comics' lore was, as noted above, enabled on one level by the increasing discourse of authorship around the graphic novel which permitted (even encouraged) a certain amount of play with the 'mythos'. Moore's *The Killing Joke* had introduced an origin for the Joker as a failed comedian who turns to crime to support his pregnant wife; Miller wrote the death of the character in a fairground Tunnel of Love. Why many fans should have sensed a betrayal of the Batman in Burton's film is, then, open to debate: I can personally only suggest the distinction between Moore and Miller's work being seen as exceptional, individual takes on the character in the context of a larger comic continuity which preserved the essential 'mythos' (these exceptions parallel the 'Imaginary Story' Umberto Eco discusses with relation to Superman, and were subsequently labelled 'Elseworld' stories by DC to distinguish them from 'continuity' narratives), while Burton's film was simply *Batman*, an 'official' version which would inevitably become the 'dominant' version for a wider audience despite its personal quirks.

Whatever their reasons, many fans of the comic protested vehemently against the film, beginning with a letter campaign to Warners from the moment Keaton's casting was announced.

In fact, the negative reaction reached such proportions that Warners' share price slumped, outraged fans tore up offending publicity material at comic conventions and the Wall Street Journal covered the crisis on page one. One appalled *aficionado* wrote in the *Los Angeles Times* that

'By casting a clown, Warner Bros and Burton have defecated on the history of Batman.'

(Salisbury 1995: 72)

Burton, by his own account, was unmoved: 'There might be something that's sacrilege in the movie....But I can't care about it....This is too big a budget movie to worry about what a fan of a comic would say.'[4]

Burton might feel a certain satisfaction to see the fans who are now defending his vision on Internet bulletin boards, even if his films are praised as the lesser of two evils, compared to Joel Schumacher's version of the character rather than that found in the comics. The following extracts are 'posts' – that is, messages from individual users to which others can reply, entering into dialogue with each other – from the *Mantle of the Bat* bulletin board during early 1997:

NIKHIL SONEJA Everybody, I'm writing WB about future Bat-Flicks...I'm sick of seeing dark, somber villains such as Two-Face portrayed as goofy idiots!! Does everybody remember the feeling during the summer of '89? It was great...

J. GRAYSON That summer of '89 was cool...I remember what it was like seeing *Batman* on opening day...Jack Nicholson's performance was clearly one of his best and Michael Keaton surprised everyone in that he pulled off the feat of making Bruce Wayne and Batman believable...the first film wasn't perfect but it was clearly the best one. And it was the one that captured the dark mood the best.

HARLEY QUINN I wish Tim Burton would return as director. His vision of Batman was much closer to the comics than Joel Schumacher's.

NIGHTWING I was floored at just how campy [*Batman and Robin*] is shaping up to be...like most of you, I felt that the original Batman was by far the best of the series...I really liked *Batman Returns* because of its even darker take on Gotham...I really prefer the darker Batman as opposed to the light campy Batman.

THE DYNAMIC TRIO Please bring Tim Burton back...Burton's Batman was dark, mysterious, shadowy and gothic. Schumacher's Batman was campy and cartoonish.

MALCOLM I still don't think Joel Schumacher is the right man as I really hate the campyness that seems to be slowly trickling into the 90s series...[5]

The oppositions being established by this fan discourse are clear, and are echoed in the critical reception of Schumacher's films, whether in reviews and previews or in the few academic approaches to the Batman franchise: Burton's vision is 'dark' and introspective, while Schumacher's is 'campy' and extroverted. The knowing moments of 'queerness' in *Batman Forever*, from the shots of Batman's buttocks to Robin's jibe about biker bars, are not mentioned in this fan forum, which elides that threat with the word 'campy'; however, they were gleefully picked up by the gay lifestyle magazine *Attitude* – 'if O'Donnell genuinely believes that dressing Robin as a leather biker will downplay his fag-appeal potential, his dumbness becomes almost heroic' (Jays 1995: n.p.) – by Paul Burston's review in *Time Out*'s gay section – 'from Batman to battyman – that's quite a leap of faith' (Burston 1995: n.p.) – and by Freya Johnson's article in the on-line journal *Bad Subjects*, which identifies a shift in Schumacher's film from 'the overtly queer *sub*text hidden beneath the surface of many Batman representations into an overtly queer *supra*text that goes right over the head of the mainstream viewing audience.'[6] *Batman and Robin*, released in June 1997, was if anything more overtly playful and was perceived as such by the *NME*: 'It starts with a lingering closeup of Batman's rubber bottom…four films in, and the Dark Knight has finally become an extra in an elongated Village People video.…In fact, short of casting John Inman as Batman and wrapping him in a pink feather boa, Schumacher couldn't really have made it any more camp' (Oldham 1997: n.p.).

Discussions on *Mantle of the Bat*, anticipating *Batman and Robin*, began to deal with this queer discourse, often reacting with barely-disguised homophobia and exhibiting what I call the 'purist' invocation of 'textual evidence' to back up an argument:

NUMBER 2 Let's get this out of the way first. Batman isn't Gay. He is a heterosexual man. Get it?

Figure 15.2 Batman and Robin (1997), directed by Joel Schumacher with George Clooney and Chris O'Donnell in the title roles

BATS Batman has fallen in love with Vicky Vale, Chase Meridian, Julie Madison, Kathy Kane and possibly at times Poison Ivy. Doesn't seem too gay to me.

BATDAN I have had this argument many times before and I can categorically assure you that it is utter bollocks. The nature of the Batman persona is such that it excludes him from regular loving relationships, but even so there is plenty of evidence to prove that Our Man is staunchly heterosexual, not that it needs to be proven.

DAWG He's not gay, unlike other superheroes he doesn't stick to one partner, every time you see him, he has a new trophy on his arm!!! He's a cool geezer.

TREX Batman is not gay but I do wonder about Schumacher. All his butt shots and crotch shots tell me that he is a little camp himself. And he keeps raving about how Val and George looked great in rubber...[7]

In one sense, as this reaction suggests, *Batman Forever* (like *Batman and Robin*) is actually a very close adaptation of an earlier text: the 1960s TV series. From explicit in-jokes like Robin's exclamation 'Holy Rusted Metal!' in *Batman Forever* to the eye-wateringly gaudy costumes, the emphasis on spectacle and the very style of performance from the guest-star villains, Schumacher's is a big-budget revisiting of the Adam West aesthetic. *Batman Forever* and *Batman and Robin* are 'adaptations', then, but adaptations from the small to the big screen, bypassing the comic book: adaptations of what was then an adaptation.

The only screen Batman left to consider is perhaps the least-known but, for many who remain dubious about Burton and Schumacher, the best-loved. As a *Mantle* post interrupts:

ANTONELLO Come on, guys! you all seem to be forgetting that marvelous animated series and the incredible people behind it. The Batman animated series should be an example to all future adaptation of comics to another medium, being faithful to the comic source, or even improving something, where necessary.[8]

This decade's animated series from Warner Brothers and the two feature-length spin-offs, *Batman: Mask of the Phantasm* (1994) and *Batman and Robin: Sub Zero* (1997), were far from being the first Saturday-morning Batman cartoon – Adam West and Burt Ward lent their voices to the *New Adventures of Batman* in the 1970s. The series was, however, the first to appeal to an adult as much as to a young audience, not for a dual address or knowingness but for its lyricism and pervading melancholy, as well as its streamlined action. This moody, stylized fusion of expressionism and gangstericity is also, as the 'post' above points out, the sole screen version of Batman to qualify strictly as an adaptation of any comic text, although in this case the comic, *Batman Adventures*, followed on the heels of the series and only later began to provide feedback into it. The animated series, then, is the Internet fangroup's 'good object' against which the screen incarnations are compared, with no flamewars over its merits; as must be obvious, I side with them here.

This is the final paradox, the Catch-22 of the adapted Batman. Those who insist on a close fidelity to the comic remain, and will always remain, a minority; those responsible for putting the character on screen, like Burton, like Schumacher, Warners, ABC and Columbia, cannot afford to care about the comic fans, however pedantic and vocal they may be, if they are ever to sell a product to the requisite mass audience. Within a narrower market, such as direct-to-video animation or half-hour cartoons, we may find a genuine 'adaptation' of a comic to film or television – as we would apply the word quite normally to, say, *The Crucible*, *Emma* or *Death and the Maiden* – that is, involving a close correspondence of plot structure, character and dialogue between the book or play and the screen. The screen texts I have discussed, though, are not adaptations of a comic so much as of a cultural moment, a societal context: their Batman belongs not to the fans, but to the world at a specific point in history.

The tendency of all screen adaptations to inflect the text, however subtly, with the *Zeitgeist* – think of the journey from Olivier's *Henry V* (1944) to Kenneth Branagh's (1989), from Zeffirelli's *Romeo and Juliet* (1968) to Baz Luhrmann's (1996) – is taken to its most visible extreme by this all-purpose icon with barely a root in the ur-text. Batman has proved himself infinitely adaptable, retaining only minimal identifying traits of appearance and personality through every incarnation as he transforms according to the needs and moods of each new period. And perhaps that's not such a bad thing. Purists might temper their protests with the reflection that their hero would, had he not been subjected to each of these mutations, be now far less complex, far less significant, far less rich in meaning; if indeed, that is, he had lasted this long. Like the work of Austen and Shakespeare, Conan Doyle and Fleming, it is through being adapted that Batman has survived.

Notes

1 There remains a degree of controversy as to the precise extent of Kane's contribution to the early Batman 'mythos'. While the signature 'Bob Kane' (or initially 'Rob't...') stood alone over every Batman story during the 1930s and 1940s, Kane himself admits in *Batman and Me* (1989) that the importance of his writer, Bill Finger, has never been fully recognized, and the young artist Jerry Robinson was also a crucial shaping influence on key aspects of Batman iconography. Kane's mark of sole authorship dominated the comic during its first three decades, yet even in the earliest years this was misleading and it continues to obscure the role others undoubtedly played in refining and developing the character and his world.

2 See Dower's example of a *Washington Post* cartoon which 'illustrates sharply contrasting American images of the enemy – an ape representing all "Japs" imitates "Hitler"' (Dower 1986: 182).

3 For instance 'Robin Dies At Dawn', first published in *Batman* #156 (1963; repr. Gold 1988).
4 Quoted in Pearson and Uricchio (1991: 184).
5 Posted on *Mantle of the Bat: The Bat-Board*, February 1997, **http://www.cire. com/batman**
6 This article was posted to the Internet as part of *Bad Subjects* #23, December 1995, **http://english-server.hss.cmu.edu/bs/23/johnson.html**
7 Posted on *Mantle of the Bat: The Bat-Board*, May 1997.
8 Posted by Antonello on *Mantle of the Bat: The Bat-Board*, 16 Feb 1997.

16

'THOU ART TRANSLATED'

Analysing animated adaptation

Paul Wells

Recovering animated adaptations

Since the very beginnings of cinema, literature has provided an extraordinary range of source materials for film texts. Writing about this relationship has been fundamentally preoccupied with the ways in which 'the word' – something you *read* – becomes 'the image' – something you *see* – raising issues about the very nature and effect of 'adaptation' itself, as a narrative moves from the primacy of the literary text into the realms of the visual (see Aycock and Schoenecke 1988; Klein and Parker 1981; Peary and Shatzkin 1978; Sinyard 1986). Generally, many writers on adaptation either suggest that nothing can usurp the literary source, or merely evaluate the various merits or drawbacks of cinematic versions. Moreover, most of this writing relates to how a novel, play or short story has become a *live-action* film, while comparatively little attention has been given to the literary adaptations in animation. Animation is, after all, a distinctive film-form which offers to the adaptation process a unique vocabulary of expression unavailable to the live-action film-maker. The following discussion seeks to partially redress this imbalance and raise some issues concerning the specific ways that animation, and its particular production processes, impact upon the interpretation of literary fictions, and text/screen debates.

Michael Klein suggests that these debates can be grounded within the larger context of literature's relationship to visual art in general. He claims that 'film is an encyclopedic and synthesizing art form' which in combining all the arts offers the opportunity for 'transposition or translation from one set of conventions for representing the world to another' (Klein and Parker 1981: 3). Interestingly, and not unreasonably, Klein includes painting and dance among his list of cinema's combinant arts, but there is no recognition that painterliness and the dynamics of expressive movement are actually more *literally* enacted within animation. Klein also speaks of literary translation as an act of metamorphosis, again without acknowledgement that animation *literally* can offer the capability of metamorphosis within its distinctive conventions – an issue I will return to later in my discussion. Klein, of course, is not unusual in absenting animation from discussions of cinematic practice, and I merely use his work as

an example of the ways in which ignoring animation refuses to properly acknowledge its ability to actually encompass the widest vocabulary of aesthetic and technical expression, and notionally its greater capacity to accommodate the broadest range of literary suggestion. Indeed, animation may be viewed as a film-form which finally liberates text/screen debates from the preoccupation with issues about 'realism', and from what Ghislaine Geloin has noted as the post-Bazin imperative to infer that cinematographic representational reality 'could restore to the literary work its ideal form, the complex fabric of the objective world' (Geloin 1988: 139).

From 'as-it-is' to 'as-it-would-be'

Principally, the act of storytelling in animation is defined by *suggestion* rather than the particularities of 'real time', plotting or the construction of narrative 'events'. Consequently, William Moritz has argued that the purest form of animation is non-linear, non-objective, abstract work, and all else is a variant on the capacity of the live-action film (in Canemaker 1988: 21–33). This view negates much of the capability of animation to caricature characters, situations, objects and so on, and exposes the limits of live-action representation. Crucially, animators can effectively critique language itself as a means of image-making. As Charles Solomon has noted, 'animation offers the artist a means of communication that transcends linguistic barriers' (Solomon 1988: 95), and it is clear that many animators when they are working on an adaptation enjoy moving beyond the limits of language to evoke feelings and establish the meanings they perceive exist within established texts. Stanley Cavell provides a useful framework by which to address this issue when he suggests that animation often moves beyond illustration to present 'drafts of the world's animism' and the essential 'circulation or metamorphosis out of and into the human organism' (Cavell 1996: xix). These shifts simultaneously encompass the movement from interiority (conscious thought, memory, dream etc.) to exteriority (verbal exchange, physical articulation etc.); from subjectivity to objectivity; from the private to the public; and crucially, as Cavell implies, from the inanimate to the animate as a mode of recognition in identifying the very 'life' within a form.

In essence this speaks to many of the rhetorical structures within literary forms – the movement from first- to third-person description; the accommodation of 'stream of consciousness' and extended dialogue; the slippage between narrational tones and styles; and the collapse of the picaresque into more abstract or self-reflexive modes. In many senses, animation most properly engages with the *imagist* agenda within literary texts, stimulating not merely the resemblance of forms but *propositional* outcomes. Jonathan Miller notes that psychologists since the early 1970s have been divided concerning the definition of 'mental images'. *Imagist* psychologists believe that these images visually echo the perceived world, while those favouring the *propositional* position believe that the 'mind's eye' generates its own imagery (Miller 1986:

220–4). Animation is the most appropriate language by which to express the mental visualizations of images suggested by literary forms because its qualities are those which incorporate the hybridity, instability and mutability of the *perception* of textual allusion. An animated film can condense material so that an image can operate simultaneously as a retrieval of image forms, as a deployment of (sometimes highly personal) symbolism and metaphor, and can provide incidence of penetration, all while effectively transposing the literary source.[1] Arguably, the ontological equivalence of the animated text accommodates the intrinsic variables of the literary stimulus. The simultaneity of what may be termed the 'incidence of objects' *as* events in animated texts, whether these 'objects' be two-dimensional lines, colours and shapes, or three-dimensional forms, legitimizes the view that each element may be reconfigured in a different way that speaks to the convergence of a mutuality or multiplicity of linguistic expressions. The most obvious way in which this is evident (though not exclusively, as I will demonstrate later), is in the mechanism of *metamorphosis.*

Interestingly, particular models of storytelling already demonstrate an affiliation with animation through this device. As Marina Warner has noted,

> Shape-shifting is one of fairy tale's dominant and characteristic wonders: hands are cut off, found and re-attached, babies' throats are slit, but are later restored to life, a rusty lamp turns into an all-powerful talisman, a humble pestle and mortar becomes the winged vehicle of the fairy enchantress Baba Yaga, the beggar changes into the powerful enchantress and the slattern in the filthy donkeyskin into a golden-haired princess. More so than the presence of fairies, the moral function, the imagined antiquity and oral anonymity of the ultimate source, and the happy ending (though all these factors help towards a definition of the genre), metamorphosis defines the fairy tale.
>
> (Warner 1994: xv–xvi)

Clearly, here 'metamorphosis' is about changes in characters or situations that may be termed 'magical' or impossible within the concept of a real world served by physiological, gravitational, or functionalist norms. Virtually all animated films play out this definition of metamorphosis as a technical and narrational orthodoxy, thus rendering the adaptation of a fairy tale on this basis, a matter of relative ease. Thus it is important to consider what 'metamorphosis' achieves beyond mere 'shape-shifting', since I wish to argue that the very 'metamorphosis' that is a developing literary narrative *per se*, is most readily encompassed by the technical ability (advanced by the conceptual freedom animation affords) to fluidly move from one (potentially discontinuous) image to another. Within the context of his analysis of comedy, Howard Jacobson has commented that the very transitions Warner cites, are 'great liberating images of a loosened world' and work as 'distorted replicas, broken reflections in a parodical mirror, humankind seeing itself in perpetual ironic flux, as-it-would-be confronting as-it-is, stagnancy eyeing metamorphosis' (Jacobson 1997: 234). It effectively articulates a conducive tension between the potential 'fixedness' of the literary text and the capability of animation (and the animator's will) to illustrate the movement from 'as-it-is' to 'as-it-would-be' as a *critical* model of address.

Animation can be achieved under a range of circumstances. An artist can work completely alone and make an animated film, while animated films may also be made under complex industrial conditions involving numerous people. Inevitably this complicates issues of authorship, especially in relation to issues arising out of adaptation. I wish to explore the distinctiveness of the animated form in relation to adaptations, therefore, through a range of case studies. First, I wish to pursue ideas concerning 'metamorphosis' and the work of the single artist through the films of Canadian animator, Caroline Leaf. Second, I will engage with some perspectives emerging out of the distinctive aspects of cartoon adaptation within the context of 'classical' animation as exemplified by the Disney model. Finally, I will make brief comparisons between three versions of Shakespeare's *A Midsummer Night's Dream* as examples of differing approaches to adaptation which use the three dominant styles of animation – *orthodox* (predominantly industrial 2-D cel animation), *developmental* (2-D and 3-D forms creatively engaging with a range of stylistic and narrational conventions) and *experimental* (principally non-objective, non-linear, avant-garde work).[2]

From 'under-the-camera' to 'out-of-the-dark'

Canadian animator Caroline Leaf cites Kafka, Genet, Ionesco and Beckett as her chief influences, and clearly inflects her work with a dark expressionist romanticism that speaks to an absurdist despair and a surrealist extrapolation of inchoate 'feeling'. Leaf's approaches – sand on glass, ink on glass, and direct scratching on to film – are essentially 'under-the-camera' techniques that support the view that particular modes of animated practice may be viewed as truly auteurist. Leaf creates and photographs every image. She comments: 'I like using my hands, I feel that I have more control; they're my best tools; [sand, for example] is a very sensuous material to be working with'.[3] Leaf views animation as a highly 'intense' medium and suggests her artisanal approach is primally driven, recalling almost archaic impulses. She insists that she must remain responsive to an instinctive and inarticulable creative feeling to sustain the intimacy, immediacy and (above all) personal nature of the work, even when adapting literary pieces. Moving easily between the figurative and the abstract, the representational and the non-objective, the given and the imagined, Leaf brings her particular signature to the animated form (ironically, in this context, the very *modernity* of her 'hands-on' technique) while engaging with literary stimulus. Kafka's *The Metamorphosis* has clearly proved an important touchstone for Leaf in the exploration of her own concerns and the development of her technique. *The Street* (1976), *The Metamorphosis of Mr Samsa* (1977) and *Two*

Sisters (1990) all aptly illustrate the ability of animation to conflate the key thematics of Kafka's work, while both literalizing and interrogating the concept of metamorphosis in its own right. Leaf recognizes that the translation from the initial stimulus of the story to its production as a film can take many years of psychological 'metamorphosing', and seeks to 'ultimately leave behind the work of literature, particularly the words, and turn them into images', an approach which clearly speaks to the movement from the imagist to the propositional.

The Street, based on Mordecai Richler's autobiographical stories about a Jewish neighbourhood in the mid-1940s, addresses what Thelma Schenkel has noted are the connections between memory and storytelling (in Canemaker 1988: 43). Leaf selects one chapter of Richler's book – the adult recollection of a grandmother's death – and essentially translates this into a stream-of-consciousness engagement with events from a little boy's point of view. Leaf brings an imagist authenticity to Jewish mores and the domestic environment, but is especially persuasive in her propositional depiction of memory – what Schenkel calls *tactility* (Canemaker 1988: 45) – in which the very materiality of ink on glass, ephemeral, liminal and ambiguous, defines the *experience* of memory beyond its description in the text. Psychological states – memory, dream, fantasy, contemplation – readily metamorphose, refuting the anticipated orthodoxies of time and space. A remembered fight between the boy and his sister, the emphasis upon the everyday detail of a mother mixing ingredients in a bowl, and the imagined hair growth of the grandmother in the hours after her death are all examples of the poignant aspects of perceived existence retained as the defining evidence of life lived: a life, like many, not defined by objectifiable spectacle but by subjective choice and selection.

It is this emphasis on the 'incoherent' yet rational subjectivity of her characters that defines Leaf's work and borrows most from Kafka's sense of surreal everydayness in *The Metamorphosis*. The family in *The Street*, like that in Kafka's short story, accept the 'supernatural' as something which must be contained within the maintenance of ordinary habit and routine. The fluid relationship between the objective world and the supernatural world is ironically *naturalized* within the animated form as one seamlessly becomes the other. Leaf further compounds this in her adaptation of Kafka's tale, *The Metamorphosis of Mr Samsa*, where she concentrates on mapping the themes of melancholia, delusionality and entrapment upon a family seeking to carry on in the light of Gregor's overnight transformation into a huge insect. The horror of Kafka's tale is its enigmatic bleakness, which Leaf captures by focusing on particular images that succeed in understating the sense of oblivion congruent with merely living everyday life. Samsa struggles to look from a window only to view falling rain; his mother laboriously winds out wool from her ball and continues to knit, and, most persuasively of all, the sound of Samsa's sister playing sad melodies on her violin is depicted as a frightening implosion into the dark hole of the shuffling insect's inner ear, anticipating similar imagery in David Lynch's *Blue Velvet* (1985). These images effectively condense Kafka's exposition of Samsa's interior monologue into silent dramatic vignettes of alienation and hopelessness. Leaf also shapes much of Kafka's preoccupation with the giving of food to Samsa into a single motif – at the moment when Samsa's sister first sees her brother as an insect she spills a bowl of milk. This symbolic, primal moment – which acknowledges the loss of innocence and 'normality' – is later developed when Samsa's sister brings him a bowl of milk to drink before fearfully leaving his room. Earlier she had echoed his attempts to see out of the bedroom keyhole; the sound of her violin is Samsa's tenuous hold on his existence; and this act of giving also recognizes the visceral nature of their relationship – a confrontation not merely with inexplicable fates, but with the 'monstrousness' beneath the surface veneer of family life.

It is this key theme which Leaf develops most fully in *Two Sisters*. Though actually based on Mikhail Bulgakov's *The Master and the Marguerita*, the film was developed over a number of years, first as a radio then as a theatre script, each time 'metamorphosing' the original tale, and finally only retaining the idea of the impact of 'a stranger' on a particular situation.[4] Leaf wanted to once more return to the intimacy of animation after seeking to work in other media, and chose to directly scratch on the surface of film stock to remove the sense of technological apparatus and fully engage with the intimacy of her piece. Looking back to *The Metamorphosis* in relation to *Two Sisters*, Leaf plays out the alienation of Samsa through the figure of Viola Ge, a disfigured novelist, who lives with her sister, Marie, in a shadowy household on an island. The relationship between Samsa and his sister is echoed in the bond between Viola and Marie, but (as Leaf has suggested) she wanted to deal with a woman as a subject, and fully examine the exchange of 'power' in relationships. The idea of Samsa's sister's obligation to her brother and her fascination with his predicament, more explicitly explored in Kafka's book, is addressed through Marie's complex relationship with Viola. As Jill McGreal has noted: 'Marie is both her sister's jailer and protector, the feelings between them a mixture of anger and defiance, pain and fear, admiration and tenderness' (McGreal 1992: 46).

While Kafka is concerned with a more supernatural agent of change, Leaf personalizes her film by using the tenets of her own gestalt therapy to explore 'action' through the figure of an admiring stranger who swims to the island and insists upon proclaiming his admiration for Viola's work, undaunted by his discovery of her facial scars. Once more Leaf takes the key theme of *The Metamorphosis*, the idea of 'exteriority' as the key aspect of the way people receive and accept others, and accentuates the problem of a sensitive psyche which seeks to be articulate. Self-evidently this also echoes Leaf's preoccupation with the contradictions between making art and living life, when the former is an extrapolation from and affectation of the latter. The outcome in *Two Sisters* is the (romantic) recognition that the Samsa-esque sense of alienation and abandonment can be cured through the knowledge that expressing oneself through art can communicate with others in a profound and life-affirming way. Leaf moves from the imagist provocations of Kafka into the fully developed propositional capability of animation, proving that adaptation is more than the translation of a text, but ultimately a statement about it. The level of interrogation involved in first drawing 'meaning' from the text, filtering it through a highly personalized creative consciousness, then redetermining the text, offers a perspective on its dominant motifs, narrative events and affecting detail. What one author originally intended has given way to what another found meaningful and inspiring. Unlike the movement from words in one linguistic form to another, in which something is often lost in translation, here something is added: a penetrating *perception* of text which is both revelatory and provocatively discursive.

From 'riffs' to 'reality'

While Leaf's work speaks to an approach drawn from a tension between fine art and the avant-garde, and epitomizes what some would argue is a more purist approach to animation, it would be remiss to neglect how more traditional cartoonal forms are also distinctive in their approach to the process of adaptation. The determining characteristics of storytelling in animation may be defined by a cursory scrutiny of the methodologies which informed the development of cartoonal animation in the United States.

Early cartoons borrowed from the sequential scenarios in comic strips, employing speech 'bubbles', and gags drawn from vaudeville performance and early silent comedy in the cinema (see Crafton 1993). Essentially 'narratives' in this context may be understood as 'riffs' in which animators extemporized a number of 'jokes' out of a limited situation or context. Best exemplified by Otto Mesmer, the creator of *Felix the Cat*, these gags would often be of a highly self-reflexive nature, in which the animator would draw attention to the creative freedoms available in exploiting the perceived assumptions of perspective drawing within the two-dimensional graphic space. These visual puns demonstrated how, by redetermining the audience's understanding of the pictorial realm, changes in narrational direction could be achieved in mere seconds. Such changes, however, were predicated more upon the creation of new gags than the development of what might be understood as a linear storyline. Crucially, this approach ensured a surreal continuity ran through the comic scenarios, before the tendency emerged (particularly in later Warner Brothers cartoons) to merely present a series of sometimes unrelated 'spot gags'.

The concentration on visual gags partially gave way to the increasing interest on the part of animators in engaging with and exploring the intricacies of animated movement *per se*. The drive towards 'full animation' – animating all aspects of the *mise en scène* – was largely instigated by the ambition of the Disney Studios to create a distinctive model of film-making which spoke both to traditions of fine art and sought to express a *populist* 'folk' sensibility. Arguably Disney's insistence on the highest standards of full animation impacted upon the medium in a way that was to misdirect some of its greatest expressive possibilities. This was largely because every innovative technological development at the studio – sound synchronization, the use of Technicolor, the three-dimensional depth afforded by the multiplane camera – drew animation increasingly into the photorealist mode. This is a contentious area because self-evidently Disney animation is not 'realistic' in its depiction of a real world, but nevertheless seeks to be persuasive on the basis of its specific attention to the 'muybridging' of anatomically correct movement cycles in its figures, and the notion of 'conviction' at the heart of even the most caricatured of its characters.[5]

This shift is of great significance because it articulates a key difference in the 'textual' interests of the animator. The 'gagman' is effectively replaced by the 'designer', though here the role of the designer is one which is not merely concerned with the 'look' of a character or background, and the authenticity of its movement, but how that design effectively *facilitates* a storytelling process.[6] Part of this change was the recognition by Disney that feature-length animation could not be sustained by gags alone, and that a narrative would need to be informed by a more conventional ethos of storytelling borrowed from the classical live-action tradition. Disney clearly felt that the complete freedoms available in animation needed grounding within an orthodox and familiar context.

An even greater factor in the emphasis upon story, however, was the impact of the Sound Era. It was only at this juncture that story departments were created at studios and 'writers' deemed to be necessary to a process that had previously resided with the creative expertise of the animator alone (see Deneroff, in Canemaker 1988: 33–9). Disney's expansive industrialization of the animation process effectively moved the medium from the kind of work done, for example, by Winsor McCay – who executed every drawing and shot every frame of his films – to an approach where director, animator, designer, in-betweener, colourist, writer, cinematographer and so on, became individual roles within a hierarchical quasi-Fordist mode of production. Inevitably, this has a major effect upon how 'authorship' of the animated text may, thereafter, be perceived. In the case of McCay, or indeed Emile Cohl and many of the other pioneers of the animated film, it is comparatively easy to conclude that as artists working independently of such an industrial context each executed the process required because they fully understood the narrational dynamics of the medium. Creating 'a story' within a studio environment required approaches by which everyone involved knew their particular function within the construction of the work, but more importantly, was working within the same narrational guide-lines and instructions as everyone else.

Such requirements necessitated that particular decisions be made in regard to the primary imperatives involved in the development of any one story. The emergence of 'the model chart', for example, in which any one character was depicted from a range of perspectives, and information was provided concerning the construction of the character, was crucial in the maintenance of consistency, but also in stressing the narrational importance of 'personality'.

'Personality' was first determined through design and the nature of the character's movement – only then did it matter in what context the character was placed, or indeed, what it actually said. The Sound Era more formally emphasized the necessity of music and dialogue, but effectively (and especially during the 'Golden Era' of Disney animation between 1933 and 1941) this was by matters of degree, and it was only with the coming of television in the 1950s, and the wholesale scaling down of animation production, that dialogue in cartoons overtook the primacy of the image.

The 'model chart' was effectively the precursor to 'storyboarding' – the process by which the story is actually conceived in images and rationalized as a form of 'proto-animation'. In order that this may be achieved there needs to be a story to work from. Walt Disney was renowned for his storytelling capabilities, and frequently performed whole stories to his animating staff, including impressions of characters (verbal and physical) and descriptions of situations. Though perhaps less flamboyantly, other writers also provided such briefs to animators, who took notes, made preliminary sketches and were finally allocated scenes or sequences within the provisional narrative. Sometimes also (particularly on cartoon shorts) writer, director and animators were charged with not merely telling the story but presenting storyboards to their colleagues (Salkin, in Canemaker 1988: 11–21). With storyboarding complete, and the narrative finalized both in relation to *what* story is to be told and *how* it is to be told in visual terms, the soundtrack (featuring vocal performances, sound effects and music) may be recorded as the essential guide for the timing and execution of the animation itself. It is sometimes the case that the recording of the soundtrack precedes the creation of a storyboard, and is predicated on the basis of a screenplay and score which corresponds more directly to the screenplays of live-action films. These processes still beg the question of sources for the material which inform these performances, sketches and scripts – all essentially acts of interpretation – and this is where my discussion refocuses upon the particular issues raised by adapting literary sources in this way, and what such a production process may distinctively add to the final outcome.

Peter Brunette, for example, has detailed how Disney translated *Snow White and the Seven Dwarfs* (1937) from the original fairy tale, effectively sanitizing the Grimms' version, changing its Oedipal message (Brunette 1980: 66–76). Karen Merritt, however, suggests that the Grimms' fairy tale is not the key source from which Disney worked, but rather that a version of *Snow White* created for Alice Minnie Herts Heniger's Children's Educational Theatre is of more importance (in Canemaker 1988: 105–23). It is in this version that overt didacticism and moral purpose is foregrounded as a message, and the darker issues of the original tale are excised or diluted. Arguably Disney actually recalls some of the terrors of the fairy tale rather than censoring them – a point reinforced at the time by film-maker and critic Pare Lorentz, who suggested that it retained 'the hate and sorrow of the old Black Forest tale' and 'Disney violence' of which he claimed 'there is no greater violence ever created on stage or screen' (Lorentz 1986: 148).

Here it is important to consider what it is that animation is enabling Disney to achieve beyond the 'literariness' of the Grimms' fairy tale, the theatricality of Heniger's production or, indeed, the live-action cinema version Walt saw as a child. Lorentz's criticism points to the view that in *literalizing* the tale in a *non-literal* image vocabulary, the deep-seated expressivity of the form connects much more viscerally with powerful emotions in the child, as well as in the adult.[7] The 'violence' here is emotional: whether in relation to the fear of the Wicked Queen in *Snow White*, or the horror of the death of the fawn's mother in *Bambi* (1941), or the sense of guilt experienced by Simba after the murder of his father in *The Lion King* (1994). Yet the 'violence' here is not *real* in the simulated sense of live-action exchanges. Animation accentuates the intended 'feeling' of the text through its very abstractness in the use of colour, form and movement. This is crucial in any attempt to adapt a literary text because animation *simultaneously* literalizes and abstracts; live action merely literalizes and fixes, speaking thereafter to issues of verisimilitude and not to inherent 'feeling' or flexibility in the text.

It is useful to recall some points from Roland Barthes' work on 'The Rhetoric of the Image' (1977: 32–46) in which he asks 'what is the signifying structure of illustration?' He suggests that it is important to take into account when images merely visualize textual description, when images add information and when a text is transformed through interpretation. The stress remains upon the 'linguistic message' to legitimate the image in many adapted texts, and indeed to retain the authority of the original literary source. This has resulted in what Barthes terms a functional model of *anchorage* and *relay* which limits the range of meanings available in the 'floating chain of signifiers' in any poly-semous image. 'Language', when related to or located within an image, essentially grounds the image within a limited frame of informational and narra-tional possibility. Consequently, as Barthes notes, meaning in advertising imagery is often 'anchored' by a caption or strap-line, but sometimes (as is often the case with early comic strips and cartoons) a 'relay' text is inspired by language within the image (for example, in speech 'bubbles' and signs). The relay text allows the possibility of alternative meanings or interpretations. I suggest that literary texts work as a primary example of an extended model of Barthes' concept of anchorage, directing the aesthetic and ideological meaning of an imagist interpretation. In effect anchorage may be viewed as the aspects of the literary source which provoke the most literal or consensual interpretations within animated imagery. Any degree of abstraction drawn out of the literary text that supports but extends the meaning of this interpretation may be under-stood as a relay text. As Barthes suggests, in prescient terms, this creates a 'plenitude of virtualities' (Barthes 1977: 42).

In order to evaluate the degree and intention in any relay text, and relate this to the imagist and propositional stances examined earlier, Barthes' ideas concerning the difference between the signifying processes of a drawing and a photograph are also useful. First, he notes that a drawing, whether based on a direct or imagined visual source, is always subject to 'rule governed transpositions' (Barthes 1977: 43). By this he means the historically determined modes of representation that precede this version of the image, and the established technical apparatus for creating an image (chiefly, for example, the role of 'perspective' in drawing, or configuration). Second, he suggests there are aspects of judgement which determine what is 'significant' and 'insignificant' in the drawn image, which ultimately amount to a recognition of 'style' above 'photorealist' authenticity/accuracy. Third, he claims that the drawing will be informed by a particular 'ethic', and thus promote its sense of purpose or meaning more readily. Accepting that these agendas inform the way in which storyboarded drawings serve to act as 'illustration' of what Barthes defines as 'description' within the original literary text, it remains to address how these ideas are compromised or developed in the act of *moving* drawings (or objects etc.), in order that the language/images become subject to Barthes' concept of 'operation'. Further, it will be possible to refine Barthes' models of anchorage and relay as helpful interrogative tools in relation to the imagist and prepositional modes as they have been applied within classical, and indeed, other forms of animation.

On these terms one need only examine *Snow White and the Seven Dwarfs* to recognize that the rotoscoped figure of Snow White speaks to a greater verisimilitude to the human form than that of the wicked queen or, more exaggeratedly, the dwarfs. By directly animating over the movements of a live-action figure, the intention is to clearly authenticate the 'humanness' of a young girl and (by extension) her very 'humanity', psychologically and emotionally. Issues of 'significance' in her design are essentially determined by enhancing pubescence rather than adolescence in the character, thus desexualizing her body in order that she can operate as a figure of innocence in what later becomes an all-male environment. Her ethical stance is clear, but later further clarified, when she is over-determined as 'mom' to completely de-eroticize any potential relationship with the differentiated dwarfs – effectively seven old men smitten with a young girl. While working within the textual anchorage of 'the beautiful, and the limits of "skin as white as snow, lips as red as blood and hair as black as ebony" child' (Lucas *et al.* 1963: 12), the Disney relay is effectively the movement towards an 'Americanization' of the character, but more crucially the fundamental creation of (character) movement from model chart to storyboard to *frame-by-frame* action. Barthes' notion of operation in animation becomes specifically the *minutiae* of finding the ways, for example, in which the character becomes 'full of terror, even of the very leaves on the trees' (Lucas *et al.* 1963: 22), made literal of course in the film by animating the environment. Snow White's gestures, actions and quality of movement come to define her character. The determining language at the core of Barthes' conception of anchorage and relay ceases to be words and becomes, first, the primacy of design and, second, the particularities of frame-by-frame execution. The act of adaptation in animation, therefore, is not predicated on the determinants of narrative events as described in a literary text but on the stimulants of function and purpose – not the fact that something happens, but the *way* it happens.

Arguably Disney animation in general is more directly governed by 'rule governed transpositions', especially with regard to the engagement with the representational apparatus of certain fine-art principles and styles. Robin Allen has located the acknowledged influences of Arthur Rackham, Ludwig Richter, Wilhelm Busch, Gustav Doré and Hermann Vogel on the paintings and drawings that inform the design of *Snow White*, noting too that Albert Hurter (the celebrated Swiss-German cartoonist) and Gustaf Tenggren (the Swedish book illustrator) working at the Disney studio, also bring their signature to this primary work.[8] The same case could be made for the ways in which Disney's insistence on anatomically correct movement in his characters formally determines their construction. Though anchorage is ultimately achieved through the combination of literary stimulus, design models and the focus upon established codes of human movement, relay – ultimately, the act of animation itself – establishes the nature of how the 'adaptable' becomes the 'adapted'. This space, which is the specific site of the adaptation process, speaks to Eisenstein's conception of *plasmaticness*: 'a rejection of once-and-forever allotted form, freedom from ossification, the ability to dynamically assume any form' (Leyda 1988: 21).

Fancy's images...

I wish to conclude this discussion by making some brief remarks about three animated adaptations of Shakespeare's *A Midsummer Night's Dream*. I have sought to establish how the free vocabulary of animation is especially responsive to the literary text because it enables a greater degree of continuity between how the text is imagined (the imagist principle) and reformed (the propositional mode), procedurally modified (effectively given a technical vocabulary of anchorage) before being subject to *literal* acts of transition (relay), and constituted as a 'plasmatic' form which resists fixedness, remaining responsive to a multiplicity of strategic movements and interpretative possibilities. The 'openness' of the animated vocabulary is especially conducive to fantastical or supernatural contexts, and more readily defines and naturalizes 'magical' conditions. Shakespeare's *Dream* is an appealing text for animators in this light, because the play constitutes what Ruth Nevo describes as 'a complex and witty exploration of the infirmities and frailties and deficiencies and possibilities of the imaginative faculty itself' where the (creative) mind 'in its aspect as the image-making and image-perceiving faculty is an errant faculty indeed, unstable, uncertain, wavering, and seeking *anchorage* among a welter of rival images and self images' (Nevo 1980: 95–8; my italics).

Animation as a language is clearly responsive to the dynamics of such a text because its plasmatic currency both retains specificity and inflection. John Canemaker's film *Bottom's Dream* (1983), for example, the most *experimental* of the three texts I am considering, merely takes two lines from the play as a point of stimulus, but nevertheless seeks to encompass the spirit of the whole text. Playing out the tension between Bottom's line 'I have had a most rare vision' and the impossibility of understanding or dissembling these images as encompassed in the line 'Man is but an ass if he go about to expound this dream', Canemaker dispenses with any storytelling orthodoxy, preferring to imagine the very delirium of Bottom's experience – here a number of metamorphoses in which he moves from pig to dog to horse to ass, coupled with the myth of a series of images that pass in front of the mind's eye of a drowning man, and the inescapable and seemingly relentless dream-chase after delusory shapes and forms. Canemaker employs a number of styles from Disney-esque line-test drawings to flowing blocks of coloured shapes (sometimes reminiscent of spider's webs, or other related flora and fauna) to impressionistic painting and charcoal sketching of 'natural' forms. He essentially abstracts Shakespeare's narrative into a visual poem, highly empathetic with the transmutation of perceptual and emotional states that is the play's chief theme. Canemaker energizes the 'Romanticism' of Shakespeare's plot, however, by emphasizing the 'animality' of passion and desire. The primal instincts aroused through Bottom's transformation are represented in the intuitive and looser formations of Canemaker's 'styles'. His free use of the plasmatic potential within the open vocabulary of animation captures and develops the 'experience' in the text and the spirit of the word.

Jiri Trnka's full-length puppet animation meets Canemaker halfway in the *developmental* style, combining established orthodoxies of voice-over storytelling and character construction with a more lyrical interpretation of the word, de-emphasizing the more primitive elements and signs of madness, and heightening the ethereal nature of the '*fairy* tale'. Trnka's *A Midsummer Night's Dream* (1959) uses an over-elaboration of design elements to heighten the supernatural abundance of the romantic context – tresses of flowers hang from every bower; figures move with balletic grace; nymphs and elves populate the lush environment. Where Canemaker's lines and forms define an interior psychic place, Trnka's fluid and highly mannered puppet movement is located in an impossibly romantic landscape, hauntingly evocative, often using soft-focus photography to mystify and render uncertain the transposition of fairy figures upon rustic spaces. The lovers – Demetrius, Lysander, Helena and Hermia – and Peter Quince's rude mechanicals, become the figures of romantic farce, subject only to the increasing realization that the more that they try and impose order and reason upon their intentions, the more they become subject to comic chaos. In Trnka's *Dream* the mortals are merely make-believing; the immortals, like the animator himself, are the agitators and provocateurs of magical and supernatural acts of imaginative juxtaposition. Trnka enjoys the orthodoxy of the 'real' events in the play only because they properly foreground the flights of fancy available to the animator. Once more text is merely anchorage for a suggestive relay of the forest scenes. Shakespeare's contextual narration is the substantive foundation of Trnka's plasmatic engagement with Puckish playfulness. Puck, when testing the potion that will later be placed on Titania's eyes, watches snails dote on each other, Athenian ruins disappear and goats become amorous. No allotted form ossifies or retains its fixedness. Trnka's developmental style insists that the inner quality of the material form reveals itself through difference. If Shakespeare's words suggest this, animation shows it.

Robert Saakiants' version of the play for the S4C/Soyuzmultfilm 'Shakespeare Project' (Osborne, in Boose and Burt 1997: 103–21), dedicated to introducing Shakespeare to a new audience and popularizing the plays in abridged animated form, works in a much more *orthodox* mode of animation in that it is much more bound up with the overt act of storytelling rather than suggestion. If Trnka's work was about the *simultaneity* of literal and imagined action, Saakiants' nevertheless distinctive piece reclaims the play's *linearity*. This is mainly because adapter Leon Garfield predicated the script on plotting and the maintenance of simple character development. Saakiants' own drawings do much to stylize the piece, matching almost cartoonal 'squash'n'stretch'[9] fairies and comic figures with highly caricatured lead characters strong in gesture and movement. The film is vibrantly coloured and uses its metamorphoses with subtle care – the omnipresence of Oberon, for example, suggested when his actual body becomes invisible leaving the flora that constituted his clothing in a Magritte-like absence that defines the forest space. As in Trnka's version, the flower from which the sight-potion is made literally grows and relinquishes its liquid, spilling on an insect, who when waking falls for another nearby bug. More concentrated on the machinations of the pairs of lovers, Saakiants' film uses animation to rejuvenate the very 'look' of the piece, drawing it away from a traditional classicism and yet not so far into the purely imaginative context offered by Canemaker or the inspiring improvisation of Trnka.

As is clear in works as diverse as those from Caroline Leaf, the Walt Disney Studios, John Canemaker, Jiri Trnka and the animators of the 'Soviet Disney' studio, Soyuzmultfilm, animation is a film-form which provides a vocabulary that enables the most sensitive response to literary texts. Animation is achieved through the specific execution of a highly detailed approach in which the smallest of factors makes a significant impact on the final work. This sense of focus and attention on each element of the process finds clear correspondence with the particularities in creating literary texts. Each 'word', 'sentence', 'paragraph' and so on, is crucial to the final outcome in the same way that any one line and its movement is overtly important in an animated film. The minutiae of detail required to create frame-by-frame movement in animation directly echoes the deep suggestion in the descriptive codes and conventions of the written word. Animation can literalize and illustrate the creative process itself as it seeks to express an interpretative outcome. A drawing, an object, a puppet moving in a specific way is evidence of the *enactment* of interpretation as it has been thought of and played out through another creative and critical consciousness *as it happens*. The perspective offered by the animator is highly responsive to the personal needs of the creative artist and the context in which the 'new' text evolves. Consequently, each version is a statement about an artist's understanding of another aesthetic artefact and its place within a broader artistic discourse, which is being added to and enhanced by what is a highly self-conscious act of redetermination. The fixedness of 'literariness' is loosened by the necessity for the animator to perceive a text as an evolving 'work-in-progress' responsive only to the mechanical and aesthetic needs of the twenty-fifth of a second in which any one displacement in movement is being executed. The simultaneous requirement of technical and artistic 'correctness' facilitates the critical idiom in which the animator is working. Above all other film-making practices, therefore, animation transfigures the literary intention and transubstantiates the reader/viewer's imagination into a visual mode that ultimately speaks louder than the words that inspired it.

Notes

1 *Condensation, symbol and metaphor* and *penetration* are concepts more fully explored in Wells (1998: 68–127).
2 I define these approaches more fully in Wells (1998: 35–68) and Nelmes (1997a: 193–221).
3 This (and all subsequent quotations and information concerning Caroline Leaf and her work) is drawn from a public interview with the author at the Museum of the Moving Image, London, held on 4 June 1997.
4 In the novel 'the stranger' is the Devil, who visits Moscow, provoking change through a series of 'magical' exchanges.
5 In interview, former Disney designer Zack Schwartz suggests that Disney animators had to necessarily caricature figures in order to facilitate the widest possible range of performative possibilities that would suggest 'reality' within this spirit of plausibility and 'conviction'. See Wells (1997b: 4–10).
6 Disney veteran Ward Kimball describes the design of Jiminy Cricket in *Pinocchio* as the movement from the 'repulsiveness' of a real cricket, with all its legs and angular features, through the influence of an earlier Disney model in *The Ant and the Grasshopper* (which effectively humanized a grasshopper by standing it upright), up to the 'Americanization' of the character in the spirit of Ben Franklin. As he suggests, 'Jiminy is only a cricket because we say he's a cricket' (interview with the author, June 1988).
7 For an analysis of audience responses to Disney films, see Wells (1998: 222–43).
8 See R. Allan, 'The Fairest Film of All', *Animator* 21 October/December 1987, pp. 18–21; 'Picture Books and Disney Pictures', Exhibition Catalogue for the Portico Library and Gallery, Manchester, 3–27 September 1990; 'EuroDisney: *Snow White, Pinocchio* and a European Artist', *Sight and Sound*, July 1994, Art in Film Supplement, 4 (7) (n.s.), pp. 8–10.
9 'Squash'n'stretch' techniques are predicated on characters who are composed of circles which may be compressed and elongated in the act of movement.

17

'A DOGGY FAIRY TALE'[1]

The film metamorphoses of *The Hundred and One Dalmatians*

Imelda Whelehan

Dodie Smith, author of *The Hundred and One Dalmatians* (1956) and better known as a playwright during the 1930s and as writer of *I Capture the Castle* (1948), was not unlike Cruella de Vil in some respects: 'All her clothes were black and white; she lived in a black and white flat, and she had often said in jest that all she needed now was a Dalmatian' (Grove 1997: 91). By 1934 her future husband had given Dodie her first Dalmatian, Pongo. Like Cruella, Smith was deeply style-conscious, being original rather than slavish to trends, and her trademark was a mink coat that she wore into her nineties. During her prolonged 'exile' in the United States from 1939 to 1953, she had intimate dealings with Hollywood and the film industry and would have been no stranger to adaptations given that she earned a great deal of money from writing screenplays and 'treatments' – although she notably refused to work on Hitchcock's *Rebecca* (Grove 1997: 128). An assiduous journal-keeper for most of her life, Smith spent much of her latter years synthesizing writings from her numerous journals into a five-volume autobiography. As her life became less dominated by humans and more colonized by dogs (and other pets), it was natural that her writing should reflect this. The central focus of the *Dalmatians* plot – the birth of fifteen puppies to Pongo and Missis and the search for a Dalmatian wet-nurse, Perdita – reflected her own experiences of puppy rearing in 1943. Moreover, a key scene retained by both animated and live-action film versions of the novel – the reviving of the 'runt' puppy by the human hero – was a true story often recounted by Smith (Grove 1997: 151).

The germs of *The Hundred and One Dalmatians* began as an idea for a children's play that was prompted by the memory of a friend's remark that her dog Pongo, when a puppy, would make a nice fur coat (Grove 1997: 232). Animal-centred and rather sentimental, *Dalmatians* had qualities which appealed to Disney, who bought the film rights to the book on the strength of the episode where the puppies roll themselves in soot as a disguise (Grove 1997: 241). When Walt Disney visited Smith in 1959 he was able to claim that they had made few changes to her essential narrative in adaptation and that he had insisted on the inclusion of the scene where cows offer their milk to the puppies against objections that this would cause offence (Grove 1997: 257). The film of *The Hundred and One Dalmatians* opened in London in 1961 and Smith attended the preview, of which on the whole she approved – her approval perhaps best indicated by the fact that she named her next Dalmatian 'Disney' (Grove 1997: 272). Despite Disney's claims about fidelity, there were many changes to the original novel, but it is fair to say that the process of animation secured faithfulness to the point of view established in the book – which is third person but focalized through Pongo, who provides the voice-over at the start of the film. This is crucial to the overall shaping of the film's narrative and marks the biggest difference between this and the 1996 live-action version.

Dodie Smith always lamented the fact that she did not get the critical acclaim for her work that she felt she deserved; moreover, she desired primarily to be recognized as a playwright and claimed: 'I was miserable over the publication of *I Capture the Castle*, and able to find little joy in its eventual success. The same applies to *Dalmatians*' (Grove 1997: 325). Ironically, the works which secured Smith a modest amount of fame and fortune were those which she felt to be subordinate to her major creative ambitions – although she complained about the puniness of her credit in the Disney film (Grove 1997: 265). The output from the Disney Corporation arguably has suffered from a similar lack of serious recognition – 'Disney film is the ugly stepsister unfit for the glass slipper of high theory' (Bell *et al.* 1995: 3) – as if it is somehow beneath artistic worth or critical attention, or because the Disney films are seen to be absorbed within a cultural identity focusing on theme parks and naked commercialism. Despite (or perhaps because of) Disney's domination and technical achievements in the field, animation remains very much the 'second cousin to mainstream cinema' (Wells 1998: 2), associated primarily with a children's audience and assumed to be therefore less structurally or thematically rich. A side-effect of this is that the Disney animation output has often been uncritically received as harmless, if trivial, and always a safe parental choice for children, which of course deflects any interrogation of the specific ideological thrust of the Disney enterprise or indeed the values filtered through the source folk tales and children's stories. As Janet Wasko asserts, Disney 'is able to remain extremely influential, if not dominant, in the marketing of children's and family entertainment' (in Curran and Gurevitch 1996: 349), offering a model experience which might be stultifying rather than expressive or liberating:

> In essence, Disney's machine was designed to shatter the two most valuable things about childhood – its secrets and its silences – thus forcing everyone to share the same formative dreams. It has placed a Mickey Mouse hat on every little developing personality in America. As capitalism, it is a work of genius; as culture, it is mostly a horror.
>
> (Schickel [1968] 1986: 18)

Although this observation might suggest some high cultural prejudice in its association of animation with industry rather than art, and its severing of capitalism and culture, it also reminds us that the tradition of feature-length animation films since *Snow White and the Seven Dwarfs* (1937) has produced certain formulaic qualities at the level of representation – particularly in the anthropomorphism of animals and things, the application of 'family values' to all situations, and consistently conservative messages about solid and timeless social values.

Dodie Smith had often been criticized for a certain child-like naivety in her work, and she brings to her children's story an investment in rigid categories of black and white that ossify rather than develop the motif of the Dalmatians' spotted coat. Cruella is from the start the two-dimensional villain of the piece, cast in the guise of the demon who thrives on fire and is physically striking: 'she had a dark skin, black eyes with a tinge of red in them, and a very pointed nose. Her hair was parted severely down the middle and one half of it was black and the other white – rather unusual' (Smith 1956: 5). When the Dearlys dine with the de Vils – a dinner which arrives in lurid colours and tastes unremittingly of pepper – Cruella has her husband stoke up the fire; if this symbolism isn't heavy-handed enough, Smith has Mr Dearly remark: 'What a strange name "de Vil" is...if you put the two words together, they make "devil". Perhaps Cruella's a lady-devil! Perhaps that's why she likes things so hot!' (Smith 1956: 12). This battle between black and white works itself out between the almost unbelievably kind Dearlys and the nurturant world of the Twilight Barking, set against the rapacious Cruella and her inept lackeys, Jasper and Saul Baddun. However, despite the pitting of innocence against evil seeming to be ideal fodder for the Disney corpus, and despite the animation containing the very recognizable core of the book's plot-structure, some ambiguities had to be evacuated to suit the Disney ideology.

Smith, unlike Disney, seeks to endow the dogs with specific and more laudable qualities of their own, rather than simply anthropomorphize animals. Nonetheless, this highly specific representation of 'Dog-dom' is upset by the dogs obeying what might loosely be termed high liberal 'Christian' definitions of partnership, marriage, family life and support for one's neighbours, symbol-ized most curiously at the close of the novel by Cadpig's memory of her epiphany in the church they took refuge in after their escape from the Badduns: 'She often remembered that building, and wondered who owned it – someone very kind, she was sure. For in front of every one of the many seats, there had been a little carpet-eared, puppy-sized dogbed' (Smith 1956: 191). Furthermore, the maternal and family instinct is demonstrated in Missis' attitude to the other puppies at Hell Hall – 'suddenly all the puppies were her puppies, she was their mother – just as Pongo had felt he was their father...she could scarcely tell where her little family ended and her larger family began' (Smith 1956: 110). The images of a natural maternal instinct in animals extend across species in the scene (keenly preserved by Disney) where cows feed the puppies (Smith 1956: 130), and female figures generally are presented as nurturant, a quality seemingly incompatible with initiative or drive.

Maleness and femaleness (presented as discrete and unchanging) polarize both the humans and the dogs, so that Pongo – described as having 'one of the keenest brains in Dogdom' (Smith 1956: 4) – is instrumental to the rescue operation, whereas Missis is only functional as a mother figure and as an object of flirtatious derision. The only way that she can be persuaded to roll in the soot as a disguise is to be complimented by Pongo: 'Why, Missis, as a black dog, you're slimmer than ever. You're positively *svelte*!' (Smith 1956: 138). Despite the fact that in Smith's novel the dogs are held up as by far the superior beings, she still imposes human social qualities upon them, with the effect of fixing gender discriminations and traditional moral strictures across species but holding up the human model as universal; this is something directly translated into the animated version, as well as being readily apparent in natural-history broadcasts from the 1960s onwards.[2] Interestingly, as in the animation, the roles of the males during the birth scene are foregrounded and in both novel and animation 'as if to underscore that males are the true generative force, the human husband brings the pup back to life' (Murphy, in Bell *et al.* 1995: 128). In the 1961 version, this scene is presaged by a thunderstorm and the moment of the puppy's revival is accompanied by a flash of lightning and a roar of thunder, offering intertextual links to Frankenstein movies as well as (more ironically) reminding us of Mary Shelley's warning of the consequences of male interference in the reproductive process. Interestingly, the thunderstorm takes on a double register, since thunder and lightning herald the arrival of Cruella in the scene in which she offers to pay upfront for the puppies.

Although the overall effect of Smith's novel is strikingly sentimental, she is decidedly unsentimental about (and possibly uninterested in) human affairs. Both film versions add a human romance element by creating a courtship scene to explain the neat pairing of dog and human. The most curious factor about the opening – and one swept over by Disney – is the fact that both couples bring to their relationship not only a dog but also a nanny: it is here that we begin to encounter one of those features that become unpalatable and unresponsive to the Disney treatment and require severe editing. Given that throughout the novel the Dearlys remain childless, the nannies decide to reinvent themselves as cook and butler (these also being their surnames), resulting in the latter wearing trousers and a frilly apron – 'it will add a note of originality' (Smith 1956: 3). While Disney synthesizes the plot to become essentially a story about couples and families, with both humans and dogs moving from courtship to partnership to parenthood, the novel contains odd couples or even threesomes who are explained away so innocently as to cause deep problems for the Disney camp. The nannies who (with the exception of the frilly apron) are effectively dressed up as the man and woman, in a sense infantilize the Dearlys by their presence, echoing the experience of the child reader whose domestic life is preordained and therefore uninteresting (and also perhaps Smith's own experiences of domesticity, for she totally relied on her husband and paid help to provide domestic services). The relationship between the Dalmatians – Pongo, his 'wife' Missis and the wet-nurse Perdita – is initially explained away by Pongo's brotherly regard for Perdita – 'he looked on Perdita as a much-loved young sister' (Smith 1956: 41) – and later by her becoming reunited with both her own 'husband' and puppies. Yet this triangle proves too thorny a problem for Disney to resolve. Meanwhile Cruella, who has kept her surname after marriage, threatens to usurp the territory usually assigned to the male (in common with Nanny Butler in her confusing outfit of trousers and frilly apron). In what may amount to a re-reading of Cruella's character for the live-action film, Cruella's parodic femininity becomes a signifier for usurpation of the 'natural' female role of nurturer and home-maker – a transgression for which she is punished in stark terms. This theme is less apparent in the animated version, but the decision to remove the figure of Cruella's furrier husband in both adaptations further excises any possibility of ambiguity in her character, supporting the ideological thrust of the Disney enterprise which embraces more clear-cut gender differentiations with obvious consequences for nonconformity.

For Disney, the book had the appeal of clear plot dynamics with its waging of good against bad, its charming animal tale at the centre and (with exceptions noted above) a family-centred moral core. As Wasko observes, some of the watchwords of the Disney enterprise are innocence, romance, reliance on gender stereotypes and individualism (in Curran and Gurevitch 1996: 358–60), all of which are employed in the two film versions of *The Hundred and One Dalmatians*. The Dearlys are presented as 'virginal' in both texts, and on both occasions it is Pongo who initiates the courtship for the dogs and humans. Even in the 1990s text, in which Anita figures as a talented designer, the women slot into traditional domestic roles with ease. Ironically, the live-action film seems to feel the need to underline the naturalness of maternal instincts and domesticity so that nanny (Joan Plowright) is able to describe 'the look every woman gets when she knows she's going to be a mother' accompanied by images of Anita's bovine passivity. As Lynda Haas asserts, 'mothers, when represented at all, are more stereotypically (and ideologically) drawn than any other character' (in Bell *et al.* 1995: 197), and motherhood is used as the measure of natural and healthy gender relations. As a complement to this, a high liberal investment in the concept of individualism is apparent in the reshaping of the male leads in the films, which simultaneously confirms that the worlds of work and responsibility are the male preserve. In the book, Mr Dearly seems effortlessly wealthy – responsible for 'getting rid of the National Debt' (Smith 1956: 2), he has been let off income tax for life – whereas Roger in both films adheres to a stricter ethic of hard work and unquenchable optimism and belief in the possibility of success. One is a struggling musician, the other a creator of video games; both owe their eventual success to the image of Cruella de Vil. In the 1961 version, Roger gets his first hit record with 'Cruella de Vil'; in the finale of the 1996 version, an animated Cruella figures in Roger's latest video game and is praised by the child who tests such games as an 'excellent villain', at once harking back to the legacy of Disney's animated success (and many adults' childhood memories of being terrified of Cruella[3]) and reminding us of the grotesque that the Glenn Close figure – ultimately effectively tarred and feathered – becomes.

Aside from the security of mainly rigid gender categories, the central Dalmatian plot allows for the representation of 'cuteness' which became a Disney staple and, offset by Cruella's grotesqueness, these figures provide the centre of narrative interest for the animation. The original story illustrators, the twins Janet and Anne Grahame-Johnstone, found the Dearlys 'rather too bland to draw' (Grove 1997: 234), and this blandness remains in the 1961 animation, successfully marginalizing the good humans to strictly functional roles. Perhaps inevitably, the Disney illustration team excelled at caricature – the stick-thin Cruella, the pear-shaped nanny and the hunched and angular Badduns – suggesting that human goodness is much more difficult to represent than human monstrosity or animal quirkiness. The focus instead remains on the delineation of doggy expressions of cuteness (often borrowed from the register of human comic expressions), slapstick via the Badduns, and the crucial screen-dominating presence of the figure of Cruella who, as an almost pantomimic stock villain, treats the audience to a range of grotesque poses and expressions made possible by her improbable skinniness and her angular skull-shaped face.

Typical of Disney, the dogs in particular suggest a close scrutiny of natural animal movement drawn from live subjects; in contrast the villainous humans contort in extravagant parodies of natural deportment, so that the binary opposition of good and evil seems to be mirrored by the delineation of grace set against the grotesque. There is a tension, therefore, in the 'hyperrealism'[4] that Disney specializes in – a tension perhaps explicable by the possibilities inherent in animation to defy the laws of gravity and to offer more complex meanings and readings of its subjects, set against the desire to demonstrate the potential of animation as capable of producing quality of movement and representational conventions close to live action. Schickel argues that 'in the late films complexity of draftsmanship [*sic*] was used to demonstrate virtuosity and often became an end in itself, a way of demonstrating what was a kind of growth in technical resourcefulness but not, unfortunately, in artfulness' (Schickel [1968] 1986: 178). It is certainly the case that opportunities are seized within the wider context of the animated film to remind us of the level of sophistication of the product we're watching, by contrasting the quality of the animation 'proper' with inferior examples. This can be witnessed in the scene where the puppies are watching the monochrome television programme featuring the dog Thunder, who has a far less rich range of movements and expressions than that evident in the watching puppies; this is further offset by what is little better than a matchstick dog animation in the Kanine Krunchies advertisement. The side-effect of this process is to suddenly remind us of the levels of artifice behind animation, whereas the main effect of viewing a Disney feature is often the reverse – the seamless naturalism in the portrayal of human movement and gesture obscuring the fact of animation's capacity to move us beyond the 'real' into the realms of the symbolic.

The process of animation (as with any adaptation) necessitates a transference of form and a reconfiguration of content, but the choice of animation of this story allows fidelity to a point of view (that of the dogs) which is naturalized by the effect of anthropomorphization, by which any object may be suddenly endowed with powers of expression – this is something in which the Disney company have excelled. Similarly the contrasts between good and evil can be perfectly played out and strengthened by visual indices of grace versus grotesque and sentiment versus slapstick. Reasons behind the animation's abiding success include the fact that the drive for cuteness avoids schmaltzy sentimentality through the narrative interest sustained by Cruella's villainy, accompanied by the pace of the chase scenes once the Dalmatians escape from Hell Hall. The romance subplot, such as it is, is accessible for comic interpretation through the voyeuristic perspective of Pongo, which reasserts the tyranny of the male gaze (most obviously dramatized by the sizing up of dog-female couples in the park) but at one remove.

Disney's decision to make a live-action version of their successful animation raises some interesting questions, as do all remakes, about what is being adapted and what the status of the original becomes. It also raises issues about whether, since this film is in some respects clearly a homage to the animated version, it also takes on some of its qualities – effecting some kind of bridge or blurring of boundaries between the live-action and animated genres. Released in 1996 and directed by Stephen Herek (of *Bill and Ted's Excellent Adventure* (1988) fame) it is, according to Jonathan Romney, 'a back-to-basics return to family values' (Romney 1997: 42) and it suffers from a sense of what it lacks – the possibilities of full animation. The decision not to give this live-action adaptation the *Babe* (1995) treatment inevitably shifts our gaze to the human subjects, since the dogs, although trained to perform, are unable to access the range of expressions and movement which underpin the hyperrealism of their animated counterparts. The sense of a lack in this version is emphasized further by the fact that the real has to be supported by the technological, and the use of animatronic creatures suggests that the film, in attempting to revisit a successful Disney formula, is 'dogged' by its own inadequacies.

In many ways the techniques adopted by the 1996 adaptation are reminiscent of the processes at work in realizing the original Hanna Barbera *Flintstones* cartoon (first appearing in 1960) into the 1994 live-action movie. Although the rendering of Fred, Wilma, Barney and Betty into flesh and blood gives the narrative overtones of the sitcom – and perhaps a return to the 'source' text, the TV series *The Honeymooners* (1955–67) – special effects are used to allow these characters the breadth to constantly flout nature's laws. This is most obviously demonstrated in the bowling alley scene when Fred takes his run-up on the very tips of his toes: the humour derives largely from our recognition of this act as an essential trope of the cartoon character. The nostalgic appeal for the audience is our memory of the cartoons, and it is clear that part of the appeal of the live-action *101 Dalmatians* is cross-generational: nudging the memories of an adult audience who first encountered the animated film (and probably not the novel) as children and perhaps suggesting a consistency of quality in the Disney product.

The Flintstones (1994), set as it is in the never-neverland of Bedrock, uses a location dependent on the fanciful settings of the cartoon, so that the live-action version remains playful with a deliberately fantastical and nostalgic portrayal of 1950s American consumer culture. The *Dalmatian* movies, on the other hand, have to confront the practical problems of representing the familiar and instantly recognizable – London – with an eye for how such a place might be constructed in the imagination of the average American. The 'British' setting of the animation instead presents us with a broad-brush representation of 'the European' – obvious London landmarks aside. Interestingly this film (also close to Disney's *Aristocats* (1970) in style) is visually reminiscent of Raoul Dufy – the broad lines and rich colour are echoed in the depiction of London streets – with one scene depicting an artist and her Afghan hound in a garret which is strikingly Parisian. This style and the classic depiction of a foggy London scene give the location – despite the depiction of modernity via the television – a date-less quality. This is in striking contrast to the live-action movie, which fetishizes London landmarks such as Trafalgar Square in the early 'courtship' scenes. The choice to opt for a contemporary setting is accompanied by the decision to update Roger's profession, but the focus on an idea of London through its landmarks, Regency houses and indicators of 'heritage' (such as Beefeaters with bulldogs and ravens looking out from the ramparts of the Tower of London) echoes the more regressive ideological thrust of the narrative.

In the 1996 version the recentring of the narrative upon the humans results in a plot which depends on its polarization between evil, represented by Cruella and her henchmen, and home and family values, represented by Anita and Roger Dearly, whose romance is as anodyne and elliptically presented as a 1950s romantic comedy. As Jonathan Romney observes: 'Roger lapses into the most ingenuous Freudian slip heard since the Doris Day comedies: "Would you like another cup of marriage?"' (Romney 1997: 42). Disney decides to further demonize Cruella through two character indices which would have remained unremarkable in the 1960s – her smoking and her love of fur. This environmentalist, eco-friendly context does not, however, reflect any modernization of the other values and (as mentioned above) a further villainous layer is added to Cruella's character through the extraordinarily vehement attack on the figure of the independent career-woman. The fur theme, which functions as a reason for the puppies' kidnap and little else, metamorphoses into an anti-cruelty theme which embraces the whole film and is further expanded by the addition of a new preamble featuring the news of the slaughter of a rare White Siberian Tiger in London Zoo. Cruella is therefore transformed into an international environmental criminal, and her constantly burning cigarette only contributes to a sense of her having a complete disregard for animal or human health. The cigarette-smoking was an addition to Cruella's character made in the 1961 version, but clearly intended at the time to set her up as chic and dangerous, rather than to be regarded as in itself a sign of 'evil' (not least because Roger smokes a pipe throughout); in the live-action film, images of revulsion and antisocial activity accompany Cruella's smoking and reflect her sadistic cruelty to others.

The live-action version's signal challenge is how to create a visually demonic presence in the form of Cruella, given that the actor Glenn Close can never be in herself as grotesque and fearsome as the animated Cruella, with her skeletal form emphasizing the skull-shape of her face dominated by large yellow eyes. Instead, Cruella's character relies heavily on the extravagant camp of Close's costumes – part pantomime dame, part *Absolutely Fabulous* (1992–6) – and contrasting white, red and black make-up, which is startlingly reminiscent of Jack Nicholson's Joker in *Batman* (1989). Close's Cruella is also a composite of past Disney villainesses, made apparent in her intoning of 'Mirror, Mirror on the wall...' as she places the pelt of the Siberian tiger against herself. Patrick Murphy notes that 'the [1961] film isolates evil as the personification of the independent woman' (in Bell *et al.* 1995: 129), but this is more true of the 1996 remake, not least because the casting of Close reminds us of her roles as lone predatory female in *Fatal Attraction* (1987) and *Dangerous Liaisons* (1988), not to mention her characterization of the doomed radical feminist in *The World According to Garp* (1982). Her evil is enhanced as the film progresses by contrasting her circumstances and behaviour with the human heroes. Cruella runs the fashion house for which Anita works and, although both might be cast as 1990s career-women, it is Cruella who is denatured in her response to Anita's assertion that she will end her career when she marries – Cruella remarks that: 'More good women are lost to marriage than to war, famine, disease and disaster. You have talent, darling. Don't squander it.' The figure of Cruella's male personal assistant, Alonso, mirrors the topsy-turvy gender performance witnessed in the figure of Nanny Butler in the book, and here it is impossible not to register the message that the world of Cruella is a world gone mad – removed from nature and the natural order of human life.

As the film progresses, the resemblances between the human figure of Cruella and her animated antecedent intensify, witnessed by the decision to often film her in hideous close-up with her mouth contorted in a maniacal laugh. At the moment of the puppies' birth she is reflected in silhouette by a flash of lightning, and the crazy outline of her shock-headed form is strictly cartoon. In the scene where Cruella learns that Horace and Jasper have success-fully stolen the dogs, she is depicted in full-length profile in her boudoir, bent backwards in an almost improbable contortion of the human form and cackling grotesquely. This woman is mad, suggests the scene, as incontrovertibly as when *Fatal Attraction*'s Alex is seen repeatedly flicking a lamp on and off in the lone-liness of her bedroom. The portrayal of an insane and possibly inhuman criminal seems to be essential to warrant her eventual punishment at the hands

Figure 17.1 Glenn Close as Cruella de Vil in *101 Dalmatians* (1996)

of the animals. In fact all the slapstick mishaps which befall the human characters – from Roger and Anita's bike crashes into the lake, through Horace and
Jasper's encounter with an electric fence, to the grand finale where Cruella is
tipped into a barrel of molasses and then rolled in straw – have much in
common with animation techniques from which we expect the characters to
emerge, intact, in the subsequent scenes. Of course continuity in the live-action
genre means that Cruella, at least, remains covered in slime and straw, and the
overriding feeling as one switches back to the recognition that this *is* a live-
action movie is that this is an image of public humiliation to excess.

The live-action *101 Dalmatians* is both a homage to the animation (with no
recourse to Smith's text other than that already contained within the 1961 film)
and an attempt to produce a hybrid form which fails because the real dogs just
look like trick performers and because 'real' villains have to be brought to the
morally appropriate forms of justice – police arrest – which doesn't sit easily
with the slapstick retribution brought against them by the animals. In this
instance the shift of perspective from dogs to humans destroys the plot
dynamics because the lead human characters do not develop appropriately
'heroic' characteristics – their representation of 'good' is inevitably static and
monotonous.

It is as if the live-action film was never meant to stand alone given the
regular re-releasing of the 1961 film, and also given the references to the 1996
film's predecessor via Roger's animated video game and a more general Disney
plug in the scene where the puppies are watching *The Aristocats* on television.

Murphy's view is that Disney's policy of re-releasing video versions of the animated classics 'depends on a belief in, and maintenance of, social stasis' (in Bell *et al.* 1995: 126). Yet the 1996 film also appears to include a plea for a return to the values of an unspecified distant past, depicted in the couple Anita and Roger. In certain respects, they are presented as out of key with 1990s living, but knowingly complicit in its material realities. Their uncomplicated lives – witnessed by the ease in which Anita 'returns' to the hearth, their passage around London on bicycles and their maintenance of a live-in domestic servant – has to be set against the fact that Roger earns his living from a high-tech, highly commercial industry, targeted at children and identified by moralists (who used to target television) as a corrupting influence and a symptom of society's moral decline. Roger's involvement in a 'debased' cultural form returns us to investigations of the reception of the animation feature, and more generally the Disney enterprise, as an equally suspect and commercially sassy cultural product. In all the Walt Disney theme parks, Main Street, USA, represents 'timeless' small-town values set in tension with its smoothly corporate, postmodern and global setting.

Interestingly, when we examine the processes of such 'multiple' adaptations, which involve little investment in either the concept of single author as guarantor of meaning or of original text as intrinsically valuable or sacrosanct, we are able to examine the concepts of authorship and authenticity with a colder eye. Here we have the work of a writer with claims to artistic excellence which were never acknowledged, and an adapter (if we can cite Walt Disney the man as having some individual agency in the decision to adapt Smith's novel five years before his death, as well as recognizing the collective creative inputs into film in general and animation in particular) who felt that artistic credibility was to be gained from 'more and more imitative realism in the movements of his characters, more and more detail (and lushness) in the backgrounds, greater and greater fidelity to nature in special effects ranging from lightning to the fall of raindrops' (Schickel [1968] 1986: 176). The matter of Smith's authorship, never the selling point of the original film, becomes obliterated under the weight of the Disney treatment in the live-action version, and authenticity becomes a question of distilling the essence of a successful formula for recycling – twofold – to a new generation of consumers.

Disney – understood as both the corporation and the *idea* of Walt the man which underpins it – appropriates authorship of *The Hundred and One Dalmatians* in such a way as to further complicate debates about the relationship of author to adaptation or the nature of the *auteur* as creator of a new and distinct artform. In the first case study in this volume, Cartmell explores the ways in which 'successful' Shakespeare adaptations must be seen to retain the idea of Shakespeare to guarantee a sense of their authentic relationship to the 'original'. Yet the identity of Shakespeare the author is no more fixed or determinate than Disney – the man, the corporation, the trademark, the guarantee of harmless children's entertainment. The 'Disney' identity is arguably more rigidly determined and less vulnerable to cultural appropriation than Shakespeare because of the activities of the corporation to prevent its 'misuse'. Further, Disney as 'low culture' is largely ignored by a critical institution which ceaselessly reappropriates the idea of Shakespeare as central to high cultural practices. In truth both, as products, are subject to the vicissitudes of the market-place and the changing modalities of taste, at the same time that as 'classics' (which in some senses define the 'high' and 'low' cultural spheres) they are ripe for reproduction and recycling.

At the time the 1996 *101 Dalmatians* was being filmed in Shepperton studios, production of Kenneth Branagh's *Hamlet* began (Jackson, in Branagh 1996: 181). Just as the respective casts of these two films might have well been able to view each other's activities across the lot, so an analysis of what happens when a little-known author is adapted by a well-known 'auteur' allows us to scrutinize the process of adapting the 'classics' with a colder eye.

Notes

1 Extract from the first notice which appeared in the *Times Literary Supplement* on 23 November 1956 (quoted in Grove 1997: 240).
2 As Rosalind Coward observes: 'many of these programmes set out with a whole series of preconceptions about male and female behaviour; they take a whole baggage of preconceptions about male aggression, bachelorhood, dominance, property, women's nesting instincts. Indeed these programmes are intensely anthropomorphic...' (Coward 1984: 213).
3 In a chapter which offers an ethnographic study of Disney audiences, Paul Wells notes that the image of Cruella de Vil recurs as a moment of fear in many individuals' viewing experiences (Wells 1998: 236).
4 This term is used by Paul Wells, following Umberto Eco, to convey the act of connoting the 'real' in an utterly 'fake' context. (For further discussion, see Wells 1998: 24–8.)

BIBLIOGRAPHY

Adams, T. (1994) Review of *Little Women*, *New York Post*, 21 December.

Adorno, T. and Horkheimer, M. (1979) *Dialectic of Enlightenment*, trans. J. Cumming, London: Verso.

Agee, J. (1946) in G. Mast and M. Cohen (eds), *Film Theory and Criticism: Introductory readings*, Oxford: Oxford University Press, p. 336.

Aitkenhead, D. (1995) 'Why did the emotionally repressed Mr Darcy send the nation's women into a swoon?', *Independent*, 26 December.

Alcott, L.M. (1868–9) *Little Women*; repr. New York: Adell Yearling Classics, 1987.

Anderson, J. (1994) Review of *Little Women*, *Newsday*, 11: 82.

Anderson, Q. (1971) *The Imperial Self*, New York: Vintage.

Andrew, D.(1984) *Concepts in Film Theory*, Oxford: Oxford University Press.

Ansen, D. (1994) Review of *Little Women*, *Newsweek*, 9 January: 57.

Appleyard, B. (1995) 'Angst? Can you buy it at the mall?', *Independent*, 24 October.

Arnheim, R. (1957) *Film as Art*, Berkeley: University of California Press.

Asherman, A. (1982) *The Making of Star Trek II: The Wrath of Khan*, New York: Pocket Books.

Austen, J. (1979) *Sense and Sensibility*, ed. T. Tanner, Harmondsworth: Penguin.

—— (1996) *Emma*, ed. F. Stafford, Harmondsworth: Penguin.

Aycock, W. and Schoenecke, M. (eds) (1988) *Film and Literature: A comparative approach to adaptation*, Texas: Texas University Press.

Bakhtin, M. (1968) *Rabelais and his World*, Cambridge, MA: MIT Press.

Balch, A. (1972) Interview, *Cinema Rising*, 1: 10–4.

Ball, R.H. (1968) *Shakespeare on Silent Film: A Strange Eventful History*, London: George Allen and Unwin.

Ballaster, R. (1996) 'Adapting Jane Austen', *The English Review*, 7 (1) September: 10–3.

Banks-Smith, N. (1995) 'A Jane reaction', *Guardian: Section 2*, 25 September: 8–9.

Barber, L. (1992) 'A little hard to swallow', *The Sydney Morning Herald*, 7 May: 34.

Barcan, R. and Fogarty, M. (1995) 'Performing *The Piano*: Feminism in five movements', *Antithesis*, 7 (1): 13–30.

Barker, D. and Kamps, I. (eds) (1996) *Shakespeare and Gender: A history*, London: Verso.

Barthes, R. (1977) *Image-Music-Text*, ed. and trans. S. Heath, Glasgow: Fontana/ Collins.

Bartov, O. (1997) 'Spielberg's Oskar: Hollywood tries evil', in Loshitzky 1997a: 41–60.

Baudrillard, J. (1983) *Simulations*, in J. Storey (ed.), *Cultural Theory and Popular Culture: A Reader*, London: Prentice Hall, 1998.

226

Bauer, Y. (1994) *Jews for Sale: Nazi–Jewish negotiations, 1933–1945*, New Haven: Yale University Press.

Baumann, Z. (1989) *Modernity and the Holocaust*, London: Polity Press.

Baym, N. (1981) 'The significance of plot in Hawthorne's romances', in G.R. Thompson and V.L. Lokke (eds), *Ruined Eden of the Present: Hawthorne, Melville and Poe*, West Lafayette: Purdue University Press.

Beckett, S. (1934) 'Proust in pieces', *Spectator*, 22 June: 975–6.

Bedell, M. (1983) Introduction to *Little Women*, New York: Modern Library College Edition.

Bell, E., Haas, L. and Sells, L. (1995) *From Mouse to Mermaid: The politics of film, gender and culture*, Bloomington: Indiana University Press.

Bell, P. (1995) 'All that Patriarchy Allows: The melodrama of *The Piano*', *Metro*, 102: 57–60.

Benjamin, W. (1969) *Illuminations*, trans. H. Zohn, New York: Schocken.

—— (1936) 'The work of art in the age of mechanical reproduction', repr. in H. Zohn (trans.), *Illuminations*, Glasgow: Fontana/Collins, 1970.

Bennett, C. (1995) 'Hype and heritage', *Guardian: Section 2*, 22 September: 4.

Berman, J. (1996) 'Feminizing the Nation: Woman as cultural icon in late James', *The Henry James Review*, 17 (1) Winter: 58–76.

Bernstein, M. (1994) 'The *Schindler's List* Effect', *The American Scholar*, 63 (3): 429–32.

—— (1998) 'Homage to the Extreme: The Shoah and the rhetoric of catastrophe', *Times Literary Supplement*, 6 March: 6–8.

Bilbrough, M. (1993) Interview with Jane Campion, *Cinema Papers*, 93 May: 4–11.

Birtwhistle, S. and Conklin, S. (1995) *The Making of 'Pride and Prejudice'*, London: Penguin/BBC Books.

Blatter, J. and Milton, S. (1982) *Art of the Holocaust*, London: Pan.

Bloom, A. (1987) *The Closing of the American Mind: How higher education has failed democracy and impoverished the souls of today's students*, Harmondsworth: Penguin.

Bloom, A. with Jaffa, H.V. (1964) *Shakespeare's Politics*, Chicago and London: University of Chicago Press; repr. 1986.

Bluestone, G. (1957) *Novels into Film*, Berkeley: University of California Press; repr. 1973.

Bockris, V. (1981) *With William Burroughs: A report from the bunker*, New York: Seaver.

Boose, L. and Burt, R. (eds) (1997) *Shakespeare the Movie: Popularizing the plays on film, TV and video*, London and New York: Routledge.

Bourdieu, P. (1984) *Distinction: A social critique of taste*, trans. R. Nice, London: Routledge.

—— (1993) *The Field of Cultural Production*, ed. and intro. R. Johnson, Cambridge: Polity Press.

Bourget, E. (1991) 'Du beidemeir au romanticisme: Les quatre filles du Docteur March', in *Positif*, December: 80–1.

Bowles, P. (1959) 'Burroughs in Tangier', *Big Table*, 2: 42–3.

Branagh, K. (1996) *'Hamlet' by William Shakespeare: Screenplay, introduction and film diary*, London: Chatto and Windus.

Bristow, J. (1997) 'Trivialising History', *Living Marxism*, February: 34–7.

Brophy, B. (1965) 'A Masterpiece, and Dreadful', *New York Times Book Review*, 17 January: 1–3.

227

Brown, G. (1994) Review, in *Village Voice*, 27 December: 68.

Brown, P. (1985) 'This thing of darkness I acknowledge mine', in J. Dollimore and A. Sinfield (eds), *Political Shakespeare*, Manchester: Manchester University Press; 2nd edn, 1994, pp. 48–71.

Brunette, P. (1980) 'Snow White and the seven dwarfs', in D. Peary and G. Peary (eds), *The American Animated Cartoon*, New York: E.P. Dutton, pp. 66–76.

Bruzzi, S. (1993) 'Bodyscape', *Sight and Sound*, October: 6–10.

—— (1994) 'Replaying *The Piano*', *Sight and Sound*, March: 64.

—— (1995) 'Tempestuous Petticoats: Costume and desire in *The Piano*', *Screen*, 36 Summer: 257–66.

—— (1996) 'Jane Campion: Costume drama and reclaiming women's past', in P. Cook and P. Dodd (eds), *Women and Film: A Sight and Sound Reader*, London: Scarlet Press.

—— (1997) *Undressing Cinema: Clothing and identity in the movies*, London: Routledge.

Bryson, N. (1983) *Vision and Painting: The logic of the gaze*, New Haven: Yale University Press.

Buchman, L.M. (1991) *Still in Movement: Shakespeare on screen*, Oxford: Oxford University Press.

Bulman, J.C. (ed.) (1996) *Shakespeare, Theory and Performance*, London and New York: Routledge.

Burchall, G. (1993) 'Filming the global village', *Age*, 1 June: 17.

Burroughs, W.S. (1959) *The Naked Lunch*, London: John Calder; repr. 1982.

—— (1961) *The Soft Machine*, London: Calder and Boyars; repr. 1968.

—— (1966) *Nova Express*, London: Jonathan Cape.

—— (1969) *The Job: Interviews with Daniel Odier*, New York: Grove; repr. 1974.

—— (1974) *Exterminator!*, London: Calder and Boyars.

—— (with Gysin, B.) (1979) *The Third Mind*, London: John Calder.

—— (1983) Foreword to H. Norse, *Beat Hotel*, San Diego: Atticus.

—— (1986) *The Adding Machine: Selected essays*, New York: Seaver.

—— (1989) *Interzone*, New York: Viking.

—— (1990) 'The Devil's Bargain', interview with N. Zurbrugg, *Art and Text* (Sydney) 35: 38–55.

—— (1991) 'Robert Wilson', in T. Fairbrother (ed.), *Robert Wilson's Vision*, Boston: Museum of Fine Arts (in association with New York: Harry N. Abrams).

—— (1992a) Introduction to I. Silverberg (ed.), *Everything is Permitted: The making of Naked Lunch*, New York: Grove Weidenfeld.

—— (1992b) '...15 questions you never asked. William S. Burroughs', interview, *The Age* (Melbourne), 1 May: 15.

—— (1993) *The Letters of William S. Burroughs: 1945–1959*, ed. O. Harris. New York: Viking.

—— (1994) 'William Burroughs: Grandpa from hell', interview with N. Zurbrugg, *World Art*, 1 (2): 68–73.

Burston, P. (1995) 'Holy Homo!', *Time Out*, 28 July.

Butler, M. (1975) *Jane Austen and the War of Ideas*, Oxford: Clarendon Press; repr. 1987.

Campion, J. (1997) 'Jane Can: Interview', *Marie Claire*, February: 72–3.

Campion, J. and Pullinger, K. (1994) *The Piano: A novel*, London: Bloomsbury.

Canemaker, J. (ed.) (1988) *Storytelling in Animation*, vol. 2, Los Angeles: AFI.

Cavell, S. (1996) 'Words of Welcome', in C. Warren (ed.), *Beyond Document: Essays on nonfiction film*, Hanover and London: Wesleyan University Press.

Chandler, R. (1940) *Farewell, My Lovely*, repr. Harmondsworth: Penguin, 1975.

Chatman, S. (1978) *Story and Discourse: Narrative structure in fiction and film*, Ithaca and London: Cornell University Press.

Chedgzoy, K. (1995) *Shakespeare's Queer Children: Sexual politics and contemporary culture*, Manchester: Manchester University Press.

Clark, R. (ed.) (1994) *'Sense and Sensibility' and 'Pride and Prejudice'*, New Casebooks series, Basingstoke: Macmillan.

Cohen, K. (1979) *Film and Fiction: The dynamics of exchange*, New Haven: Yale University Press.

Coleman, T. (1983) 'The Terry Coleman interview', *Guardian*, 5 September.

Collick, J. (1989) *Shakespeare, Cinema and Society*, Manchester: Manchester University Press.

Condé, M. (1986) *I, Tituba, Black Witch of Salem*, trans. R. Philcox, New York: Ballantine, 1994.

Connolly, K. (1993) 'Playing for keeps', *Age*, 15 August: 7.

Conomos, J. (1992) 'A fascinating and phantasmagoric universe', *Filmnews* (Sydney) 22 (4): 16.

Cotta Vaz, M. (1989) *Tales of the Dark Knight: Batman's first fifty years*, London: Futura.

Coward, R. (1984) *Female Desire*, London: Paladin.

Crafton, D. (1993) *Before Mickey: The animated film 1898–1928*, Chicago and London: University of Chicago Press.

Craig, S. (ed.) (1980) *Dreams and Deconstructions: Alternative theatre in Britain*, Ambergate: Amber Lane Press.

Creed, B. (1987) 'From here to modernity', *Screen*, 28 (2): 47–67; repr. in P. Brooker and W. Brooker (eds), *Postmodern After-Images: A reader in film, television and video*, London: Arnold, 1997, 43–54.

Cronenberg, D. (1997) *Cronenberg on Cronenberg*, ed. C. Rodley, London: Faber and Faber.

Cummings, R. (1994) 'The Piano revisited', *Sight and Sound*, February: 72.

Curran, J. and Gurevitch, M. (eds) (1996) *Mass Media and Society*, 2nd edn, London: Arnold.

Davies, A. (1988) *Filming Shakespeare's Plays: The adaptations of Laurence Olivier, Orson Welles, Peter Brook and Akira Kurosawa*, Cambridge: Cambridge University Press.

Davies, A. and Wells, S. (eds) (1994) *Shakespeare and the Moving Image: The plays on film and television*, Cambridge: Cambridge University Press.

Davis, M. (1995) 'Reworking women', *Village Voice*, 3 January: 66.

DeMatteis, J.M. and Giffen, K. *et al.* (1989) *Justice League: A new beginning*, New York: DC Comics.

Denzin, N. (1988) *'Blue Velvet*: Postmodern contradictions', *Theory, Culture and Society – Postmodernism*, 5 (2–3) June: 461–3.

Dickens, H. (1971) *The Films of Katharine Hepburn*, New York: The Citadel Press.

Dillard, J.M. (1996) *Star Trek: First Contact*, New York: Pocket Books.

Dior, C. (1958) *Dior by Dior: The autobiography of Christian Dior*, trans. A. Fraser, Harmondsworth: Penguin.

Doane, J. and Hodges, D. (1987) *Nostalgia and Sexual Difference*, New York and London: Methuen.

Doane, M. (1982) 'Film and the masquerade: Theorising the female spectator', *Screen*, 23: 74–87.

Doherty, T. (1988) *Teenagers and Teenpics: The juvenilization of American movies in the 1950s*, Boston and London: Unwin Hyman.

Donaldson, P.S. (1990) *Shakespearean Films/Shakespearean Directors*, Boston and London: Unwin Hyman.

Dower, J.W. (1986) *War Without Mercy: Race and power in the Pacific war*, New York: Pantheon.

During, S. (1997) 'Popular culture on a global scale: A challenge for cultural studies?', *Critical Inquiry*, 23 (1) Summer: 808–33.

Dyer, R. (1977) 'Entertainment and utopia', *Movie*, 24: 2–13.

—— (1993) 'Rock: The last guy you'd have figured', in P. Kirkham and J. Thumin (eds), *You Tarzan: Men, masculinity and the movies*, London: Routledge, pp. 27–34.

Dyson, L. (1995) 'The return of the repressed?: Whiteness, femininity and colonialism in *The Piano*', *Screen*, 36 (Summer): 267–76.

Eisner, J. (1987) *The Official Batman Batbook*, London: Titan.

Ellis, J. (1992) *Visible Fictions*, revised edn, London: Routledge.

Epstein, J. (1993) '*The Piano*', *The Melburnian*, August: 20–1.

Evron, B. (1983) 'The Holocaust reinterpreted: An indictment of Israel', *Granta* 6: 54–73.

Falk, P. (1994) *The Consuming Body*, London: Sage.

Falk, P. and Campbell, C. (eds) (1997) *The Shopping Experience*, London: Sage.

Featherstone, M. (1991) *Consumer Culture and Postmodernism*, London: Sage.

Feiffer, J. (1965) *The Great Comic Book Heroes*, New York: Dial Press.

Feldman, A. (1991) *Formations of Violence*, Chicago: University of Chicago Press.

Felman, S. (1991) 'In an era of testimony: Claude Lanzmann's *Shoah*', in C. Nouvet (ed.), *Literature and the Ethical Question*, Yale French Studies no. 79, New Haven: Yale University Press, pp. 39–81.

Fensch, T. (ed.) (1995) *Oskar Schindler and his List*, Forest Dale: Paul S. Eriksson.

Fetterley, J. (1979) '*Little Women*: Alcott's Civil War', in *Feminist Studies*, 5: 369–83.

Field, M. (1994) '*The Piano* becomes an industry', *Canberra Times*, 30 April: 8.

Foucault, M. (1978) *The History of Sexuality, vol. 1, An Introduction*, trans. R. Hurley, Harmondsworth: Penguin.

—— (1982) 'Sexuality and solitude', *Humanities in Review*, vol. 1, New York: Cambridge University Press.

—— (1984) 'The body of the condemned', repr. in P. Rabinow (ed.), *The Foucault Reader: An introduction to Foucault's thought*, London: Penguin, 1991.

Fowler, B. (1997) *Pierre Bourdieu and Cultural Theory: Critical investigations*, London: Sage.

Frank, A. (1991) 'For a sociology of the body: An analytical review', in M. Featherstone, M. Hepworth and B.Turner (eds), *The Body*, London: Sage.

Franke, L. (1996) 'On the brink', *Sight and Sound*, November: 6–9.

Friedberg, A. (1993) *Window Shopping: Cinema and the postmodern*, Berkeley and Los Angeles: University of California Press.

Gaines, J. (1990) 'Introduction: Fabricating the female body', in J. Herzog and C. Herzog (eds), *Fabrications: Costume and the female body*, London: Routledge, pp. 23–7.

Gardiner, D. and Walker, K.S. (eds) (1984) *Raymond Chandler Speaking*, London: Allison and Busby.

Garner, H. (1993), 'A New Zealand genius', *Independent Monthly*, August: 32.

Garrett, R. (1995) 'Costume drama and counter memory: Sally Potter's *Orlando*', in J. Dowson and S. Earnshaw (eds), *Postmodern Subjects/Postmodern Texts*, Amsterdam and Atlanta: Rodopi, pp. 89–99.

Geloin, G. (1988) 'The plight of film adaptation in France: Toward dialogic process in auteur film', in Aycock and Schoenecke 1988: 135–148.

Giddings, R., Selby, K. and Wensley, C. (1990) *Screening the Novel: The theory and practice of literary dramatization*, Basingstoke: Macmillan.

Gilbert, M. (1985) *The Holocaust: The Jewish tragedy*, London: Collins.

Gilbert, S.M. and Gubar, S. (1979) *The Madwoman in the Attic: The woman writer and the nineteenth-century literary imagination*, New Haven: Yale University Press.

Gillespie, N. (1994) 'Reclaiming the vast wasteland', *Reason*, 26 (3): 53–5.

Gillett, S. (1995) 'Lips and fingers: Jane Campion's *The Piano*', *Screen*, 36, Summer: 277–87.

Ginsberg, A. (1963) *Reality Sandwiches (1953–60)*, San Francisco: City Lights; repr. 1993.

Gold, M. (ed.) (1988) *The Greatest Batman Stories Ever Told*, New York: DC Comics.

Goldsworthy, K. (1993) 'What music is', *Arena Magazine*, October–November: 46–8.

Greig, D. (1997) 'Notes and queries 4', *Studies in Theatre Production* 15, June: 99–103.

Grimes, W. and Barber, L. (1994) 'Critics sing sour tune in emerging backlash to acclaim of *The Piano*', *The Age*, 15 March: 3.

Grove, V. (1997) *Dear Dodie: The life of Dodie Smith*, London: Pimlico.

Gutman, I. (ed.) (1990) *Encyclopaedia of the Holocaust*, 4 vols, New York: Macmillan.

Gysin, B. (1997) 'Interview with Arthur and Corinne Cantrill', in J. Sargeant, *The Naked Lens: An illustrated history of beat cinema*, London: Creation, pp. 177–83.

Halliwell, L. (1991) 'Review of 1949 film adaptation of *Little Women*', in J. Walker (ed.), *Halliwell's Film Guide*, 8th edn, London: Harper Collins, p. 655.

Halttunen, K. (1984) 'The domestic drama of Louisa May Alcott', in *Feminist Studies*, 10: 233–54.

Hansen, M.B. (1996) '*Schindler's List* is not *Shoah*: The second commandment, popular modernism and public memory', *Critical Inquiry*, 22 (2): 292–312.

Hanson, C. (1994) *Virginia Woolf*, Basingstoke and London: Macmillan.

Harper, S. (1994) *Picturing the Past: The rise and fall of the British costume film*, London: BFI Publishing.

Hattersley, R. (1995) 'Watch without prejudice', *The Times Magazine*, 26 August: 18–19, 21.

Hawthorne, N. (1850) *The Scarlet Letter*, repr. London: Penguin, 1986.

Hayes, P. (ed.) (1991) *Lessons and Legacies: The meaning of the Holocaust in a changing world*, Evanston: Northwestern University Press.

Herald Tribune (1933) Advertisement for McCreary's, Fifth Avenue, New York, 1 December.

Héritier-Augé, F. (1989) 'Semen and blood: Some ancient theories concerning their genesis and relationship', in *Fragments Three*.

Herzog, C. (1990) ' "Powder puff" promotion: The fashion show-in-the-film', in J. Gaines, J. Herzog and C. Herzog (eds), *Fabrications: Costume and the female body*, London: Routledge, pp. 134–59.

Higham, C. (1975) *Kate: The life of Katharine Hepburn*, New York: Signet.

Hilberg, R. (1985) *The Destruction of the European Jews*, revised and definitive edn, 3 vols, New York: Holmes and Meier.

Hipsky, M. (1989) 'Anglophil(m)ia: Why does America watch Merchant–Ivory movies?', *Journal of Popular Film and Television*, 17 (1): 99–107.

Hobsbawm, E. and Ranger, T. (eds) (1984) *The Invention of Tradition*, Oxford: Oxford University Press.

Hodge, J. (1996) *Trainspotting and Shallow Grave*, London: Faber and Faber.

Hollander, A. (1980) 'Reflections on *Little Women*', in *Children's Literature*, 9: 28–39.

—— (1995) '*Little Women* through the ages: Each in its own fashion', *The New York Times*, 15 January: 20–1.

Horne, P. (1997) 'Valuing the honour of the thing', *Times Literary Supplement*, 7 March: 20.

Horowitz, S.R. (1997) 'But is it good for the Jews?: Spielberg's Schindler and the aesthetics of atrocity', in Loshitzky 1997a: 119–39.

Humm, M. (1997) *Feminism and Film*, Edinburgh: Edinburgh University Press.

Insdorf, A. (1989) *Indelible Shadows: Film and the Holocaust*, 2nd edn, Cambridge: Cambridge University Press.

Itzin, C. (1980) *Stages in the Revolution: Political theatre in Britain since 1968*, London: Eyre Methuen.

Jacobson, H. (1997) *Seriously Funny: From the ridiculous to the sublime*, London: New York *et al.*: Viking/Channel Four.

James, H. (1997) *The Portrait of a Lady*, intro. R. Barreca, London: Penguin.

James, K. (1994) 'Amy had golden curls; Jo has a rat. Who would you rather be?', *New York Times*, 25 December: 3, 17 and 34.

Jameson, F. (1981), *The Political Unconscious*, London: Methuen.

—— (1983) 'Postmodernism and consumer culture', in H. Foster (ed.), *Postmodern Culture*, London: Pluto, pp. 111–25.

—— (1984) 'Postmodernism, or the cultural logic of late capitalism', *New Left Review*, 146, July–August: 53–92.

—— (1991) 'Nostalgia for the present' from *Postmodernism, or the Cultural Logic of Late Capitalism*, in P. Brooker and W. Brooker (eds), *Postmodern After-Images: A reader in film, television and video*, London: Arnold, 1997, pp. 25–35.

Jarman, D. (1984) *Dancing Ledge*; repr. London: Quartet, 1991.

Jays, D. (1995) 'Camp Crusaders', interview with Chris O'Donnell, *Attitude*, July.

Jenkins, H. (1992) *Textual Poachers: Television fans and participatory culture*, London: Routlege.

Johnson, F. (1995) 'Holy Homosexuality Batman! Camp and Corporate Capitalism in Batman Forever', *Bad Subjects*, December: on-line journal.

Jones, E. (1949) *Hamlet and Oedipus*, New York: Norton; repr. 1976.

Jones, L. (1996) '*The Portrait of a Lady*: The screenplay based on the novel by Henry James*, London: Penguin.

Jorgens, J. (1977) *Shakespeare on Film*, Indiana: Indiana University Press.

Kane, B. (1990) *Batman Archives: Volume one*, New York: DC Comics.

Kane, B. with Andrae, T. (1989) *Batman and Me*, California: Eclipse.

Keneally, T. (1983) *Schindler's Ark*, London: Coronet.

Kerr, H., Eaden, R. and Mitton, M. (eds) (1996) *Shakespeare: World Views*, Delaware: University of Delaware Press.

Keyser, E.L. (1988) '*A Bloodsmoor Romance*: Joyce Carol Oates's *Little Women*', in *Women's Studies*, 14: 211–23.

Kirkham, P. (1995) 'Dress, dance, dreams and desire: Fashion and fantasy in *Dance Hall*', *Journal of Design History*, 8 (3): 195–214.

—— (1996) 'Fashioning the feminine: Dress, appearance and femininity in wartime Britain', in C. Gledhill and G. Swanson (eds), *Nationalising Femininity: Culture, sexuality and British cinema in the Second World War*, Manchester: Manchester University Press, pp. 152–74.

Kirkham, P. and Skeggs, B. (1998) '*Absolutely Fabulous*: Absolutely feminist?', in C. Geraghty and D. Lusted (eds), *The Television Studies Book*, London: Arnold.

Kirkham, P. and Thumin, J. (1995) 'Me Jane', in P. Kirkham and J. Thumin (eds), *Me Jane: Masculinity, movies and women*, New York: St Martin's Press, pp. 11–35.

Klein, M. and Parker, G. (eds) (1981) *The English Novel and the Movies*, New York: Frederick Ungar.

Kracauer, S. (1960) *Theory of Film: The redemption of physical reality*, London: Oxford University Press.

Kushner, T. (1994) *The Holocaust and the Liberal Imagination: A social and cultural history*, Oxford: Blackwell.

Langer, L.L. (1991) *Holocaust Testimony*, New Haven: Yale University Press.

Lanier, D. (1996) 'Drowning the book: *Prospero's Books* and the textual Shakespeare', in J.C. Bulman (ed.), *Shakespeare, Theory and Performance*, London and New York: Routledge, pp. 187–209.

Lanzmann, C. *et al.* (1991) 'Seminar with Claude Lanzmann', in C. Nouvet (ed.), *Literature and the Ethical Question*, Yale French Studies no. 79, New Haven: Yale University Press, pp. 82–99.

Le Faye, D. (ed.) (1995) *Jane Austen's Letters*, 3rd edn, Oxford: Oxford University Press.

Leighton, A. (1983) 'Sense and silences: Reading Jane Austen again', in J. Todd (ed.), *Jane Austen: New perspectives*, New York: Holmes and Meier, pp. 129–41.

Levi, P. (1987) *If This is a Man and The Truce*, trans. S. Woolf, London: Abacus.

—— (1989) *The Drowned and the Saved*, trans. R. Rosenthal, London: Abacus.

Leyda, J. (ed.) (1988) *Eisenstein on Disney*, London and New York: Methuen.

Lipman, A. (1995) Review of *Little Women*, *Sight and Sound*, March: 42.

Lippart, L.R. *et al.* (1966) *Pop Art*, London: Thames and Hudson.

Lorentz, P. (1986) *Lorentz on Film: Movies 1927–1941*, Norman and London: University of Oklahoma Press.

Los Angeles Times (1934) 6 March, New York Public Library, Performing Arts Research Collections.

Loshitzky, Y. (ed.) (1997a) *Spielberg's Holocaust: Critical perspectives on 'Schindler's List'*, Bloomington and Indianapolis: Indiana University Press.

—— (1997b) 'Holocaust others: Spielberg's *Schindler's List* versus Lanzmann's *Shoah*', in Loshitzky 1997a: 104–18.

Lovell, T. (1976) 'Jane Austen and gentry society', in F. Barker *et al.* (eds), *Literature, Society and the Sociology of Literature*, Essex: University of Essex Press, pp. 118–32.

Lucas, E.V., Crane, L. and Edwardes, M. (trans.) (1963) *Companion Library Collection: Grimms*, New York: Grosset and Dunlap.

Lurie, A. (1995) 'She had it all', *New York Review*, 2 March: 3–5.

Lyttle, J. (1996) 'All dressed up for the movies', *Independent: Section 2*, 26 August: 2–3.

MacComb, D. (1996) 'Divorce of a nation; or can Isabel Archer resist history?', *The Henry James Review*, 17 (2) Spring: 129–49.

Mailer, N. (1965) 'The Boston trial of *Naked Lunch*', *Evergreen Review*, 36: 40–49, 87–8.

Major, J. (1994) Quoted in *Guardian*, 22 January: 23.

Mander, J. (1920) *The Story of a New Zealand River*, Auckland and London: Whitcombe and Tombs; repr. 1938.

Manvell, R. (1979) *Shakespeare and the Film*, New York: A.S. Barnes.

Marrus, M. (1995) 'Jewish resistance to the Holocaust', *Journal of Contemporary History*, 30 (1): 83–110.

Mars Jones, A. (1997) *Independent Tabloid*, 13 February: 5.

Marshall, L. (1997) 'What Jane Campion did next', *The Age*, 18 January: 9.

Martin, A. (1994) 'Piano falls between two stools', *The Australian*, 12 May: 14.

Matthews, G. (1987) *'Just a Housewife': The rise and fall of domesticity in America*, Oxford: Oxford University Press.

Maynard, M. (1995) ' "The wishful feeling about curves': Fashion, femininity, and the 'New Look', in Australia', *Journal of Design History*, 8 (3): 43–59.

McCarthy, M. (1963) 'Burroughs' *Naked Lunch*'; repr. in *New York Review of Books*, 1991, 1 (1): 4–5.

McFarlane, B. (1996) *Novel to Film: An introduction to the theory of adaptation*, Oxford: Clarendon Press.

—— (1997) '*The Portrait of a Lady*', *Cinema Papers*, 115: 35–7.

McGrath, J. (1981) *A Good Night Out – Popular Theatre: Audience, class and form*, London: Eyre Methuen.

McGreal, J. (1992) '*Two Sisters*', *Sight and Sound*, May/Spring: 42.

McIntyre, V.N. (1982) '*Star Trek': The Wrath of Khan*, New York: Pocket Books.

McKenna, K. (1995) 'The Women behind *Little Women*', *Newsday*, 1 January: 20, 36.

McLuhan, M. (1964) *Understanding Media*, New York: McGraw-Hill.

Medhurst, A. (1991) 'Batman, deviance and camp', in R. Pearson and W. Uricchio (eds), *The Many Lives of Batman: Critical approaches to a superhero and his media*, London: Routledge, pp. 161–2.

Meehan, E. (1991) ' "Holy Commodity Fetish, Batman!": The political economy of a commercial intertext', in R. Pearson and W. Uricchio (eds), *The Many Lives of Batman: Critical approaches to a superhero and his media*, London: Routledge, pp. 41–65.

Merritt, K. (1988) 'The little girl/little mother transformation: The American evolution of *Snow White and the Seven Dwarfs*', in Canemaker (1988): vol. 2, pp. 105–23.

Miles, B. (1992) *William Burroughs: El hombre invisible*, London: Virgin.

Miller, F. *et al.* (1986) *Batman: The dark knight returns*, intro. A. Moore, London: Titan.

Miller, G. (1980) *Screening the Novel: Rediscovered American fiction in film*, New York: Frederick Ungar.

Miller, J. (1986) *Subsequent Performances*, London: Faber and Faber.

Moore, A. and Bolland, B. (1988) *The Killing Joke*, New York: DC Comics.

Morgan, T. (1988) *Literary Outlaw: The life and times of William S. Burroughs*, New York: Henry Holt.

Moritz, W. (1988) 'Some observations on non-objective and non-linear animation', in Canemaker 1988: vol. 2, pp. 21–33.

Morrison, G. and McKean, D. (1989) *Arkham Asylum: A Serious House on Serious Earth*, New York: DC Comics.

Mulvey, L. (1975) 'Visual pleasure and narrative cinema', *Screen* 16 (3): 6–18.

Murfin, R.C. (ed.) (1991) *Nathaniel Hawthorne, The Scarlet Letter: case studies in contemporary criticism*, Boston: Bedford/St Martin's Press.

Murray, T. (1997) *Drama Trauma: Specters of race and sexuality in performance, video and art*, London: Routledge.

Neale, S. (1983) 'Masculinity as spectacle: Reflections on men and masculinity', in Kirkham and Thumin 1995: 9–19.

Nelmes, J. (ed.) (1997) *Introduction to Film Studies*, London and New York: Routledge.

Nevo, R. (1980) *Comic Transformations in Shakespeare*, London and New York: Methuen.

New York Sun (1932) 19 September, New York Public Library, Performing Arts Research Collections.

News (1933) 26 November, New York Public Library, Performing Arts Research Collections.

Nicholls, M. (1997) 'She who gets slapped: Jane Campion's *Portrait of a Lady*', *Metro*, 111: 43–7.

Nuttall, J. (1968) *Bomb Culture*, London: Paladin; repr. 1970.

Okuda, M., Okuda, D. and Mirek, D. (1994) *The Star Trek Encyclopedia*, New York: Pocket Books.

Oldham, J. (1997) 'Bun Lovin' Criminal', *New Musical Express*, 28 June.

Oliner, S.P. and Oliner, P.M. (1988) *The Altruistic Personality: Rescuers of Jews in Nazi Europe*, New York: Free Press.

Olivier, L. (1984) *Laurence Olivier's Henry V*, New York: Lorrimer.

Orr, J. and Nicholson, C. (1992) *Cinema and Fiction: New modes of adapting, 1950–1990*, Edinburgh: Edinburgh University Press.

Pearson, R. and Uricchio, W. (eds) (1991) *The Many Lives of the Batman: Critical approaches to a superhero and his media*, London: Routledge.

Peary, G. and Shatzkin, R. (eds) (1978) *The Modern American Novel and the Movies*, New York: Frederick Ungar.

Penley, C. (1991) 'Brownian motion: Women, tactics and technology', in C. Penley and A. Ross (eds), *Technoculture*, Minneapolis: University of Minnesota Press.

Poovey, M. (1984) *The Proper Lady and the Woman Writer: Ideology as style in the works of Mary Wollstonecraft, Mary Shelley and Jane Austen*, Chicago: University of Chicago Press.

Porter, H. (1996) 'Trivial pursuit', *Guardian*, 1 February: 2.

Powdermaker, H. (1951) *Hollywood the Dream Factory: An anthropologist looks at the movie makers*, London: Secker and Warburg.

Press Book A (1933) *Little Women*, New York Public Library, Performing Arts Research Collections.

Press Book B (1949) *Little Women*, New York Public Library, Performing Arts Research Collections.

Pryor, I. (1993) 'Piano lessons', *Onfilm*, October 1993: 25.

Reeves-Stevens, J. and Reeves-Stevens, G. (1994) *Federation*, New York: Pocket Books.

—— (1997) '*Star Trek Phase II*': *The lost series*, New York: Pocket Books.

Reynolds, P. (ed.) (1993) *Novel Images: Literature in performance*, London: Routledge.

Richardson, R. (1969) *Literature and Film*, Bloomington: Indiana University Press.

Riley, V. (1995) 'Ancestor worship: The earthly paradise of Jane Campion's universe', *Metro*, 102: 61–4.

Robertson, C. (1987) 'House and home in the arts and crafts era: Reforms for simpler living', in W. Kaplan (ed.), *'The Art that is Life': The arts and crafts movement in America, 1875–1920*, Boston: Little Brown, pp. 336–57.

Roeder, G.H. (1993) *The Censored War: American visual experience during World War Two*, New Haven: Yale University Press.

Romney, J. (1993) 'Cinema appassionata', *New Statesman and Society*, 29 October: 33–4.

—— (1997) *Sight and Sound*, 7 (1) January: 42.

Rose, A. (1981) *Transcendentalism as a Social Movement: 1830–1850*, New Haven: Yale University Press.

Roth, L. (1987) 'Death and rebirth in *Star Trek II: The Wrath of Khan*', *Extrapolation* 28 (2): 159–66.

Rubinstein, W.D. (1997) *The Myth of Rescue: Why the democracies could not have saved more Jews from the Nazis*, London: Routledge.

Ryan, M. and Kellner, D. (1988) *Camera Politica: The politics and ideology of contemporary Hollywood film*, Bloomington and Indiana: Indiana University Press; repr. 1990.

Salisbury, M. (ed.) (1995) *Burton on Burton*, London: Faber and Faber.

Salway, J. (1991) ' "Veritable negroes" and "circumcized dogs": Racial disturbances in Shakespeare', in L. Aers and N. Wheale (eds), *Shakespeare in the Changing Curriculum*, London: Routledge, pp. 108–24.

Saxton, M. (1977) *Louisa May: A Modern Biography of Louisa May Alcott*, Boston: Houghton Mifflin.

Schaeffer, S. (1994) '*Little Women* comes of age', *New York Post*, 20 December: 37.

Schembri, J. (1993) 'Me Jane', *The Age*, 6 August: 13.

Schickel, R. (1968) *The Disney Version: The life, times, art and commerce of Walt Disney*, London: Pavillion; revised and repr. 1986.

Seigel, S. and Seigel, B. (eds) (1997) *The Winona Ryder Scrapbook*, Secaucus: Citadel Press Book.

Shakespeare, W. (1988) *The Complete Works*, eds S. Wells, G. Taylor, J. Jowett and W. Montgomery, Oxford: Clarendon Press.

Shaughnessy, N. (1996) 'Is s/he or isn't s/he? Screening *Orlando*', in D. Cartmell, I.Q. Hunter, H. Kaye and I. Whelehan (eds), *Pulping Fictions: Consuming culture across the literature/media divide*, London: Pluto.

Shaughnessy, R. (ed.) (1998) *Shakespeare on Film*, New Casebooks, Basingstoke and London: Macmillan.

Showalter, E. (1991) *Sisters' Choice: Tradition and change in American women's writing*, Oxford: Oxford University Press.

—— (1995) 'Meg, Jo, Beth and Me', *London Review of Books*, 23 March: 19.

Shorter Oxford English Dictionary (1993), Oxford: Clarendon Press.

Silverberg, I. (ed.) (1992) *Everything is Permitted: The making of 'Naked Lunch'*, New York: Grove Weidenfeld.

Sinyard, N. (1986) *Filming Literature: The art of screen adaptation*, London and Sydney: Croom Helm.

Skeggs, B. (1997) *Formations of Class and Gender: Becoming respectable*, London: Sage.

Slavin, J. (1993) 'The films of Jane Campion', *Metro*, 95: 28–30.

Smith, D. (1956) *The Hundred and One Dalmatians*, Oxford: Heinemann.

Smoodin, E. (ed.) (1994) *Disney Discourse: Producing the magic kingdom*, London: Routledge.

Solomon, C. (1988) 'Animation is a visual medium', in J. Canemaker (ed.), *Storytelling in Animation : The art of the animated image*, Los Angeles: AFI, vol. 2, p. 95.

Sparke, P. (1995) *As Long As It's Pink: The sexual politics of taste*, London: Polity Press.

Spiegel, A. (1976) *Fiction and the Camera Eye: Visual consciousness in film and the modern novel*, Charlottesville: University Press of Virginia.

Stevenson, L. (1995) '*Little Women?* The female mind at work in antebellum America', *History Today*, March: 26–31.

Tasker, Y. (1993) *Spectacular Bodies: gender, genre and the action cinema*, London: Routledge.

Taylor, C. (1989) *Sources of the Self*, Cambridge, MA: Harvard University Press.

Theweleit, K. (1987) *Male Fantasies*, Cambridge: Polity Press.

Thomas, K. (1994) *New York Post*, 21 December: 1.

Thompson, E. (1995) *Jane Austen's Sense and Sensibility: The screenplay*, London: Bloomsbury; repr. 1996.

Thompson, J.O. (1996) 'Film adaptation and the mystery of the original', in D. Cartmell, H. Kaye, I.Q. Hunter and I. Whelehan (eds), *Pulping Fictions: Consuming culture across the literature/media divide*, London: Pluto.

Uricchio, W. and Pearson, R. (1993) *Reframing Culture: The case of the vitagraph quality films*, Princeton: Princeton University Press.

Virilio, P. (1993) *The Art of the Motor*, trans. J. Rose, Minneapolis: University of Minnesota Press, 1995.

Wagner, G. (1975) *The Novel and the Cinema*, Cranbury: Associated University Presses.

Ward, D. (1995) 'Darcy's wet shirt draws visitors', *Guardian*, 7 November: 10.

Warner, M. (1994) *From the Beast to the Blonde: On fairytales and their tellers*, London: Chatto and Windus.

Warren, S. (1997) 'Four *Little Women*: L.M. Alcott's *Little Women* and three film adaptations', unpublished B.A. thesis, Department of English and Media Studies, De Montfort University, Leicester.

Washington, P. (1996) 'This Last *Tempest*: Shakespeare, postmodernity and *Prospero's Books*', in H. Kerr, R. Eaden and M. Mitton (eds), *Shakespeare, World Views*, Delaware: Associated University Presses and University of Delaware Press, pp. 237–48.

Weldon, F. (1995) 'Star of age and screen', *Guardian: Section 2*, 12 April: 2–3, 12.

Wellbery, D. (1990) Foreword to F.A. Kittler, *Discourse Networks 1800/1900*, Stanford: Stanford University Press.

Wells, P. (1996) *Around the World in Animation*, London: BFI/MOMI.

—— (1997a) 'Animation: Forms and meanings', in J. Nelmes (ed.), *Introduction to Film Studies*, London and New York: Routledge, pp. 193–221.

—— (ed.) (1997b) *Art and Animation*, London: John Wiley/Academy Group.

—— (1998) *Understanding Animation*, London and New York: Routledge.

Welsh, I. (1996a) *Trainspotting*, London: Minerva.

—— (1996b) *Trainspotting and Headstate*, London: Minerva.

Welter, B. (1966) 'The cult of true womanhood: 1820–1860', *American Quarterly*, 18: 151–74.

Whelehan, I. and Cartmell, D. (1995) 'Through a painted curtain: Laurence Olivier's *Henry V*', in P. Kirkham and D. Thoms (eds), *War Culture: Social change and changing experience in World War Two*, London: Lawrence and Wishart.

Williams, E. (1965) Untitled sleeve notes for the LP *Call Me Burroughs*, Paris: The English Bookshop.

Willson, R.F., Jr (ed.) (1995) *Entering the Maze: Shakespeare's art of beginning*, New York: Peter Lang.

Wilson, R. (1992) Interview with N. Zurbrugg, *The Tempest* (Leeds), 1–2: 48–52.

Wishart, K. (1997) 'Drugs and art meet on campus', *Times Higher Education Supplement*, 30 May, p. 18.

Wodehouse, P.G. (1935) *Blandings Castle and Elsewhere*, London: Penguin; repr. 1954.

Woolf, V. (1928) *Orlando*; repr. Harmondsworth: Penguin, 1945.

—— (1929) *A Room of One's Own*; repr. London: Hogarth and London: Granada, 1977.

—— (1938) *Three Guineas*; repr. London: Hogarth and Harmondsworth: Penguin, 1977.

—— (1981) *A Reflection of the Other Person: The letters of Virginia Woolf – Volume IV: 1929–1931*, ed. N. Nicolson, London: Chatto and Windus.

—— (1982) *The Diary of Virginia Woolf – Volume III: 1925–30*, ed. A. Oliver Bell, Harmondsworth: Penguin.

—— (1994) *The Essays of Virginia Woolf – Volume IV: 1924–28*, ed. A. McNeillie, London: Hogarth.

Wroe, M. (1996) 'Hard drugs and heroine addiction', *Observer*, 10 March, p. 13.

The Year's Work in English Studies (1996–), Oxford: Blackwell.

Zelizer, B. (1997) 'Every once in a while: *Schindler's List* and the shaping of history', in Loshitzky 1997a: 18–35.

Internet references

>Mrmunterworldonline.nl= (1997) >Re: *First Contact* = **dejanews.com** [Downloaded 12 June]

Brown, J. (1991) >*The Addams Family* = **washingtonpost.com** [Downloaded 21 November]

Iannicca, D. (1997) >Re: *Star Trek: First Contact* = **rec.arts.startrek.current** [Downloaded 12 June]

Johnson, B. (1992) >*The Addams Family* = **rec.arts.movies.reviews** [Downloaded 15 April]

Maloney, F. (1991) >*The Addams Family* = **rec.arts.movies.reviews** [Downloaded 15 April]

INDEX